Paul Jennings' Companion to

BRITAIN

The Schweppes Leisure Library

Already published:

Travel
America (Nigel Buxton)
Australia (Vicki Peterson)
China (Sarah Allan & Cherry Barnett)

Sport
Rugby (John Hopkins)

By the same author

Humour
Oddly Enough
Even Oddlier
Oddly Bodlikens
Next to Oddliness
Model Oddlies
Iddly Oddly
I Said Oddly, Diddle I?
Oddles of Oddlies
The Jenguin Pennings
Oddly Ad Lib
I Was Joking, Of Course
It's An Odd Thing But
I Must Have Imagined It
Britain As She Is Visit

Documentary
The Living Village
Just A Few Lines
The English Difference

Novel
And Now For Something Exactly The Same

Anthology
The Book Of Nonsense

For Children
The Hopping Basket
The Great Jelly Of London
The Train To Yesterday

Paul Jennings'Companion to
BRITAIN

Cassell

LONDON

CASSELL LTD.
35 Red Lion Square, London WC1R 4SG
and at Sydney, Auckland, Toronto, Johannesburg,
an affiliate of
Macmillan Publishing Co., Inc.,
New York.

Text copyright © Paul Jennings 1981
Photographs copyright © Olive Smith

First published 1981

ISBN 0 304 30459 X

Typeset by Inforum Ltd, Portsmouth
Printed and bound in Great Britain by
Fakenham Press Limited, Fakenham, Norfolk

All photographs by Edwin Smith

Acknowledgements

The publishers would like to thank the following for permission to quote extracts:

Faber & Faber for the lines from T.S. Eliot's *The Waste Land* on pages 54 and 63, and W.B. Yeat's 'Meditations in Time of Civil War: Ancestral Houses' on page 60.

John Murray for the lines from John Betjeman's 'Devonshire Street, WI' on page 24.

Max Reinhardt for Paul Jennings's 'Unorthography' on page 6.

The Sunday Times for the verses by Paul Jennings which appear on pages 37–38.

A.D. Peters for the verses by Rose Macaulay on pages 109–110.

In addition, the author thanks Hodder and Stoughton for occasional short extracts from his book *The Living Village*, and the Shell magazine for extracts quoted from his previously published articles on Bristol and Chester.

Contents

Unorthography

(A Rhyming Guide to Britain, although it may not look like it)

Tourists are hopers. In some Other place
They hope to find some wondrous Other race;
Their heads are cameras, which they hope can be
Loaded with memory-film in bright 3-D.

The easiest Other race to be among
Is surely Britain's with its common tongue –
    tourists' attention! Nor forthwith assume
You say as spelt each little town (like Frome);
The Welsh have funny names your tongue to twist with,
Like Penmaenmawr and Gwlch and Aberystwyth –
That you expect. But when in England, how
Dare any tourist ask the way to Slough
Who yesterday put someone in a huff
By thinking *brow* homophonous with Brough?
Though Glyndebourne opera for the cultured few is
How can they get there but by way of Lewes?
(Under the Sussex Downs, where snug they both lie
Are many other gems – for instance, Hoathly.)
What lord of maps, what orthographic jouster
Grapples with Bicester and its sicester, Towcester
And never gets in something like a panic
If blank stares greet him when he asks for Alnwick
Nor ends by thinking people downright spooky
Who makes a place spelt 'Stiffkey' rhyme with Newquay?

Tourists! You needn't be alarmed unduly
By England's treatment of a word like Beaulieu.
These Norman names (*or* Saxon ones, like Wrotham)
Unlettered men have modified to suit 'em
And pundits long since gave up trying to teach 'em
How you should really say a name like Beauchamp.
Our names and views hold unexpected joy;
Seaward, Atlantic views (as seen at Fowey);
Views over sands, or rocky views and pebbly;
Pastoral views, near inland towns like Weobley;
East Anglian views, with churches old and mossy,
Each as unique as disyllabic Costessy.

Tourists! Take heart! You won't go really wrong;
Most of our names are what they seem to be,
Often euphonious, almost never harsh,
Thus: Souldrop: Beer; or Moreton-in-the-Marsh;
Winterbourne Whitechurch: Milton Abbas: Deal;
Birdlip; Uttoxeter: Piddletrenthide: Seal;
Gussage All Saints; Sea Houses; Wantage; Diss
(All useful padding in a verse like this)
Just now and then our names, our doubtful skies,
Give that most precious tourist gift: surprise.

Introduction

The great secret of Britain is that its people have conquered Inner Space.

Consider the figures. England and Wales, 58,340 square miles; add another 30,405 for Scotland (when the tide is out), and that's 88,745 altogether. Now in Africa, Asia, Australia, Russia, both parts of the American continent, there are areas where you could cut out one of those rectangular states or indeed countries that they used to make in the 19th century by drawing straight dotted lines across the map, 300 miles by 300, usually rectangular except for Antarctica where they tended to be shaped like slices of pie and have names like Van Heflin's Land or Queen Muriel's Land. They wouldn't be missed, and you'd have an area bigger than our whole country.

You could make such areas, of course, with majestic mountain landscape far surpassing anything this country has to offer (highest in Scotland, Ben Nevis, 4,406 feet; in Wales, Snowdon, 3,560 feet; in England, Scafell Pike, 3,210. These are mountains? La Paz, the capital of Bolivia, is 11,916 feet, for goodness' sake. Ah, but when you *see* Ben Nevis or Snowdon . . .). You could cut them out to contain cities with more skyscrapers, great bridges, etc., than London—although, come to think of it, we have just built the longest single-span bridge in the world. Where? Across the Humber, a river not really famous in song and story. This bridge goes from Hull (only place in England with *green* telephone kiosks; a busy port, makes chemicals, paint, machine belting, starch, serious stuff like that, miles from the sweeping, romantic, glamorous parts of Yorkshire) to, well, nobody knows really, just a lot of potato fields in Lincolnshire. Hell of a bridge though.

Now, as a matter of fact there are plenty of far, high moors and silent, forested valleys, and multitudinous creeks with a view of blue promontories and islands, places where you are as far from the rhythms of commuter and industrial life as you would be in the Gobi Desert, only a great deal more beautiful. If you go up the famous road, never really out of sight of water, from Oban (by Loch Linnhe, roadstead to the Inner Hebrides), through Fort William (Ben Nevis on your right, on your left the river Lochy, then *Loch* Lochy, then the Caledonian Canal, then Loch Ness (Gregorian chant, or what's left of it, at Fort Augustus Benedictine Abbey near home of famous invisible monster)) to grey-stoned, splendid-new-theatred Inverness, your journey north-eastwards has only bisected the Highlands. The really famous parts, no doubt, are south of you; the Cairngorms, the Grampians. But you can look at a huge expanse still remaining to the north, with no town of any size (and, now only one railway), dotted with mysterious, lonely-sounding names of places that you know you will never see; that most Englishmen, probably most *Scots*, will never see. Meall Nan Con (3,154 feet), Glencanisp Forest, Rumsdale Water, Skullomie, Coldbackie . . . and even as my eye roams over the map I see there is a little dot below Mull called Frank Lockwood's Island.

Who was, or is, Frank Lockwood? A world authority on seals, a retired pop star, a hermit known to everyone but me? He must remain something else unknown, in that so small yet so sky-huge, lonely, bird-haunted, atmospheric country. I have this book to write, and you, dear reader, have the essence of these magical and historical islands (I hope) to extract from it.

You can get the same real isolation in Wales. I remember a dream-like drive from Llandrindod Wells through Builth Wells, in what used to be Radnorshire but is now some bureaucratically more convenient area called Powys, and into orcharded Herefordshire. At first, after the lacy Edwardian-spa architecture, with a lot of woodwork, of the elegant little towns, it was more like flying than riding, since on this autumn morning I was just above the top of a level white sea of mist. Then it dissolved and (surrealistic thought, I was about fifty crow-flight miles from *Birmingham*) I was clearly the only human being in the paradise-tinted woods of the upper Wye Valley.

Birmingham, cities; now we are coming closer to the heart of the matter, to the British, and more specifically the English conquest of Inner Space. England now has more people to the square mile than India. But you don't even have to go an hour or so down the M4 motorway into the bare solitudes of Wiltshire, where you can walk along neolithic paths and feel as insignificant in a huge landscape as neolithic man did. There are amazingly lonely lanes in Kent the moment you are past the outer London street lighting. The immense silence of beech woods called Epping Forest drives a wedge into the formless sprawl of north London. Come to that, there are bits of Hampstead Heath that look much the same as they did when Constable painted them before railways had been invented, but you walk another twenty yards and you can see not only St Paul's but a hundred (or so it seems) post-war semi-skyscraper office blocks.

We have our wilds, but we also have the most man-made landscape in the world. Everyone says, Ah, yes, those hedges; and it is true that the intimate, subdivided landscape, the fields with strange old names like *Jinhodgson, Little Wild Carrots, Nutbins, North America, Top Hat* (these and many more are to be found in just one village, the picture-postcard, tile-hung and white-weatherboard Kentish village of Smarden) owe a lot to 18th-century enclosures, the development of scientific crop-rotation farming (and the aggrandisation of gentlemen's parks). Though not everything. You will find huge, hedge-lined ditches which turn out to be parish boundaries established a thousand years ago, in Saxon times. Indeed the curious fact has recently been scientifically proved that you can date an old hedge by counting the number of tree species in a thirty-yard stretch of it. By some mysterious, always-obeyed law of nature, it is one per century (whatever the original composition of the hedge).

As a matter of fact you are likely to notice changes from this traditional pattern, as 5,000 miles of hedge disappear each year to make room for the kind of prairie farming which modern machinery finds more suitable; obviously more in corn-growing East Anglia and parts of the Midlands than in the hilly north country with its stone walls marching straight up to the top of high fells. And unless you are in one of Britain's twelve national parks, where there are regulations about this kind of thing, you may also notice another change, in fact you'd have to be blind not to—the appearance everywhere of could-be-anywhere bungalows and housing estates which break from the centuries-old way of using local materials.

This, incidentally, is one of the reasons for the amazing diversity of Britain, its division into sharply defined areas. Why should this be so? There is

A Cotswold stone manor house.

nothing unique to Britain in the fact that, for example, you don't see slate roofs on any houses in East Anglia built before the railway age (and not all that many after), since it had to come from Wales. Obviously people used the material that was close to hand all over Europe.

Yet there it is. You could be driven blindfold to almost any region in England and guess where you were from the material and the style of architecture, not so much in the increasingly standardised towns, naturally, as in the villages. If the houses were of stone you would know for a start you were in the south-west, or in the stone belt that sweeps up through the Cotswolds (*honey*-coloured, absolutely unavoidable adjective) or the darker iron-brown of Oxfordshire and Northamptonshire, up through the East Midlands to Northumberland. If the stone had a fat, rich, Georgian quality you would be in Yorkshire, knowing from a certain openness that you were not in the cosy (for all their airy uplands) Cotswolds; if there were mountains about, you would be in the north-west, unless there were a lot of sheep about as well and the people, or many of them, didn't seem to be speaking English at all, in which case you would be in Wales. If every church seemed to be made of flint you would either be in coastal Suffolk, or in a great sweep that goes from north Norfolk, skirts London to its north-west, then bends east again in two great south-country swathes reaching to the coasts of Sussex and east Kent; although in these latter parts it would be the houses you noticed, not the churches. They couldn't hold a candle to Suffolk when it comes to churches, amazing semi-cathedrals rising sometimes from lonely marshes and hidden fields miles, apparently, from anywhere.

There would be lots of other pointers to help you know where you were, and indeed the study of these indicators is perfectly capable of growing into such a consuming passion that you wouldn't have time to be interested in the towns, the fantastic great houses and parks, the cathedrals, which for so many tourists are the places to be seen, and just happen to have all this country between them.

But when you are actually in any of these areas it has such sharply defined characteristics, it is so different from the next one you come to, that you tend to think it bigger than it actually is. In the Fens, which are more primevally English than—than Shakespeare (it was there that Hereward the Wake headed the forlorn resistance to the Normans) yet were also invented by the 17th-century Dutchman Vermuyden, you can sometimes get the feeling that this must go on for hundreds of miles, England's answer to the prairie, even though the prairie wouldn't almost invariably have a distant wirescape bringing electricity to the tight little concentrations of yellow-brick villages standing slightly above dyke level—and certainly would not have, lifted above the wide and skyey flatlands, a marvel such as Ely Cathedral, with its octagonal lantern (appropriate word for that raised light shining out over the wild marshes for centuries), a magical geometry of huge timbers, 400 tons raised, no one quite knows how, 600 years ago. Let alone the (for my money) queen of them all, Lincoln with its Angel Choir, crowning a rare hill, a city at its base; a crown, a focal point, a living dream of human aspiration in stone, turning all those matter-of-fact lives scattered through the miles and the centuries into glory.

Or you can go half an hour's drive or so from Southampton through the New Forest, with its June splendour of rhododendrons, its sudden open spaces, its glades, its wild ponies, and find yourself on a Hardy heath . . . 'the face of the heath by its mere complexion added half an hour to evening; it could in like manner retard the dawn . . . every night its Titanic form seemed to await something, but it had waited thus, unmoved, during so many centuries, through the crises of so many things, that it could only be imagined to await one last crisis—the final overthrow.'

That's from *The Return of the Native*, but of course Hardy was not alone in using a sharply-defined English region to express human feelings. It is a peculiarly English tradition, born somehow from the landscape. It reaches from Shakespeare (take *King Lear*, for example, where the huge drama of the king's madness, of the passing away of things, is paralleled by an actual storm and an actual heath.

There's a great thesis waiting to be written, in fact, with some such title as *The Heath and its Significance in English Literature*. From grim northern industrial cities it is never far to curlew-haunted, windblown moors; they are an essential part of the passionate stormy drama of *Wuthering Heights* or *Jane Eyre*. There's the *Lorna Doone* country, so sharply defined, again, that you might almost think the novel was written by R. D. Exmoor rather than R. D. Blackmore. There's the Walter Scott border country, where you still see over shop doors names like Strong-i'-th'arm; the instantly recognisable D. H. Lawrence rural Nottinghamshire scarred by pitheads, the start of a genre which comes right down to all those modern novels about northern young men ashamed of their new-found middle-class literacy.

In short, we have conquered Inner Space. In summer my route from Suffolk to London was sometimes blocked by a notorious four-mile traffic block, now happily by-passed. This traffic block was sometimes featured in photographs from helicopters on fine Sundays; but I would go to or return from London through a deserted, private little valley full of waving corn, through spacious and sleepy small towns (in one of which, however, there is a nylon research laboratory) and sometimes stopped off at a little round church, hidden among meadows, which is one of the only five surviving round churches built after the Crusades on the model of the church of the Holy Sepulchre at Jerusalem. Little Maplestead dates from 1355. I crossed defunct railway lines, now simply tracks that march into woods. I found another lane, into another valley containing more manor houses, lakes, fords, churches, pubs, woods, hedges, roof dispositions at the ends of culs-de-sac and subdivisions, hump-backed bridges over streams, old grand houses, unsmart or smart cottages, bungalows, and open fields, than there is, on paper, actually room for.

And everywhere, men in shirt-sleeves in the evening sunlight making paths, rockeries, arbours and flower-beds, mowing lawns. Even from trains you can see such men, oblivious of your hurtling, clattering passage on the embankment through their suburb, as they trim the edges of their tiny lawns, carefully tie bits of paper to miles of cotton to keep birds away from seedlings, burn neat bonfires, lay crazy paving in straight lines or in wild baroque sweeps curving through all of ten yards, build tiny fountains and ponds, lean-to conservatories for tomatoes and chrysanthemums; and everywhere, trellis arches and pergolas for roses. They are only doing in little what the great classical English landscapers of the 18th century did in large. They are obeying the same instinct, to create ever more diversified Inner Space.

It is a mistake in any country to regard its landscape as something that you just happen to go through on your way to famous towns or buildings or even Beauty Spots. But it is more of a mistake in England, where the slow, invasion-free growth of almost a thousand years after a previous invasion-absorbing period going back beyond Stonehenge, and taking in a lot of Rome on the way, has caused most towns to be simply a refinement of, a concentration of and an added grace to what already surrounds them.

This is another way of saying that the other dimension of any visit to Britain is history. As you move about this incredibly various land, obviously the more you know that (for instance) Norman arches were round, Early English were delicately pointed (Salisbury), the Black Death (1348) carried off many craftsmen among perhaps a third of the population so that the Decorated style which you see in many a curlicued east window gave way to straight-up Perpendicular, the 'box of light' (but what a box; wait till you see Bath Abbey!), a unique English style which we continued a century after the rest of Europe had gone on to Renaissance domes—the more you know that the scarcity of timber used for shipbuilding and other purposes in the 16th century made them stop building houses with lots of uprights carrying a *wider* upper storey with an 'oversail' and use instead an integrated frame—the more you know, the more you will enjoy.

Or will you? Perhaps this is like saying you can't enjoy Beethoven unless you know all that stuff about binary form, second subjects being ushered in on the oboe, and the rest of it. Of *course* you can enjoy it.

And obviously the place to start enjoying it, the heart and centre of it all, is **London**. The flower of cities all, said the poet (the *Scots* poet, what is more: William Dunbar). There is, whatever the present condition or the future of Britain (or, for that matter, of the world) a huge *inevitability* about London. Just look at the map. Where is the most important river? And where is the lowest point at which early man could easily cross it?

Britain may no longer be the centre of an empire. She may have abandoned her ancient duodecimal money system, which like our method of counting time (at least there are still twenty-four hours in the day, and sixty minutes, not a hundred, in the hour) goes back to the Sumerians, and you can't go much farther than that; they knew a thing or two, such as that you can divide 12 by 2, 3, 4 and 6, whereas you can only divide 10 by 2 and 5; she may appear to spend a lot of her time arguing with EEC countries about fish, or the regulation of juggernaut lorries. But until something really catastrophic happens, the zero meridian from which the world measures its longitude passes through our capital. I belong to what must be surely the fairly small club of those who have stood with one foot on either side of it at Greenwich (of which more later) *and* also, in a very different place (in my case, Uganda) with one foot on either side of the Equator.

You mustn't think this is just some kind of imperialistic boasting. It's just that it's perfectly easy to observe certain vast historical trends after they have happened (if a trend can happen, but never mind). The indisputable facts, *so far*, are that the dynamic (and this concept includes that of colonising, good or bad) centres of power moved westwards for over three thousand years. Sumeria, Egypt, Greece, Rome, Norman-French, Iberian-Atlantic, British-Atlantic. In the words of the poet Auden, Britain 'trousered Africa'. Never mind that he went on to say that Africa might now be getting its 'revenge', I'm not going into the morals of all this, either to speak of the slave trade or of Amin and Bokassa. I point out merely that London, with its tumultuous, race-mixing history behind it, was the point through which it was agreed, at an international conference in Washington in 1878 (by which time it was perfectly clear that the whole world was ultimately going to be trousered and industralised, no longer necessarily by us, though we started it) that the line of zero longitude should be measured from London. From Greenwich, in fact, site of the Royal Observatory, completed in 1676 but moved to Herstmonceux in Sussex in 1946 because the London atmosphere, even after the Clean Air Act banned coal fires and smoke and revolutionised the place, banishing the pea-soup fogs which most foreigners still assume to last throughout the winter and to be like the one so vividly described by Dickens at the famous beginning of *Bleak House*, was not ideal for looking at the heavens.

London, as a matter of fact, gives a more immediate impression of being a focal point than it did when it was the centre of an empire. And although of course a great deal of this has to do with the great post-war emergence of the tourist *industry*, this I advise every tourist to forget, since the more ordinary people he talks to who are not connected with this industry, the truer the idea he will get of the country and its amazingly talkative, not at all stereotyped or taciturn people. A surprisingly large number of them turn out to be students, even if all they have come to learn is the English language. (Very difficult. Two examples from essays. (1) 'Hitch-hiking is a way of getting from place to place without spending a penny.' (2) Said to a girl: 'you have a beautiful corpse'. Mind you, most British people don't even know enough of other languages even to make mistakes in them.)

London

The Approaches

How much you instantly absorb this always exciting 'focal point' feeling may well depend on the method by which you approach London for the first time. If you arrive from Southampton, having come on that old-fashioned thing called a ship, you will arrive at **Waterloo station**, immediately next to a footbridge over the Thames, from which you can get a marvellous instant panorama: on the north bank, from the familiar, so-*there*-it-is, million-times-photographed Victorian Gothic Houses of Parliament and Big Ben (bong bong bong BONG, bong bong bong BONG, bong bong bong BONG . . . BRRRWOOONGGG, BRRRWOOONGGG, and can it be really only that high, and are you dreaming or is it ever so slightly leaning over?).

If you have come from the West Country (and even nowadays a few must make their landfall at Plymouth, to say nothing of Welsh ports), you will have come into **Paddington station**, through a flatter, rather more industrial suburbia, in spite of its many-railinged municipal parks and cemeteries, than the formless brick hills of the south London through which Waterloo is approached. There will be vestigial reminders, behind the standard blue-and-white British Rail livery, that you are on what was the literally *Great* Western Railway (GWR), with its chocolate-and-cream coaches, its unique combination of romance (Cornish fishing villages, Land's End, Dartmoor, Welsh mountains), history (Exeter, Bristol) and commerce (also Bristol, Welsh heavy industry—or nowadays ex-miners making alarm clocks and brassières) and snug, efficient service.

At Paddington you are, well, just on the fringe of the West End, you step out into an area of big white stuccoed houses, with big front doors up a flight of steps, which though now all offices or hotels, still give you the sense that you are in an area where the metropolitan rich once sallied forth in their top-hats and crinolines to take the air in the great parks, Regent's or Hyde.

To come from the north means **Euston**, once the HQ of the LMS (London Midland & Scottish), father of all railways in the world, remembering George Stephenson, Liverpool, the manufacturing north, Lancashire, the Lakes, Scotland. Until 'rebuilt' as a kind of suburban version of—well, of a station in a prosperous but impersonal suburb—it had a magnificent Doric arch, actually known as the Propylaeum, after the one leading to the Acropolis. Or it could mean the many-splendoured **St Pancras**, where from the street you can see huge Victorian windows now cut horizontally in half by mean little office-floor subdivisions. (It was Sir George Gilbert Scott's design and contained a lot of the ideas in his rejected plan for a new Foreign Office in Whitehall. 'It would have been a noble building', he said sadly. Still is.) The approach is through enormous sidings and yards, fringed by processed-food and domestic appliance factories; and once at Euston you are separated from the beating central heart of London by the Intellectual Belt—London University, Russell Square, under the great plane trees of which the late T. S. Eliot used to be seen walking to the old offices of Faber & Faber (the publishing firm of which he was, improbably, a director), Bloomsbury, the British Museum, Dillons (bookshop to London University).

If you have the misfortune to approach from the east it is better not to look out of the window at all for at least ten miles before you get to **Liverpool Street**, that shabby old cathedral; for you will see nothing but dismal Victorian factories, scrapyards, canals and blank-sided warehouses. You would be wrong, however, to judge us by this. It's just that we've never quite made up our minds what to do with old factories (and after all we've got more of them than anyone else. You will get the same feeling, only more so, looking out of a train window around, say, Manchester). The new ones tend to be in different locations. On this line, for instance, you may well have come through Chelmsford, not on the tourist route, but home of, for instance, the Marconi factory where there are some very clever gentlemen indeed.

Indeed it must not be deduced from the foregoing that all British railways and all British people are incapable of looking forwards and won't change anything because they are haunted by a great past. It is merely meant to show how everything here *is* layered by history, even a railway system which is capable of spectacular new high-speed (125 m.p.h.) trains and, at the last count, had more restaurant and refreshment cars than all the railways of continental Europe put together (no doubt you can get a splendid—and expensive—meal on the train from Paris to Brussels, but you try and get something on the continental equivalent of London to Ipswich!).

At whatever terminus you alight (and I see I haven't mentioned **Victoria**, which more or less connects the White Cliffs of Dover with the gardens of Buckingham Palace) you are connected to an Underground railway system which, with two lines built since the war and another building, is still the most complex and most used, if no longer the cheapest or even most efficient city network in the world. It also, incidentally, contains what is still the longest tunnel in the world, on the Northern line.

But of course with every year that passes a larger majority of those coming to London for the first time see it from the air. Here their impression may very well be that it is entirely surrounded by large square ponds full of green-looking water, but this is only because Heathrow Airport happens to be near a lot of reservoirs. Many will be lucky enough, either on approach or soon after take-off, to see under the wing an unmistakable group of towers, battlements, courtyards, on the edge of a town and a winding river which are on the edge of a clear green park with great avenues and woods. Windsor. The Queen is in official residence here during April, and parts of March, May, June and December. More of Windsor later.

The Monarchy

With the Queen we come, obviously, to the person, and the institution, whence the special, the uniquely focal quality of London ultimately derives. Most of the time it is a traffic-roaring capital city like any other (except for the double-decker red buses, the sudden quiet squares with huge trees, the amazing classical Wren churches tucked in among new glass towers . . .).

All capital cities are by definition focal points. But they do not have, preserved by a marvellously illogical logic into the democratic (in part of the world anyway) 20th century, a monarchy going back more than a thousand years—and incidentally only interrupted for eleven years, Cromwell's Commonwealth, 1649–1660—long before any other European country ventured on such experiments.

A plaque in the wall of Bath Abbey says 'Edgar, first King of all England, was crowned by Dunstan, Archbishop of Canterbury, in the Saxon Abbey on this site on Whit Sunday, A.D. 970'. But in fact the form and order of the British Coronation Service goes back to Egbert, King of Wessex (800–836). The Investing with the Armill and Royal Robe; the Delivery of the Orb; the Investiture *per Annulum et Baculum* (that is, by Ring and Sceptre)—and, perhaps above all, the Anointing—go back even further, to Biblical times. The Coronation Stone, dramatically stolen and recovered in the 1950s, is *Lia Fail*, the Stone of Destiny, traditionally the pillow of Jacob, carried to Ireland in the 5th century BC, thence to Scotland, thence to England by Edward I (which of course is why it was pinched by a Scot).

These things, where physical objects and procedures have a non-material (or symbolic, or magical, or spiritual, according to your viewpoint) significance, have survived into an age when you can see, when people are getting married, that they are often faintly embarrassed by *any* kind of symbolism, such as the simple act of putting a ring on a finger and saying 'with this ring I thee wed'.

People can, and do (especially if they are a Scottish Member of Parliament called William Hamilton, who any day now will be given some such official title as Objector-Serjeant to the Royal Household) argue that by now these are simply ancient ceremonial façades behind which there is a great nothing. Well, it is true that the Sovereign reigns but does not rule. It is true that one member of the House of Lords, Lord Milford, is a Communist. A Communist Lord, an ultimate and beautiful paradox.

It is also true that the tank succeeded the horse some time ago. This does not alter the fact that you do not need to be in the crowd on that famous ceremonial route, up the broad tree-lined Mall, through Admiralty Arch, past Trafalgar Square and Nelson on his column, and right turn down Whitehall to Westminster, whether Abbey or Parliament, for an actual ceremony, to be surprised by one of the most romantic sounds—to many people *the* most romantic sound—imaginable in a modern city: the amazing multiple *clop-clop-clop* of many horses' hooves.

The Editor of *Punch*, Alan Coren, tells how he was walking down Constitution Hill (wall of Buckingham Palace's garden on one side, Green Park on the other, leading to summer-deck-chaired, ponded, great-treed, often band-resounding St James's Park further down) with the late lamented S. J. Perelman, when they heard this magical noise. 'Run for your life,' shouted Perelman, 'Cossacks!'

Nobody comes more sophisticated than a man who wrote scripts for the Marx Brothers, but of course that great humorist found the whole thing just as exciting as anyone else, indeed a great deal more exciting than many Londoners for whom the Queen's Household Cavalry—the Life Guards with their splendid red tunics (cloaks in winter) or the Royal Horse Guards (the Blues)—are an everyday sight.

There are of course state occasions when not only the crowds specially assembled but people in outer space see it, via satellite. But as surely everyone knows by now, the splendid free spectacle of the **Changing of the Guard** happens every day of the week. In fact it happens twice, since those horses are bound for the Horse Guards in Whitehall (just up the road from the cul-de-sac where the Prime Minister lives, 10 Downing Street; a sober, perfectly Georgian façade in a block like hundreds of others in London, and often claimed in the past as an example of democratic unpretentiousness, although this claim was mildly diluted a few years ago when the interior was renovated at a cost of two or three million pounds). The Changing of the Guard that most people see is of course the one at **Buckingham Palace**, with the Foot Guards, and of course the bands.

From time to time other regiments guard the Palace, but basically this is the privilege of the **Guards**—five regiments of them. With the obvious exception of the ones in kilts, to most onlookers the Foot Guard of the Household Troops, to give them their full title, are simply an undifferentiated lot of marvellously well-drilled soldiers in red coats and busbies, now such a tourist-photograph target that the ones actually left on guard after the bands and the crowds have dispersed do their periodical marching-towards-each-other and foot-stamping about-turn to and from sentry boxes that are *inside* the railings of Buckingham Palace, although they can be seen outside on the ordinary pavement outside **St James's Palace**, a comparatively modest dark-red-brick Tudor building just up the Mall (an ex-monastery characteristically appropriated by Henry VIII, no longer lived in by royalty but still officially the 'Court' to which embassadors are accredited). But there are always policemen there to guard *them* from the over-curious.

They are, it is hardly necessary to say, extremely well-trained functional soldiers as well as ornamental ones, and the military exploits of the Grenadiers, the Coldstream, Scots, Welsh and Irish Guards (having in their respective busbies a white, red, none, green-and-white or blue plume) have filled many books a great deal thicker than this one.

The Changing of the Guard (11.30 a.m. at Buckingham Palace, 11 a.m. at Horse Guards, 10 a.m. Sundays, but all times subject to revision) is something to which you can either make your own way or do in a coach tour; London Transport, for instance, do one which leaves Victoria Coach Station at 10 a.m., takes in the whole thing, shows you the West End—Parliament Square, Trafalgar Square, Piccadilly Circus and Marble Arch—gets you back at 1 p.m., and costs, at the time of writing, £4.30 (under 14's, £3.20).

But however you do it you will have a strong sense of witnessing something central, focal. This has been a century of increasing violence compared, at least, with its immediate predecessor. There has been a great deal of talk about power growing from the end of a gun. Well, of course, the British have had a fair amount to do with guns in the past, like anyone else (it was just their good luck that a lot of *their* guns happened to be on ships). But they have also thought a great deal, in that peculiarly British unthinking way, about power, its ultimate sanction. Shakespeare is full of it ('there is a divinity doth hedge a king'; 'uneasy lies the head that wears a crown', etc. etc.). It is conceivable, in such a century (but only just conceivable) that the Queen of England will be in exile in Honolulu or somewhere while a mob of somewhat mature-looking students, acting on the orders of a mad archdeacon with a beard, hold the entire staff of the US Embassy hostage in Grosvenor Square.

It is *slightly* more conceivable that there will be a Marxist takeover of some kind. If so, it is also quite conceivable that the order of the ancient Coronation Service may be altered; *then, the Chrism having been poured by the Secretary of the British Humanist Association, the Orb shall be presented to the Archbishop by the Unknown Miner . . . a fanfare being sounded the Monarch shall present himself to the People at the West Door. Twelve Armature Winders, being Members of the Electrical Trades Union, shall then bring forth the Golden Bicycle of State . . .*

Meanwhile, there is still the Changing of the Guard. Do not be deceived. It is a good deal older than the tourist trade. It is not just flummery. It is powerful magic.

When a new Sovereign accedes to the throne, it isn't just announced from loudspeakers at street corners. Various gentlemen attired more like court cards than you would think possible (though sometimes spoiling the effect with horn-rimmed glasses; in my opinion Heralds with weak eyesight should be compelled to wear contact lenses) appear in places like the courtyard of the aforementioned St James's Palace and declare the thing in round periods:

> We, therefore, the Lords Spiritual and Temporal, Members of His Late Majesty's Most Honourable Privy Council, the Lord Mayor of London, together with other gentlemen of quality, with one heart and voice do publish and proclaim that the high and mighty Princess Elizabeth Alexandra Mary is now become our Sovereign Liege Lady Elizabeth the Second, by the Grace of God Queen of Great Britain and Northern Ireland, and of all her other realms and territories, Defender of the Faith. God Save The Queen.

Westminster Abbey

Very little is known about King Sebert. *Who?* King Sebert. But a great deal is known about the church which now occupies the site where he is said to have built the first one, in 616. The present Westminster Abbey was built as an enormous Romanesque church (the Benedictine abbey having been established in the 8th century) by Edward the Confessor, and this was consecrated in 1065, just in time for the Norman invasion, and in fact the English kings and queens have been crowned here, and many buried, since William the Conqueror (who was also, like Richard I, crowned at Winchester). Like most major churches it has undergone various stages of gothicisation, starting in 1245 and not ending, in fact, till the 18th century, since the two towers of the great west front are by Wren (1632–1723) and Hawksmoor (1661–1736).

> Mortality, behold and fear
> What a change of flesh is here!
> Think how many royal bones
> Sleep within these heaps of stones

wrote the Jacobean poet Beaumont, falling off somewhat in the last two lines. But you don't need much imagination to feel what is concentrated here over the centuries since Sebert (who later went back to paganism; lot of it about) on what was Thorney *Island* between the Thames and armlets of the fens now Chelsea and Battersea. As so often in French-influenced churches there is an enormous sense of height. The nave is actually 105 feet, nothing by the standards of the Pan-Am building or even such a curious post-war white elephant (doubtless making money for *somebody*) as the thing called Centre Point at the end of Tottenham Court Road. These things are relative. There is a point, a focus to this height, to this building, to these proportions; to the lovely building which replaced the original Lady Chapel, the Henry VII chapel, with its marvellous fan vaulting; to the equally marvellous triforium (the high bit, a gallery or arcade, above choir and nave arches and mingled with these architectural splendours though they are only a beginning if you are planning a real cathedral-hop in England—wait till you see Ely, or Durham!); to this unmistakable feeling of centrality. Here is the Tomb of the Unknown Warrior, at which some weep, some shudder, some pray, some

Westminster Abbey.

sneer, some manage a combination of all four; here (in the south transept) is the famous Poets' Corner (a uniquely English idea, but then we have a unique corpus of poetry); and it was here that the thrilling trebles of the boys from the adjacent Westminster School rang out at the Coronation. *Vivat, vivat, vivat!*

There are notices outside in the summer requesting people not to take ice-cream into the church, so be warned; three o'clock on a summer afternoon is not the best time to absorb all this. If you can't manage some nice sunny day in January, you can always try Holy Communion at 8.00 a.m., or, more reflectively and passively perhaps, Matins at 9.20. *They* don't all come quite so early.

We will come to the *City* of London, the original Roman, then Norman, now commercial heart of London, a mile or so down the Thames, in more detail after having a good look at the West End (a phrase of which I must here enlarge the narrow connotation of mere Mayfair to include Westminster, the huge South Bank complex facing it across the river, the Strand, theatreland, and in general the part where the *life* is). But it is logical at this point to balance Westminster Abbey with its secular counterpart at the centre of British history—

The Tower of London

It is more than a counterpart; it is, if you like, an *opposite*. One could go further than saying that Westminster Abbey stands for the spiritual and the Tower for the physical aspects of power. Better theologians than the writer of this book have pointed out that man mixes good and bad, he can be angel and devil. Now, it's perfectly possible to come away from a day at the Tower with nothing more than a recollection of the Yeomen of the Guard (whom you are more likely to see in their undress blue tunics than the full pike-carrying scarlet Tudor ceremonial splendour, and who take parties round with commentaries containing quite enough history for the half-day tourist, and do not spurn a little collection at the end), of the huge-steel-door-guarded, glass-protected dazzling splendour of the Crown Jewels. But for anyone with any sensitivity at all it must surely represent what might be called the unacceptable face of authority.

It really is haunted by screams of pain and spurts of blood and force and treachery. Obviously time has softened it. The great central fortress, the roughly square White Tower or Keep, standing alone on its island site in the middle of the 18-acre complex of towered walls, started by William the Conqueror and finished by Rufus, gives an overpowering impression of brute Norman strength for all that most of the windows were replaced with something more classical by (who else!) Christopher Wren—and for all that the highest part of it accessible to the tourist is the sudden marvellous thick-stone round-arched quiet of the perfect St John's Chapel, where those about to be made knights once kept a night-long vigil before the day of their honour; a custom which seems to have lapsed.

Of course the one legend everyone knows about is the murder by Richard III of young Edward V and his young brother Richard (Duke of York; Richard III was *Gloucester*, not that it is possible to remember such details unless (a) you have just seen the Shakespeare, (b) are a historian and/or (c) actually belong to the actual Society, with a secretary and committee and everything, which exists for the sole purpose of saying it's all lies, lies about Richard III, even though others say he did for Henry VI as well).

It was in the Wakefield Tower that Henry was found dead. There are a whole lot of Towers; the Middle, the Bell, the Lanthorn, the Salt, the Broad Arrow, the Constable, the Martin, the Brick, the Bowyer, the Flint, the Devereux, the Beauchamp, the Cradle, the Well, the Develin, the Wardrobe—and of course the Bloody.

It was in the Bloody that Sir Walter Raleigh, the inventor of Virginia (named after the Virgin Queen, who then arrested him for loving, let alone marrying, the lady-in-waiting Elizabeth Throckmorton), pirate, Spaniard-wrecker, poet, did something you don't usually associate with pirates, even poetical ones; he wrote a History of the World, of which let a Frenchman, Emile Legouis, be the critic: 'his shortcomings as a historian are redeemed by superb pages. About 1593 he had been suspected of sympathy for Marlowe's atheism, although he was, in point of fact, a deist with his own philosophy who ended his life absorbed in grave religious thought. In the work of this amateur there is something at once strange and passionate which compels attraction.'

King James I, who very much disliked this work if only because 'it is too saucy in censuring the acts of princes' and who thought it was one of the world's ten great puns to say he 'thought rawly of him' let him out of prison for an expedition (financed by Raleigh himself with what money he had left) to Guiana, which he was fairly sure would fail since he, James, let the Spaniards have all the details in advance. Then it was back to the Tower. James had got him now. On the morning they took him to be beheaded in Old Palace Yard, at Westminster, a servant noticed that his now white hair was not combed. 'Let them comb it that have it,' he said. 'Peter, dost thou know of any plaister to set a man's head on again when it is cut off?'

No wonder Orlando Gibbons (resounding Jacobethan name!) composed one of the noblest and gravest madrigals in the world, *What Is Our Life?*, to Raleigh words. And on the night before his death he wrote:

> Even such is time! who takes in trust
> Our youth, our joys, and all we have,
> And pays us but with earth and dust:
> Who in the dark and silent grave,
> When we have wandered all our ways,
> Shuts up the story of our days.
> But from that earth, that grave, that dust,
> The Lord shall raise me up I trust.

That's the sort of man you think about, in the Tower. Or St Thomas More, or (on the other side, so to speak; or could it be the *same* side?) Cranmer, Latimer, Ridley; not to mention the women: Anne Boleyn, Catherine Howard—and of course Lady Jane Grey.

Many prisoners left poems or signatures or rebuses scratched on the walls. But there is nothing by Lady Jane Grey, although she was 'an exceedingly accomplished scholar, was well versed in feminine arts and was of a gentle and happy disposition'. She had, however, the double misfortune of being the great-granddaughter of Henry VII and of having been compelled to marry Lord Guildford Dudley, fourth son of the Earl of Northumberland (formerly, in that confusing way they had, Warwick), a great promoter of the Protestant way of life. He persuaded Edward VI, before he died in 1553 at the age of fifteen, to 'devise' the throne to Lady Jane, his cousin.

She was queen for nine days. England believed (correctly as a matter of fact) that Mary, Henry VIII's daughter by, ah yes, Catherine of Aragon, had a

stronger claim to the throne. Lady Jane was, on 10 July of that year, pro-
claimed Queen Jane. On 19 July she was a prisoner in the Tower. On 12
February the next year she was beheaded. There is a plaque on the ground in
the pleasant bit of lawn outside the Chapel of St Peter ad Vincula where this
happened. She is buried in the Chapel. Before the high altar lie 'two dukes
between two queens, to wit, the Duke of Somerset and the Duke of Northumberland, between Queen Anne [Boleyn] and Queen Katharine, all
beheaded'.

'Bloody Mary', says everyone, and it's true, as the historian Sir George
Clark remarks, that the 'name of religious persecution has never been affixed
to any other episode in English history' (although it was no fun being a
Catholic in Elizabeth's reign either), but 'it was not due to cruelty on the part
of individuals such as Gardiner [her Chancellor] who died soon after it began,
or of Mary herself; but to a belief which was shared by rigorous thinkers on
the protestant side. Many of the bystanders valued their human instincts
above theology.'

They also valued a nice public hanging, drawing and quartering, as you
may see in innumerable woodcuts of them standing close-packed, all wearing
solemn hats, to watch. In fact the medieval sentence of hanging (till not
actually dead), drawing (cutting out the entrails and burning them in front of
your eyes, if you could still see) and quartering was pronounced in the 18th
century on the five Jacobite Lords captured in the 1715 rebellion, although
two were pardoned. The crowds who turned up to see the mere beheading of
the other three only saw two die, Lord Derwentwater and Lord Kenmure.
The third, Lord Nithsdale, had escaped a few hours earlier with the help of his
amazing wife.

This lady, having found there was so much snow that no coach was leaving
York, *rode* to London with her Welsh maid Evans. She got into a 'drawing-
room' held by George I and clung to his coat tails with her petition so tightly
that she was pulled across the room by him. When it was rejected she went to
the Tower with her friend Mrs Morgan, who was wearing a dress belonging
to Lady Nithsdale's landlady, Mrs Mills, over her own. Lady Nithsdale and
Mrs Morgan went to the prisoner's room and put the dress on him, then Mrs
Morgan was despatched as if to fetch Evans. Lady Nithsdale then called to
Mrs Mills, whom she had instructed to be crying, and 'took him into my
lord's chamber', then took her out *not* crying, and with a different hood, so
that when the Earl should come out, weeping into his hood (she had 'rouged
his face and cheeks, to conceal his beard which he had not had time to shave.
All this provision I had before left in the Tower') everybody would think *he*
was Mrs Mills, whom she first took out (not crying, remember) telling her
also to hurry up and get Evans, as this was the last night for trying her petition
again. Then she took the Earl out and delivered him to the faithful Evans and
Mr Mills, who got him away. Then, since she was supposed to have sent the
young lady on an errand, she went back through the guards, still complaining
loudly about Evans, and into her husband's room where 'I talked as if he had
been really present. I answered my own questions in my lord's voice, as
nearly as I could imitate it, and walked up and down as if we were conversing
together, till I thought they had time to clear themselves of the guards'.

The Earl got away to Europe disguised as a footman in the Venetian
Ambassador's suite, but she wasn't finished yet. She went up to retrieve vital
family papers to protect the estate for her *son*, and by the time the authorities
at Dumfries were on to her she had dug them up and got away again. She and
her husband (and, one likes to think, the faithful Evans) lived happily for

many years in Rome . . .

History, history. I said to myself a thousand words back that I would just describe the Tower, and here we've had these stories already. But then the Tower *is* stories. There are more stories, grim, or less frequently just exciting, like that of Lady Nithsdale, or of 'Colonel' Blood who dropped the Crown in the gutter during the struggle in which he nearly got away with the Crown Jewels (he did, mysteriously, get away not only with his life but a pension of £500 a year and estates in Ireland from Charles II. He is said to have died a Quaker. Even more mysterious).

There are marvellous displays of armour, and if you had the time you could get a pretty comprehensive knowledge from the explanatory cards in the show cases of how it developed (and perhaps be struck by the curious affinity between armour and today's space-suits), and then go on to firearms, and get clear in your mind the difference between flintlock and matchlock—and perhaps be struck by the artistic fantasy which often decorated weapons of death: human figures, animals or motifs from nature incorporated into the mechanisms in a way you simply don't get with the Armalite or the Kalashnikov.

You might even see the Yeoman Ravenmaster attending to the surprisingly large-looking black birds of which legend says that the Tower will never fall while they are there. And you will find it odd to come out from these buildings so radio-active with history that the most philistine can feel it, into the rather tatty surroundings of souvenir shops selling plastic London policemen, guardsman gonks, Winston Churchill ashtrays and the rest of the junk. But even before you get to the roaring traffic passing along the north bank of a Thames from which the dock and shipping element is ebbing relentlessly down-river, away from the city, you find plenty of reminders that you are in unique, ancient, twentieth-century London. The last time I was there there was a crowd of jeering City workers, during their lunch break, surrounding an earnest young Canadian in jeans on a soap-box at Tower Hill, the City's free-speech answer to the better-known Hyde Park Corner. 'What does a man want most out of life?' he demanded. 'A good f—', said the crowd wit. 'We cannot live by bread alone . . .' (drowned by equally witty retorts). In short, back from history, fixed for ever, into modern life, very unfixed indeed.

Just across the road you can see a confident, turn-of-the-century building decorated with various bearded, trident-holding male, or classically female, marine figures decorating its cornices the way those saints decorate the skyline of St Peter's in Rome. It was the home of the **Port of London Authority**, in the old pre-container, pre-Rotterdam, pre-strike days when London *was* a port. Symbolically, it is now occupied by a large insurance firm, and the PLA now occupies a less grand building a little downstream.

Adjoining it, however, is the home of a very much older institution, **Trinity House**, which has been the body regulating pilotage since a charter of 1514. Today it still is, and is also responsible for 92 lighthouses, reaching to Gibraltar, and some 700 buoys and other seamarks. One of Winston Churchill's favourite uniforms (which is saying something) was that of the Elder Brethren of Trinity House. It seems appropriate that on a small garden site, with a few benches, there should be a series of curved walls and steps with bronze tablets containing thousands upon thousands of names of merchant seamen lost in two world wars. Some of them, like Zablonski, Cristoforides, Bhattacharjee, would perhaps surprise the men of 1514 . . .

Nodal Points

It is now even more pages since I said we would pay this brief, *preliminary* visit to the City, the secular Tower counterbalancing the spiritual Westminster Abbey. The fact that I now have to tear myself away from describing the famous church of All-Hallows-by-the-Tower, with its hanging model ships, its activity as a London brass rubbing centre, its lunchtime concerts, is simply another example of London's extraordinary capacity for leading you off on another trail, revealing another treasure (especially perhaps, in the City, even though post-war rebuilding has demolished a lot of Dickensian out of-the-way corners) the moment you step a few yards out of your way. All great cities, whatever they look like on a street map, could be psychologically better represented by what I shall have to describe as an interest map. This would look like a lot of spiders' webs, not the same size or shape, but each having a nodal point, a centre. It is a good way to get to know a city, to have these points in mind. It's not simply a matter of orientating yourself geographically on the map, although of course that's part of it. It's a matter of knowing where the focal points are, so that you can skip the boring bits . . .

I was about to give, as an example of a boring bit, or at any rate a bit not worth exploring if you have to do London in a day, or even a week, the oblong section, almost entirely inhabited by very expensive medical specialists and their now mainly Arab patients, which lies between Great Portland Street, Marylebone Road, Marylebone High Street (*it's* not boring, it is a fascinating street with some very good specialist shops selling everything from authentic Nazi helmets to old books and Rolls-Royces, and the magnificent Wallace Collection with Frans Hals's *Laughing Cavalier* is just off it; I'm speaking of the area inside this oblong) and Wigmore Street (very good small concert hall there, you might just catch the best guitarist in the world, or something, before the world knows this) and its continuation Cavendish Street which runs into Great Portland Street, with which we started some way back. (A complicated paragraph, but worth the effort, like London itself.)

And then I thought of Wimpole Street, which runs right across this area, and certainly wouldn't be boring for anyone interested in Mrs Browning, née Elizabeth Barrett, or for anyone who knows the poem by Betjeman called *Devonshire Street W.1.*:

> The heavy mahogany door with its wrought-iron screen
> Shuts. And the sound is rich, sympathetic, discreet.
> The sun still shines on this eighteenth-century scene
> With Edwardian faience adornments—Devonshire Street.
>
> No hope. And the X-ray photographs under his arm
> Confirm the message. His wife stands timidly by.
> The opposite brick-built house looks lofty and calm
> Its chimneys steady against a mackerel sky.
>
> No hope. And the iron knob of this palisade
> So cold to the touch, is luckier now than he . . .

And I thought even more of the Heart-lifting Door-Knobs. I'm sorry if that sounds like the title of a whimsical mystical detective story, by somebody like G. K. Chesterton or (more likely) Lord Dunsany, The Case of the

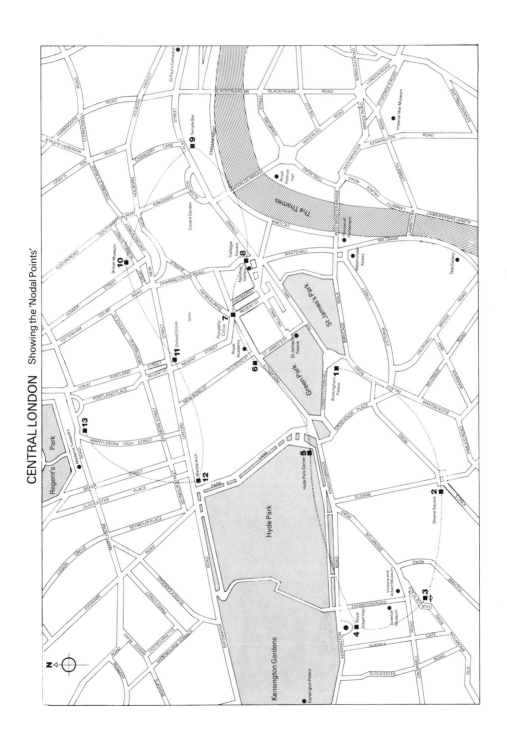

CENTRAL LONDON   Showing the 'Nodal Points'

Heart-lifting Door-knobs. But there it is. I am never, but never, on foot in Cavendish Square, passing the Convent which commissioned a Madonna and Child from Epstein, a great bronze on the wall noticed by about one per cent of the passers-by, without going to look at the enchanting door-knobs, cherubs, full of joy and life and innocence and energy. Epstein, a Jew of course, threw these in as a gift to the nuns. And they certainly lift *my* heart. Boring, indeed! You see what I mean about London surprising you the moment you step a few yards out of the way.

Do not, however, in the unlikely event of being able to get your car into the park underneath Cavendish Square, think you will have much change out of £3 for the fee if you're away for even a modest bit of shopping.

Buckingham Palace

But to get back to these nodal points. Clearly the most nodal of the lot is the one where we started. As we have seen, whenever there is a real intensification of national feeling, whether joyful or ominous, Buckingham Palace is an instinctive, natural focus. You can't actually go into Buckingham Palace or even its gardens, unless you have been a midwife or a mayor or a trade union official for thirty-five years and get an invitation to one of the famous summer garden parties, with about four thousand other people. But you can get into the adjoining **Royal Mews** and see the legendary royal and state coaches and equipage; a very good 15p worth (5p for children). Mind you, it's only 2 to 4 p.m. on Wednesdays and Thursdays, and not even then during Ascot Week in June, for obvious reasons. Well, not obvious if you don't know about Royal Ascot, which is the grandest and most social race meeting in England, at which the Queen drives down the course in an open carriage.

Adjoining, and opening much more (including Sunday afternoons, in fact only closed on Mondays) in the **Queen's Gallery**, which has a selection, periodically changed, from the fabulous store of royal pictures.

Even if there is only a lot of traffic swirling about you, and not the Changing of the Guard crowds, there is a very nodal feeling about the **Queen Victoria Memorial**, 2,300 tons of Carrara marble; round the Old Queen there are Victory, Courage and Constancy, with Justice on the north, Truth on the south and Motherhood on the west. The broad, reddish stone processional way, the Mall, points straight up to Admiralty Arch and Trafalgar Square beyond. But for the moment, assuming that you are holding a map correctly facing north, with the Thames flowing eastwards from Chelsea in the bottom left-hand corner, turning north at Vauxhall, right and east again, after passing Westminster, as it curves under Hungerford (pedestrian, leading to Charing Cross) and Waterloo Bridges, let us look south and west from Buckingham Palace. London does not actually name its streets after compass points as New York does, but you don't really get the feel of London until expressions like 'West End', 'East End' or 'South Bank' actually mean something to you.

Still within range of Nodal Point 1, Buckingham Palace, is **Victoria Street**. If you walk through to it you will pass through a curious *mélange* of still *quite* residential streets, with the odd extremely elegant pub, flower baskets outside hanging above pavement tables in the summer, a huge office block alleged to be known to Prince Philip as Paris Match Tower, since the photographers of that enterprising French magazine, forever seeking out British Royal Family stories (usually wrong; I remember one about a young man squiring Princess Alexandra, in which they said his ancestors had fought at 'la bataille de Flobben' and that she asked him in with the traditional English invitation 'have a night cup, old chap') use its roof for their telephoto snooping into the gardens of Buckingham Palace. But the thing to see in, or just off Victoria Street, is **Westminster Cathedral**, the headquarters of the Roman Catholic church in Britain.

It is a fine, gloomy Byzantine building, large areas of its noble brick interior not yet covered with the mosaics which, if they ever are *all* finished, will make it look more like a millionaire's bathroom. At the moment it is just right. There are some characteristically clean-lined Stations of the Cross carved by the remarkable Eric Gill, sculptor, anti-big-business Catholic apologist; he maintained that Francis Bentley's design for the Cathedral, though a masterpiece, did not result in a *sacred* building because the men who actually built it were wage-slaves under the capitalist system. He was not terribly cared for by a lot of the clergy, being an artist, not to mention a world-famous typographer (the type-face called Gill Sans was his creation). They are marvellous Stations. There is a fine musical tradition, in some danger now after Vatican II. The 270-foot tower is still an excellent place for a helicopter's-eye view of central London. Recent development has meant the opening-up of a piazza, so that the cathedral, originally hidden among Victorian mansion flats, can now be seen end-on from Victoria Street.

This same redevelopment has meant the replacement of the many old head offices of civil engineering firms (it was here that I once saw the magnificently polished brass name-plate of a firm called Activated Sludge Ltd) by the usual glass cubes. But the other glory of Victoria Street, the **Army and Navy Stores**, is still very much there. This famous old shop has, in fact, been rebuilt and now has a very strong fashion side aimed at the girls who work in those cubes, as well as the usual furniture and the rest of the range of a modern department store (very good book department too). But something of the old tradition lingers; this was the shop where, in the days of the British Empire, people going off to serve in it went to buy their tropical kit, their camp beds, solar topees, elephant guns, canvas baths and the rest of it. Readers of Evelyn Waugh's delicious novel *Scoop* will remember William Boot, the nature correspondent sent in error to cover the Abyssinian War, thinking vaguely that he might need some cleft sticks for sending secret messages, and being told at the Army and Navy Stores that they could cleave some for him.

Sloane Square

It is only a few hundred yards down Victoria Street to Parliament Square and what we must call Nodal Point Zero, Westminster itself. Instead, let us move south-west, along the boring part of **King's Road** through boring Belgravia, just a lot of big white rich houses, Rolls-Royces and the kind of people who *have* Rolls-Royces, to Nodal Point 2, Sloane Square, where the King's Road suddenly gets very interesting indeed.

At one corner, the Royal Court Theatre, which now looks back with some nostalgia to the days when John Osborne Looked Back In Anger and, some say, revolutionised the British threatre. Diagonally opposite, the excellent department store of Peter Jones, like some definitive statement about ordinary bourgeois up-to-date department-store shopping amid the wild semi-bazaars, half trash and half genuine bargains—no, perhaps a *tenth* genuine bargains, a lot of them are on the look-out for you in King's Road—of the trendy young. Actually the best bargain is King's Road·itself. At no time could a walk down it ever be described as dull.

At the Sloane Street end you need only turn off and walk a few yards in the direction of the Thames (which the King's Road approaches diagonally till at its farther end you actually come to within a few yards of it, to find a colony of houseboats and a bit known appropriately as World's End) to step into another world; a change from the pop and bustle and trendiness of King's Road to the classical calm of the 18th, indeed the 17th century; for **Chelsea Royal Hospital**, that elegant home for old soldiers with their famous and distinctive uniform, was opened in 1694. It is an island of quiet in spacious gardens which face the equal repose of the equally historically resonant-sounding Ranelagh Gardens (oh, the great, long-vanished rotunda holding 6,000 people, the promenades, the musick of Handel, the visits by Johnson, Reynolds, Goldsmith, Walpole . . .). These are the south grounds of the Royal Hospital, offering a refreshing sight at any time, but especially in early summer when the famous Flower Show is on (and it's no good trying to get in on the first day unless you Know Somebody) at once the joy and the despair of all gardeners (which is to say pretty well all Englishmen at heart—or, once you get out of London and move across the country, obviously all Englishmen in *fact*).

Go north up Flood Street and you are still only in the middle of the interesting part of King's Road, in fact Chelsea Town Hall is on the corner. This is, among other things, the place where the Chelsea Opera Group have a habit of discovering and promoting works which no one has ever heard of before the rest of the world recognises them as masterpieces. I'm not speaking of far-out gong-and-cymbal pseudo-Balinese pieces or four-hour, four-orchestra-and-electronic-workshop marathons, but of works like *The Trojans* of Berlioz. *Music*.

South Kensington

About half a mile north of here is Nodal Point 3, which we might as well make South Kensington tube station. There are some interesting antique, special-book, stamp and other speciality shops in the immediate vicinity. But what this is really a nodal point for is the most amazing and comprehensive collection of museums in the world. When you come out of the station and walk the short distance up Cromwell Place to Cromwell Road (itself merely a dismal thoroughfare choked with traffic impatient to get to the M4 or Heathrow, the great western exit of London) your eye is met by nothing but museums.

And they are the kind of museums that are very good for us in these dismal and pessimistic days, exuding as they do the inexhaustible Victorian faith in work, science, art, progress, the romance of the past and the perfectibility of the future. The very road at the junction of which with Cromwell Road stands the huge rambling pile of the **Victoria and Albert Museum** (never mentioned in speech as anything but 'the V and A') gives you the sketch straight away; for it is actually called Exhibition Road. The nucleus of the V and A was in fact a selection of objects bought for £5,000 for the Great Exhibition of 1851 which, illustrating different styles, was to be devoted to 'the application of fine art to the objects of utility and the improvement of the public taste in design'.

It would be perfectly possible to spend your whole life in the V and A. I myself once went in intending to look at the splendid collection of Constables they have there and I spent the whole afternoon on the ground floor, never in fact very far from the entrance, looking at netsuke, tiny little Oriental joke carvings of people and animals doing everything conceivable. I'd only just got from them to a tremendous array of Spanish furniture when to my astonishment the bell went for closing time. There's a wonderful Indian section (needless to say!), in fact it's very strong on Oriental art altogether, not to mention post-classical sculpture, British water-colours and miniatures. And the famous Raphael Cartoons. And Ceramics. And Metalwork. And Woodwork. (It all sounds like a night-school syllabus, but just you see some of those altar-pieces!) And Prints and Drawings . . .

The V and A is only an outpost of this vast assemblage, like a colossal 3D encyclopaedia, like a succession of grammar schools for giants, and before we consider them briefly, just a few yards further into London, where the Cromwell Road becomes Brompton Road, there is, appropriately, just about the most un-Cromwellian, flamboyant, building you could imagine—**Brompton Oratory**, chief church of the Counter-Reformation order introduced to England by Cardinal Newman, of whom there is a statue in the forecourt. Its strong musical tradition has enabled it to survive the sub-Cromwellian liturgical depredations of the otherwise admirable Vatican II better than most; a young friend of mine was married there recently with a Latin mass, and Haydn with full choir and orchestra.

To get back to the museums. The **Science Museum**, to which every parent in the south of England worth his (or more usually her) salt has taken a child or children at half-term, contains everything from marvellous old beam steam engines and pristine Puffing Billys to space capsules and bits of moon rock—and a special children's gallery. The Natural History Museum has everything from unbelievable birds and insects and models of vanished or exotic landscapes to (of course) reconstructed dinosaurs.

And what non-geologist would have thought a **Geological Museum** could be interesting? Hear E. V. Lucas on the subject:

> One has naturally come to suppose that anything in a museum that is beautiful or gloriously coloured must come from a foreign land. That is the general rule. But here are delicate quartzes and prismatic stones, transparent or opaque, all in their own way mysteriously beautiful, whether purple fluorites or agates or stilbites, and all English: all found in our own unromantic country. Ordinarily, it is understood, beauty and romance begin at Dieppe, but here it is proved that the visitor to Matlock, for instance, if he only knew it, has his feet just above exquisite treasure. Matlock [it is in Derbyshire, a great pot-holing centre, and they also mine the beautiful semi-precious stone called Blue John there] seems to be builded upon subterranean loveliness . . . and . . . by means of pins' heads of varying sizes, to the scale of one foot to a million miles (nothing more difficult to realise than that) and a gilt globe the size of a football at the far end of a room, the visitor is playfully put in possession of a fit of cosmic dizziness, and reminded more forcibly than usual that this planet on which we fret our little lives away for seventy years or so is not precisely all.

When E. V. Lucas wrote that he was referring to a geological museum in Jermyn Street; a comparatively small affair. Today the Geological Museum in Exhibition Road is 'the largest exhibition on basic earth science in the world, telling the 5,000-million-year history of our planet'.

It is a natural transition from here, via the Imperial College of Science, a very high-powered collection of boffins indeed and Britain's not entirely inaudible reply to the Massachusetts Institute of Technology, to our Nodal Point 4—

The Albert Hall

(Actually it is the *Royal* Albert Hall, like its neighbours the Royal Geographical Society on one side, and the Royal College of Organists and the Royal College of Music and the new Royal College of Art on the other—in fact the whole outfit is in the Royal Borough of Kensington; but no one ever *says* anything but 'the Albert Hall' except BBC men announcing programmes).

There has always been a mysterious connection between science and music. Borodin got his doctorate for a thesis on 'The Analogy of Arsenical with Phosphoric Acid'. The English bass John Shirley-Quirk used to teach chemistry. All physicists can play the flute. It was two splendid madmen from the Imperial College of Science who conceived the idea of '*Messiah* from Scratch' in which anyone who can play or sing in this mighty work just comes along and they all perform it, after about an hour's rehearsal. Indeed I once myself presented a BBC TV programme about this in the Albert Hall, in which some 4,000 of us (there were certainly well over 2,000 sopranos) performed it to an understandably embarrassed-looking audience of about 500.

Most people know the old joke about the Albert Hall being the only place where the works of British composers get a second performance—the echo. There was indeed a long period—in fact from the opening in 1871 till after World War II—when there were many seats in it where no counterpoint or musical finesse could be appreciated at all because of the ultra-reverberant acoustics. The famous 'flying saucers' now su⌐ pended from the roof of this vast, 10,000-capacity circular hall have achieved a near-miracle. The building which has heard Caruso and Melba, not to mention Gladstone and Churchill or the stage grunts of all-in wrestlers or the thwack of a serve by Bjorn Borg, is now fitting acoustically, as well as traditionally since the wartime destruction of the Queen's Hall, to serve as the home of the greatest, cheapest and longest-running music festival in the world, the famous **Promenade Concerts**.

Any season of the Proms, a non-stop concert series beginning in mid-July and ending in September, would serve as a basic education in music. In their great, formative inter-war years, the Proms followed a definite pattern. A verse in the magazine *Musical Opinion* by someone using the *nom-de-plume* 'Diogenes the Younger' encapsulated this nicely:

> The week begins with Wagner's frenzy:
> Perchance the Overture *Rienzi*.
> Anon we trace the subtle line
> Of Siegfried's *Journey to the Rhine*;
> Some tenor earns a great ovation
> For singing *Lohengrin's Narration*.
>
> On Tuesday night our taste we widen
> With Mozart and the genial Haydn.
> Now everybody's blythe and matey,
> We're sure to have *Voi che sapete*;
> Or (to dispel all notions tragic)
> An aria from the *Flute* that's *Magic* . . .

Doggerel, of course. But the words *blythe and matey* in the second verse (even though we should spell *blythe* with an *i* now), indeed the whole thing, does convey the unique club atmosphere of the Proms. But not an exclusive club, anyone can join. It's just that somehow the Proms are more than just

The Royal Albert Hall, photographed from the Albert Memorial.

concerts, isolated cultural events slipping into the past of your life even as you are coming out of the building. Their scope has now widened; several orchestras take part, usually with visiting ones also, of the stature of, say, the Chicago Symphony, and there are events in other venues—a Monteverdi Vespers in Westminster Cathedral, Stockhausen in the Roundhouse (a converted Victorian train shed in Camden Town which now houses anything from surrealist French circus to pop shows). But the hard-core Prommers, (the ones who queue for hours or even camp out overnight) are the nucleus of a young and knowledgeable audience, the noisiest in the world, throwing streamers, bursting balloons, shouting orchestrated wisecracks to the tuning-up orchestra before the music begins—and, miraculously, the most deeply, silently attentive and responsive in the world once it begins. Lifelong friendships, marriages have originated in Prom queues. On the famous Last Night (not a chance of getting in *there* unless you're lucky in the ballot) some of them, known as Prince Albert's Flying Circus (they have their own magazine too) perform a—well, an entertainment on the steps behind the hall. One year it was called *Die Meistersinger von Kensington*.

The Albert Hall is also, of course, the Nodal Point for *the* great breathing-space of London, **Hyde Park**, and the logical entry into this from the Albert Hall would be via the **Albert Memorial**, which has survived a great deal of ridicule to emerge—well, one cannot say as a great work of art; rather an amazing example of what you get when giants have fantasies. The Victorians *were* giants.

You can't ignore the Albert Memorial. It has a lot of figures besides the seated, 15-foot Prince Consort himself, reading what many have taken to be the Bible but is in fact a catalogue of the Great Exhibition. There are 178 figures altogether, ranging from what appear to be angels in tin hats to Faith, Hope, Charity, Astronomy, Chemistry, Geometry, Rhetoric, Medicine . . . four tableaux with a bull representing Europe, a camel Africa, a bison America, an elephant Asia . . . Physiology with an infant on her left arm, 'the highest and most perfect of physiological forms', while her finger points to a microscope 'for the investigation of the minuter forms of animal and vegetable organisms'. Sir George Gilbert Scott, the designer, said: 'my idea in designing the Memorial was to erect a kind of ciborium to protect a statue of the Prince'.

You are now facing the largest green space in London. As a matter of fact if you started at the north-western corner of **Kensington Gardens**, the Bayswater corner, you could walk nearly 2½ miles on grass (if you discount crossing the road at the south-eastern Hyde Park Corner and subsequently The Mall) through **Green Park** and **St James's Park** to Parliament Square and practically the Thames at Westminster. And marvellously rural, tree-shaded, flower-scented and bird-loud a lot of it would be.

In Kensington Gardens, a royal palace with orangery and sunken garden; the Round Pond where you may see boys up to 80 years old with model boats; a wild richness of crocuses in the formal gardens nearer the Albert Memorial, followed by seasonal splendours up to chrysanthemum time. It is actually officially Hyde Park on the other side of the bisecting road which crosses the Serpentine, in summer a mass of near-naked bodies at the Lido, and overlooked by a perfectly delicious star-shaped restaurant and bar, like something left over from a carefree millionaire's party.

Whether you row or swim or just eat and drink here, you are now in one of the best bits of London for—well, for just *being*, not actually pursuing some tourist 'must'. Once you are in the thick of London there aren't many places where you can sit down (though it's better than some capital cities, there are at least seats in places like Berkeley or Grosvenor Squares and indeed, nowadays, down Oxford Street). There you are on this well-landscaped Middlesex country estate (on the right days you can even see sheep-dog trials) but the immense sound of a great city is all round you, you can absorb a curious metropolitan excitement simply from the air. And it is always possible that while you are thinking what to do or where to go next some marvellously unexpected sight or sound could delight you: a troop of the Household Cavalry jingling back to nearby Wellington Barracks, or the civilian riders in Rotten Row (corruption of *route du roi*, as everyone says, although there's always someone with another explanation, such as *rattan-reigh*, a Celtic word meaning a good mountain path. *Mountain?* But you know what philologists are), or the amazing sudden film-set glory (*but it's real*) of the Honourable Artillery Company dashing on with highly-polished and doubtless outmoded guns, wheeling into position, number one kneeling down or whatever it is, and firing off tremendous salutes (Fire! Bang! Smoke!) for some official reason like the birth of a royal infant or the visit of someone really *important* (most routine salutes are fired from the Tower Wharf); or music from a bandstand surrounded by deck-chairs.

You are most likely, from this area, to feel yourself moving eastward (the Albert Hall was the westernmost of our nodal points) to Nodal Point 5—

Hyde Park Corner

In terms of traffic this is the nearest thing London has to Paris's Place de la Concorde; all the lorries from the north of England trying to get to Dover avoiding the City, all the people from the west of England trying to get into London and vice versa, engaged in a fearful each-man-for-himself maelstrom round the Artillery Monument on its island site.

Unless you are actually staying at the Hilton or the Dorchester or Grosvenor House or the Inn on the Park there's not much point in actually walking northwards up **Park Lane**, unless it's to get to another nodal point, Marble Arch (we'll come to that later). *Spring in Park Lane* was a romantic film title, but all it means now is the smell of exhaust fumes and noise, even though in spring you can actually see lots of crocuses across the road. But there's scarcely one shop window the whole length of it; just ex-front-gardens covered over with crazy paving and reserved for Rolls-Royces. Park Lane reminds you what the word 'exclusive' means: it excludes you.

At Hyde Park Corner you can find No. 2 in the list of London's Most Concentrated, Intimate, Least-visited Worthwhile Museums (No. 1 is the Soane Museum, see p. 51). This is **Apsley House**, where the Duke of Wellington lived, behind bullet-proof shutters, as opposition to the Reform Bill crystallised round him. The lovely house, built from designs by Robert Adam and faced with Bath stone by Wyatt, is full of pictures, plate, china and memorabilia of the man who not only saved Europe from the first dictator of them all (and the inventor of conscription), but said, on seeing the first Reformed Parliament, 'I never saw so many shocking bad hats in my life'. Oh, and when they asked him who should be put in charge of the expedition to Burma he said instantly 'Lord Combermere', and when they said 'but we have always understood your Grace thought Lord Combermere a fool', he replied 'So he is, and a damned fool; but he can take Rangoon'. What a man!

Still, for every visitor who thinks of Hyde Park Corner as the home of the Duke of Wellington there will be twenty who think of it as the start of

Knightsbridge, leading down to one of London's classic shopping areas. As you go down to Harvey Nichols, an up-market fashion and household store on the corner with Sloane Street, you will be faced with the terrrible decision whether to turn left and go down Sloane Street; Bally Shoes, Truslove and Hanson Books, Bendicks, one of those chocolate and confectionery shops where they pick out the hand-made pieces you want with tongs, Jaeger, Laura Ashley, Casa Pupo interior decoration, a splendid place called the Jewel House full of crystalline minerals, the surely not overcrowded Iran Information and Tourist Centre, *two* Vidal Sassoons—the man seems to be everywhere, there's another one in Brompton road—and many other tempters right on down to the General Trading Company where you are practically back at Nodal Point 2 (Sloane Square) . . . or should you go straight on down Brompton Road? Very jolly little Brompton Arcade on your left, almost immediately opposite the Scotch House, full of soft wools and tartans. Shops shops shops shops, till you come to the greatest of them all, the largest department store in Europe, Harrods.

Harrods is in a way commerce's answer to the V and A (at Nodal Point 3 just down the road, if you remember. I *said* they would overlap). They have 240 departments, including a magnificent Art Nouveau Food Hall, full of amusing tile designs. You couldn't call anything so magnificent as this a mere Department, it is a Food *Hall*, where you can buy not only quite ordinary good meat for the weekend joint but caviare, and chocolate-coated ants, and practically anything you can think of.

Pianos, Persian carpets, diamonds, little wooden things for the kitchen . . . to come out of Harrods without buying anything at all is like coming out of St Peter's, Rome, without saying a prayer, and is probably done by about the same proportion of either crowd.

There used to be a legend that you could buy aircraft at Harrods. They get a bit sniffy when you ring them up about this kind of thing. ('We don't sell aircraft, but it doesn't matter what people ask us for, we can always help them to get it. But we'd like to check what you print about us . . .'). Well, sorry, Harrods, no time for that, got to get this book out, but I've been round, several times, like everyone else, and this is all true. Perhaps the horns have been drawn in a tiny bit since the aircraft days (if such there were). Certainly there used to be more than a pets department, it was a *zoo*, but now they only sell dogs, cats and fish. Their motto is *omnibus ubique* which means 'for everybody, everywhere', and they seem to like to paraphrase this, in terms of what they sell rather than to whom they sell it, as 'everything from a pin to an elephant'. Curious, really. You couldn't get one ordinary pin or one elephant at Harrods. But you could pretty well anything else. To paraphrase Dr Johnson, the man who is tired of Harrods is tired of London. Harrods is Shopping as Theatre.

Even nearer to Nodal Point 4, just past Harrods in Brompton Road, there is a turning to the left called Beauchamp Place, like a kind of open-air arcade, since every one of the pretty Regency houses has been turned into a shop; antiques (and two of them sell chimney-breasts), model horses, jewellery, fashion, doll's house furniture, a shop called Reject China, Scandinavian country furniture, British-only crafts from a shop aptly name Boadicea; and of course those shoes, two suppliers being Gamba and the equally aptly named Shoosissima.

Piccadilly

If you go the other way from Hyde Park Corner towards Nodal Point 6 you

St. James's Park.

will of course be going down (or more strictly speaking, up) Piccadilly to Nodal Point 7, Piccadilly Circus. For the English this was for many years the centre of the universe, definitely Nodal Point 1. In a mad sort of way it still *is* the centre of the social, and nowadays even more the tourist life of London. But it is perhaps better to approach it for the first time by coming down Piccadilly itself, which still retains *some* of the metropolitan chic of old. It is certainly better to approach it this way than from **Leicester Square**, which the literary gentleman Cyril Connolly at least thirty years ago described as the place where the village idiot is to be found, rather than the village, and which pedestrianisation has only made even more vulgar.

As you come eastwards down Piccadilly, then, you are, as you leave Hyde Park Corner behind you, in the part most likely to remind you of (or, I'm prepared to bet in the case of 93.47% of you, dear readers, to cause you to discover for the first time, otherwise what's the *point* of researching for yet another book, eh?) the origin of the word *Piccadilly*. 'Piccadill', says the *Oxford English Dictionary*, '1607, the seueral diuisions or peeces fastened together about the brimme of the collar of a doublet, app. repr. a Spanish *picadillo*, dim of *picado* pricked, pierced, slashed. Hence the name of the street called Piccadilly . . .'

I like that 'hence'. Some say it's because a lot of roads met at the Circus, like those peeces and diuisions of the collar, some say there was a 17th-century tailor there whose piccadills gave the road its name. Whatever the reason, the name and the road have been at the centre of things for a long time, and you get the sense of it as you go down this shopless western end. On your left rather secret and grand façades, some of them clubs like the Army and Navy, known as the In and Out because it has a drive-in, no doubt in these days worth about £1,000 a square foot, bearing these words. On your right, the widening expanse of **Green Park**, separated by railings which seem to bear a permanent outdoor art exhibition which ranges from artists prepared to draw you on the spot, galleons etched on copper, very literal seascape, animal and flower paintings, to the odd one worth buying.

Then buildings on both sides. On your right the Ritz, still a secure haven of curiously comforting Thirties-type luxury. Below and behind it, but well worth seeking out (and sacred for ever to me as the place where I first met James Thurber) is another park-edge hotel, the Stafford Court. A little way down Dover Street on your left is Brown's Hotel, a creditable version of a comfortable English country house right in the middle of London, much loved by certain Americans, including the late S. J. Perelman. On your right **St James's Street**, leading down to Pall Mall and the Mall, and really only of interest either to professional insiders, the famous Clubmen of famous (and of course unlabelled) Clubs who would all, in their hearts, like to follow the example of the Duke who sat in the bow window because he liked to 'see the damned people getting wet' or professional outsiders, i.e. tourists, who will find in the HQ of the British Tourist Authority a very helpful staff (and a mass of free leaflets and paid-for brochures).

You are in airline office and car showroom country now, and it is sad to write that Jackson's, a marvellous gourmet grocer's and wine merchant's shop which one was somehow glad to know was *there* even if one could never afford it, has closed; but its even more famous neighbour, Fortnum and Mason ('Purveyors of Food to the Royal Family') are still there, closely followed by the middlebrows'-delight bookshop of Hatchards. Just before you get there, however, there are three elegant little **arcades**. The slightly more pop ones, Piccadilly and Princes Arcades, are on your right. On your left it is the elegant Burlington Arcade, lined on both sides with beautiful little speciality shops, and patrolled by its own beadles (ex-soldiers of the 10th Hussars).

Burlington—now we come to the great Piccadilly name. Burlington House is the home of the **Royal Academy of Art**, and it is one of the few remaining institutions of this kind in the world that have somehow managed to avoid some at least of the intellectuals' scorn at the very word *academy*. Its primary treasure is the priceless Michelangelo Tondo (simply Italian for 'round' since it is in fact a circular bas-relief of the Madonna and Child, one of those marvellous works where you seem almost to be privileged to observe its creation, as you look at the chisel marks still plainly visible). But it has, in its long history since its foundation by Sir Joshua Reynolds in 1768, acquired many masterpieces if only through the fact that anyone elected a Royal Academician (RA) presents one of his paintings. So there are Constable's *Leaping Horse*, and *Boat Passing a Lock*, and Reynolds's *George III*, and many others. The Academy still maintains its tradition of free art classes (it was here that Constable learnt the basics of life drawing). Its annual Summer Show of new paintings though not the immense social occasion it once was (and all the better for *that*), somehow manages to be up-to-date without being far out, no mean achievement. Its current President, Sir Hugh Casson, an architect by profession, recently said in a television interview that some avant-garde artists 'climb above the snowline, then in the end they reach the peak, and there's nobody to talk to except other artists that they shout to on other peaks'. Its Loan Exhibitions, arranged usually round a country or a period or a school, are of the kind to draw visitors not only from Britain but from other countries.

Above all, entrance to it (though not to specific exhibitions) is *free. All* public museums in Britain are free. It is a great glory. Admirable though the Royal Academy is, it is absurd to be mentioning it before the amazing, all-embracing riches of the **National Gallery** in Trafalgar Square (Nodal Point 8, some pages before we get there). In the last three months of Mr Heath's government there *was* an entry charge, since heaven knows they don't make a profit. But there was a terrible outcry, in which I am proud to have taken a part. In fact it was fairly certainly the only time I am likely to be quoted in Hansard, the official parliamentary record, when a bit of the following verse which I wrote in *The Sunday Times* was quoted in the debate:

LINES WRITTEN IN DESPONDENCY IN TRAFALGAR SQUARE
Through portico-pillars, up stately stone steps ascending,
Harmless-for-once humanity smiles,
Admiring, inspired, untiring at vistas unending
Of modes and madonnas, of statues and styles,
Of dreams and dimensions, angelical lineaments captured,
Severe Sienese with a stiffness of stuff,
Gabriel-gaudium, wonder of wings to a virgin enraptured,
Velvet or vestment, a veil or a ruff
Framing ferocious or foxified, water-eyed fellows,
Eyes of the miser, the loser, the proud,
Lances and lines of perspective-exultant Uccellos. . . .

Museums, so magic and marvellous, making us wonder
Daily in dalliance with real and ideal,
What is this mumble and marching, this threat as of thunder?
Who dares to say *You shall not feel*
Unless you pay?

> O God, a dreadful army comes
> Of foopish hardhats, po-faced bowlered bums
> Whose mealy minds, whose souls of dust and ash
> Chafe for the chance of turning art to cash.

The word *foopish* is not a misprint. I made it up. *Foopish*.

If we actually make the intersection of St James's Street with Piccadilly our Nodal Point 6, it just about rates this because if shortly after it we turn left, just *before* Burlington Arcade and the Royal Academy, we shall be in **Old Bond Street**, and eventually **New Bond Street**. This, again, is not the ultra-chic luxury-only shopping street it once was, although it is still pretty smart. There is *another* Vidal Sassoon in New Bond Street, but probably its greatest distinction nowadays is in the art field. Apart from **Sotheby's**—or to give them their full modern global name, Sotheby Parke Bernet—who are in New Bond Street, you will also find the Wildenstein Galleries and the Fine Art Society, with Partridge Fine Art and the Antique Porcelain Company on either side of them, and next to Partridge one of the most elegant shop fronts, that of Savory and Moore, said to be the oldest chemist's shop in London, visited by the Duke of Wellington, Nelson (one never thinks of him in a chemist's, does one?) and Lady Hamilton (well, perhaps he was buying *her* something).

In Old Bond Street (that's the part nearer Piccadilly, you remember) you have other famous art names: Agnew, Leger, the Folio Society (old books), Marlborough, and a few doors away from them a shop called Sac Frères which can do you practically anything in amber. Not far away in Dover Street **Christie's** have their contemporary art gallery. *Their* auction rooms are in King Street, off St James's Street. They, like Sotheby's, smell as much of money as of art, indeed more so. All the same, if you like Auction as Theatre (and there is always a certain pleasure in merely watching rich people paying too much for something) you can have some fine entertainment for the price of a catalogue, and that's all nonsense about people scratching their noses absent-mindedly and finding they've bought a Fragonard.

If you actually join up the nodal points as I am numbering them (and there's no earthly reason why you should, except that they will show you a continuous path roughly resembling a double S-bend; a logical way to explore the map but not to explore London itself, since you can obviously start from *any* nodal point, that's what the word means) you will see that the next one is—

Piccadilly Circus

Well, of course for a great many people that is Nodal Point 1, not 7. Never mind. How extraordinary that within living memory it was a cliché to call this the Hub of the Empire. As a matter of fact it is altogether a more vulgar and crowded and traffic-plagued, let's-get-out-of-here spot than in the days when there *was* an Empire. It is, of course, still the place people think of first if they want to meet in London. 'See you outside Swan and Edgar' must have been the first words spoken in countless affairs and marriages. Sorry, marriages and affairs. Must have been the thought of nearby Soho that suggested that order. We'll come to Soho in a minute, more's the pity. Well, Swan and Edgar is of course the corner-site department store (mainly fashion) facing **Eros**.

Since that famous statue was itself based on a pun, it may not be totally out of place to recall here that *Time and Tide*, a now sadly defunct magazine, once had a competition for suggestions about the *real* meaning of London shop and company names, and one entry for Swan and Edgar was 'an Anglo-Saxon epic'. Others were Robinson & Cleaver, 'a notorious pair of Victorian murderers'; Bourne & Hollingsworth in Oxford Street, 'a wayside station in the Thames valley'; and Faber & Faber, the famous publishers, now of Queen Square, 'twin blacksmiths in the Roman Empire', and . . .

. . . ah yes, the pun about Eros. Well, as everybody knows, Eros, *alias* Cupid, *alias* Amor, is the God of Love. And as almost everybody knows, the statue was put up in honour of Anthony Ashley Cooper, 7th Earl of Shaftes-bury (1801–1885), a reformer and philanthropist whose Ten Hours Act of 1847 stopped the worst abuses of child and other labour. But hardly anybody seems to know that Eros is actually pointing his bow downwards, so as to *bury* the *shaft*. Oh, well.

A marvellous way to start branching out from Piccadilly Circus, especially if you are interested in cheese, is to go a few yards down Lower Regent Street, turn right into **Jermyn Street** (unless it happens to be mid-afternoon and you feel like having the best cup of tea in London, with or without service, with or without sandwiches and cakes and stuff to go with it, in which case you turn left to the other corner site where you will find the **Tea Centre**, staffed by delightful ladies in saris who *never hurry you*) and, as I was saying before we had all that about tea, go down Jermyn Street a few yards. Here you will find a true temple of cheese, a noble silence of Stilton and Cheddar—for these are the two upon which Paxton and Whitfield have built their 200-year-old tradition. They have about 300 other kinds of cheese as well, two-thirds of them from the Continent, although once you've had real Stilton you wonder why they bother. Still, it's a grand shop in a grand street, full of grand discreet shops where you can buy grand sponges or have grand shirts made to measure.

If you retrace your steps you can go into St James's, Piccadilly, and instantly find yourself part of an estimated (by me) 0.0000011 per cent of the daily passers-by who are suddenly removed from the world (though not entirely from its noise) in this calmly beautiful Renaissance interior with its magnificent Grinling Gibbons carving showing the Pelican feeding its young with its blood. Such instant contrasts are the essence of London, and the more of them you experience the more you will enjoy it.

Regent Street still begins with a noble curve and retains some of the grandeur intended by John Nash when he designed it as a kind of Royal Mile from the Prince Regent's Carlton House to Regent's Park (you wouldn't think this best of all the parks is only a mile away, but it is); but it is now perhaps the Main Street of the Nation of Shopkeepers, the one where the Switching On of the Illuminations is today's equivalent of the First Sunday of Advent as the official harbinger of Christmas.

Hamley's is here, absolutely the biggest and best-known toyshop in Bri-tain (although I'm not so sure when I think of the one in Bath, Tridias, where the manager took me round and I bought, for my wife's birthday, a wooden heart with a sounding-board, and eight wires stretched over it against which you can jangle eight little hanging wooden balls, like a Balinese orchestra in your own home, it had a northern-European folk look about it but even the manager didn't know where it had come from. They know where everything has come from in Hamley's). And there's Aquascutum, and some very grand jewellers, in one of whose windows I once saw a *gold egg-timer*, with red-looking sand in it. Crushed rubies, perhaps. There is Austin Reed, chief shop of a now nation-wide chain of Gentlemen's Outfitters, or if you want to be even grander, just west of and parallel to Regent Street is **Savile Row**, where if you have a letter of introduction from two noblemen you can go in and have the keel laid for the trousers, and come back six weeks later for another fitting for the coat, and eventually collect, for God knows how much now (but you certainly needn't look for any change out of £300, if that) one of those suits which tell *everybody* you're a gentleman.

Regent Street goes roughly north from Piccadilly Circus. Going roughly west is **Shaftesbury** (remember him?) **Avenue**; the Heart, as they always say, of London's Theatreland. Well it is true that here, more or less next door to each other, are the Lyric, the Apollo, the Globe, and Queen's' not to mention the Piccadilly just off, and the Criterion actually *in* Piccadilly Circus itself. Two grander ones, which often have good middlebrow plays with titled actors, or good foreign imports, are in Haymarket (that's the one further on from the Circus where the traffic all goes down. It comes *up* Lower Regent Street). Long time since you could buy hay there, but one absolute must in this street is the **Design Centre**, where you can see the best—well, the best-designed things made in this country, from pens to hi-fi, furniture to bicycles (hurry, while we still make those. Before we started to think quite so consciously about design we used to make our own motorcycles, too). The only snag about this fascinating place is that whenever you see something that you would like (and there's always been something *I* wanted) you can't actually buy it there. There's just a list telling you who makes it and where you *can* buy it. But if you are doing some serious shopping in London it's not at all a bad idea to look in here first.

Well, to get back to Shaftesbury Avenue. This is also the southern boundary of **Soho**, now almost entirely known as the strip-show magnet for Dirty Old, Middle-aged or Young Men who, wherever they come from, always tell you it's full of people from somewhere else. Oh, it's all Yorkshiremen, all Welsh rugby fans, all Scottish soccer fans (what, when there isn't a match?), it's all Japanese businessmen, it's all *Manchester* businessmen (why? There's plenty of strip entertainment in Manchester). In fact the customers are just men, or *nearly* all men, come to look at women. *They're Naked, and They Dance*, said the sign outside one place. Well of course, what would one expect them to do? No, that's a silly question. As far as I know, though, they haven't got to wrestling in mud yet, though I may be wrong. Things keep changing.

A curious area. Even now you can see serious Italian families eating decorous dinners with their families, behind the lace curtains of old apartment blocks. There are famous expense-account restaurants and discreet, very good, old-fashioned ones, still giving nothing away behind the curtains, brass-ring-suspended, that cover the lower halves of their windows. There are always people to be seen walking about with cans of film, for the place is also honeycombed with cutting-rooms, dubbing suites and viewing theatres, in a way the modern successor to the serious old trade of music engraving and publishing still also flourishing.

Soho between the wars was mainly Italian, but before 1900 it was mainly French. When the district was first laid out in the 17th century more than half the residents were Huguenot refugees. So it's not surprising that there's the French Protestant Church, looking across Soho Square to St Patrick's (and you can guess what religion *that* is), which stands on the site of Carlisle House, in 1760 taken over by one Madame Cornelys, who had had a child by Casanova when she was an opera singer in Venice. The nobility and gentry turned up for balls and masquerades there. Later, when she was just a poor old woman selling asses' milk for invalids on the little green at

Knightsbridge the occupant of a carriage going to Kensington Palace would avert her eyes, for she was that same daughter now become the Queen's Almoner, not caring to recall, as James Laver remarks, that charity begins at home.

Dryden lived at what became No. 43 Gerrard Street. The Literary Club, to which Johnson had some difficulty in getting Boswell elected, met at No. 9. The philosopher Hume lived in Lisle Street. Sheridan and Hazlitt lived in Frith Street. Oh, there's a lot to be seen in Soho besides naked women (and they *dance*. Oooh). In the daytime, anyway.

You can get a similar sense of pretty well submerged history if you move eastwards from Piccadilly Circus to **Leicester Square**—or, if you did actually go to the end of Shaftesbury Avenue, coming the few yards southwards again through an interesting little street-market and junk-and-old-record-etc.-shop area.

This is now a pedestrianised square entirely surrounded by cinemas showing either pornographic films or ones that you want to see and then discover to your rage aren't continuous, you can't just walk in, you have to book (*book*! For a *cinema*! What next!), so you just go away again, or at least I do. About the only interesting thing (and strictly speaking it isn't even quite *in* Leicester Square) is the Swiss Centre, where you can get absolutely splendid coffee and lots of other, more expensive Swiss goodies. And—heavens, I nearly forgot—if you come west a bit, past some dismal peepshow or other, and look very carefully for a door saying *Eglise Française*, do open that door and go down the little corridor and you will suddenly find yourself in a charming, graceful, quiet modern Catholic church, built in a circular shape but conveying the pristine sense of excitement the architect must have felt at this, before the liturgical reforms, if that is the word, where now the narrowest and most oblong of churches have somehow to pretend that they are circular too. It has a nice altar cloth making the most of the fact that *Marie* is an anagram of *aimer*.

Still, neither of these is what could be described as Typically English. And yet, and yet. You can sit on benches on the little grass green At The Heart of London's Entertainment World and reflect that when the busts of Hogarth, Reynolds, Isaac Newton and John Hunter, called by some the founder of scientific surgery, who all lived round here, were put up in 1874, this was for a re-opening some time after the Earl of Leicester in 1636 built Leicester House in the fields above the royal mews (where Trafalgar Square now is. And naturally the Hay Market was where they got their fodder). It became smart in Hanoverian times. Frederick, Prince of Wales, who like all the Hanoverians did not like his father, George II, put up a statue of his grandfather George I (whom of course George II had not liked) just to spite him (George II).

It became a great place for duels. In the 18th century various Panoramas and Exhibitions more or less started the entertainment tradition. In 1851 the statue of George I was buried to make room for Wyld's Great Globe, within which was constructed a giant relief map of the world. Lectures were given to groups of visitors who viewed these marvels from platforms in the middle. Then there was the Alhambra Music Hall, where men on leave from World War I crowded to see George Robey in the 'Bing Boys' shows . . .

Goodbye, Piccadilly; farewell, Leicester Square. In the middle of the little green now there is a statue of Shakespeare. Well, which quotation comes to mind first? 'O! wither'd is the garland of the war, The soldier's pole is fall'n'? 'All the world's a stage'? For me it is

> These our actors,
> As I foretold you, were all spirits and
> Are melted into air, into thin air:
> And, like the baseless fabric of this vision,
> The cloud-capp'd towers, the gorgeous palaces,
> The solemn temples, the great globe itself,
> Yea, all which it inherit, shall dissolve
> And like this insubstantial pageant faded,
> Leave not a rack behind. We are such stuff
> As dreams are made on, and our little life
> Is rounded with a sleep.

My God, what a speech, what a poet! That's one Empire, of the imagination, on which the sun is never going to set.

Our revels, however, are not ended. Indeed, they have scarcely begun, since from the bottom corner of Leicester Square it is a minute's walk to Nodal Point 8—

Trafalgar Square

It has almost as good a claim to be Nodal Point 1 as Buckingham Palace. Piccadilly Circus is nothing to it. Even now in these diminished days it has a sense of space, history, great things, national life. Obviously the thing that takes your eye first, as it is meant to, is **Nelson's Column**, as well it might, since if it hadn't been for him we might well have had a William-the-Conqueror act all over again early in the 19th century, and *then* the world would have been different, wouldn't it?

The column is 182 feet high so you might not realise that the statue, placed in position on 4 November 1843, is itself 18 feet high. A few days before it was placed there 'fourteen persons ate a dinner of rump steak on the summit'. The Landseer Lions were added in 1868. The bronzes at the base of the column, which hardly anyone except visitors ever looks at, represent scenes from Nelson's life, and it is the one facing Whitehall which shows his death and bears the words of the famous message, 'England expects . . .'

The square is full of pigeons, fountains and (in summer) tourists and (in the weeks before Christmas) carol singers of varying skill, and (on New Year's Eve) many thousands of people who gather with that residual hope that the next year can't be any worse, at any rate. It has been the scene of huge recruiting rallies, of all kinds of political rallies, the starting point of innumerable marches.

It also is bounded on the north by the noble façade of one of the greatest, and certainly *the* greatest free (see p. 44) art collection in the world, the **National Gallery**. Well, either you go there and get the copious books and catalogues and slides and cards they have and know what you want to see yourself (the wonderful Sienese ones, the famous Mantegna *Agony in the Garden* with the amazing foreshortened Apostles, the Uccello *Rout of San Romano*, and, oh yes, *St George and the Dragon*, so beautiful like a kind of formal nightmare, the huge voluptuous Titians, the Veroneses, and oh, that Botticelli *Nativity* with the angels dancing in a ring of solemn music above the stable in their blues and pinks and greens; the Rembrandts and Ruysdaels, the Cuyps and Constables including of course *The Hay Wain*); or you perhaps just settle for one picture and stare at it the whole morning. Now there's a Masaccio (in fact the *only* Masaccio), a Madonna and Child, with small, rather serious, angel heads looking from behind the triangular shape of that mys-

Trafalgar Square at night. In the background can be seen the church of St. Martin-in-the-Fields.

teriously satisfying blue cloak, that has on me the effect that I keep reading drugs have on their devotees: the more you look, the more real it becomes, the more you are in it, a kind of magic . . . oh, what's the use? As Dr Johnson observed, if a man has experienced the unutterable, let him not attempt to utter it. But do please look at the Masaccio. That calm face. That blue . . .

And it's all free.

It's all free. What a glory. Well, sir, how would you define civilisation? Well, I'd say it is a state reached by mankind when you can have a capital city with a building like the National Gallery in the middle of it where you can go in free and look at the Masaccio Madonna and Child for as long as you like. Thank you.

I really must go again and have another look, so I can recall it *exactly* whenever I want if They come and I'm in this prison camp.

Well, you see what I mean about all this really being Nodal Point 1. And I haven't even mentioned yet the **National Portrait Gallery**, which you will have passed on your way to the Nat Gall, as its habitués call it, if you came down from Leicester Square. It has the most diverse assemblage of faces imaginable, Kings from Richard II, not to mention Chaucer, Cromwell, Shakespeare. By artists including Van Dyck, Reynolds, Gainsborough, Raeburn, Lawrence (recently rediscovered, after a superb exhibition, in the *Annexe* to the National Portrait Gallery, which is rather a long way away for an annexe, being in Carlton House Terrace—bottom of Lower Regent Street, turn right and it's on your left)—to be an exuberant, life-giving virtuoso of paint).

The National Portrait Gallery is practically opposite **St Martin-in-the-Fields**, a church which, although it has given its name to a now world-famous chamber orchestra (The Academy of St etc.), and with its beautiful James Gibb (1726) design and fretted Italian ceiling is also well known as the place where famous actors come to read the lesson at memorial services for other famous actors, does also instantly give you the feeling that it is a parish church, right here in the middle of impersonal London, with as coherent and constant a congregation as if it were the only one in some small town in Somerset.

'Let's all go down the **Strand**', said the old music-hall song (never been quite sure why, since the presumed crowd of revellers would be going away from the West End first towards Fleet Street and then towards the empty, darkened, night-lifeless City. Surely it ought to have been 'Let's all go *up* the Strand'). You could of course go on northwards from the National Portrait Gallery up **Charing Cross Road**, notable for its second-hand books, special-ist new books, and, as you get past the point where it crosses Shaftesbury Avenue, Foyles (The Biggest Bookshop In The World), the music (both sheets of and instruments for) of Tin Pan Alley, and shops selling various devices alleged to make sex more interesting, or in some cases possible, than the human race has found it in the past.

But the Strand does give a feeling of arterial importance. For all the huge important metropolitan sprawl of London it is the *only* real road between the West End and the City. I discount the **Embankment** itself, a 19th-century development, as a bronze plaque on the river wall just above Charing Cross Bridge announces, beneath an image of a moustachioed Victorian face:

Flumini Vincula Posuit
Sir Joseph Bazalgette, C.B.
Engineer of London Main Drainage
System and this Embankment.

Flumini Vincula Posuit, he literally 'put chains on' the river. Now we are not so sure. At the moment of writing They are hastening to complete a £600 million scheme of huge barriers against the disastrous effects a North Sea 'surge' could have (there have been plenty in the past, and as the south-east of England is sinking at the rate of a foot a century there will be more; let us hope not before 1982, when they hope to get the scheme completed).

Now traffic roars along the Embankment, but unless you are walking along the side nearest the river (and the only reason you are likely to be doing that is that you are thinking of a river trip, see p. 59), it is not a real, human-life, let alone historic thoroughfare, like the Strand. In the early days it was more appropriately named, and you could actually see the Thames from it.

As a matter of fact, such is the mysterious attraction of water, that whenever I am around there on foot I find myself turning riverwards soon after it starts, to look at what is left of the **Adelphi**, a classic example of High Georgian architecture by Robert Adam. There were four streets, three of them named after his brothers John, James and William (that's why it is called the Adelphi, *adelphoi* being the Greek for brothers). There was a 1936 demolition scheme about which some people are still angry (before my time. Well, I was alive, but it was before my time). You can, however, still see John Adam Street, which contains among other things the classical, elegant premises of the Royal Society of Arts.

If you go from the western end of this down Villiers Street, a curious little road half conscious of tourists, with those open-booth shops selling plastic aprons, and nude posters, and printed signs bearing such legends as CARNABY STREET, and other essentials, and half of the commuters hurrying to and from Charing Cross (British Rail) station at its upper end and Embankment (Underground) at its lower end, you will come upon another of London's jolly little hidden surprises; the **Victoria Embankment Gardens**.

Here there is a covered stage facing on to an enclosure filled with deck-chairs on any summer day, but you can hear just as well, sitting on the grass without paying, music by a military band or (said the notices for the week the last time I was there) the band of the London Fire Brigade, the Max Collier Rhythm Aces, the Blackbottom Stompers or (the ones I heard, and very good too), the Mike Ward Southern Sound.

Well, to get back to the Strand, as you Go Down it you will pass such landmarks (on your right) as the Savoy Hotel, not to mention the adjoining Savoy Theatre, built from the profits of Gilbert and Sullivan, and another famous restaurant, Simpsons of (naturally) The Strand, no place for a vegetarian.

Just past the end of Waterloo Bridge you come to **Somerset House**, elegant 18th-century (Sir William Chambers between 1776 and 86) replacement of an earlier palace. It is best appreciated if you walk on to the bridge and admire its river frontage, which will probably make you join the ranks of those who think that, useful though it is as the home of such gentry as the Inland Revenue and, even more, the department of the Registrar-General which houses wills after 1858, (for earlier ones you have to visit the Public Record office in Chancery Lane, where you may see, among others, Shakespeare's) it's a pity the original idea, that it should house the Royal Academy and its pictures (now, as we have seen, at Burlington House in Piccadilly) was abandoned.

You will now have to go (on the map, I mean, not necessarily physically) round the huge block of Bush House, labyrinthine home of the BBC's World

Service, that's a Voice From The West talking loud and clear from there in spite of endless threats of economic cutbacks, to turn north to our next-but-one nodal point. But before you do, it is logical (and this book is nothing if not logical) to go a few yards on, past the church on its island site made famous by the nursery rhyme ('Oranges and lemons, the bells of St Clement's') to what is this book's Nodal Point 9 but is by any standards a classic boundary—

Temple Bar

This is the official boundary of the City. When the Sovereign passes this point the procession stops to receive formal permission of the Lord Mayor, there is a great business of fanfares and the handing over of a sword. Until 1878 there was an archway across the road, by Wren, then this was deemed to hold up the traffic. It finished up at a place called Theobald's Park, Waltham Cross, where it still is. From time to time one reads articles about restoring it or even moving it back, but nothing seems to happen and probably will.

As you face the City the **Law Courts** are on your left, the public galleries a splendid free drama, although more likely to be complicated tax cases than the more sensational trials to be observed farther into the City at the **Central Criminal Court**, the **Old Bailey**. The Strand now becomes Fleet Street, the narrow sounding-board of England, running through those legal districts, one of the unique charms of London, which we'll come to later. For the moment let us go back to our S-bend.

It's worthwhile going a little way up the otherwise boring Kingsway to take the first turn right, Portugal Street, and thence into Portsmouth street to see what some say is Dickens's **Old Curiosity Shop** (not so, say others, it used to be in Charing Cross Road. Never mind, it looks like everybody's picture of the Old Curiosity Shop). But it's much more interesting then to go back, along curved Aldwych westward again, and take the *next* turn north, **Drury Lane**, where you are on your way to two of the most famous theatres in the world.

The first, of course, is the Theatre Royal, Drury Lane itself, haunted by the glories of Garrick, Peg Woffington, Mrs Siddons, Kemble (who made his first appearance as Hamlet there in 1784), Sheridan; burnt down twice, the scene of riots over prices, now the home of musicals. The other, which involves turning westward (i.e. left), is **Covent Garden**, though not before you have seen the marvellous shop in Drury Lane which is a kind of Temple of the Pen, in the days when pens were pens, with nibs. There are marvellous formal patterns of nibs on display cards, and old inkstands, and the elegant sample cases of stationery of commercial travellers in the good old days. Some things are for exhibition only, but it is a shop, a magical shop.

This wonderful opera house, so red-plush grand, chandeliered, metropolitan yet somehow simultaneously so comfortable and welcoming, the home both of the Royal Ballet and of the Royal Opera, is one of the glories of London; the more so because, although it has always been one of the world's great venues for what Dr Johnson defined as 'an exotic and irrational entertainment', the light which it kept burning by assembling international casts when opera *was* indeed the most un-British form of music has helped bring us to the state when British opera singers are found in every other European opera house, there is so much native talent that another (and sometimes better) organisation, the English National Opera, based at the Coliseum, has burst into flourishing life.

The British Museum

The best spot, theoretically, for Nodal Point 10 would be the centre of the grandest room in London, the British Library, still more familiar to most people by its old name, the Reading Room of the British Museum. I myself am always slightly surprised to be reminded that Panizzi's Dome (the very words have a 17th-century sound about them, as one might say 'Bernini's Colonnade') was only built in 1857. This great circular building, walled with books, with radial lines of desks at which sit people working at anything from a master's thesis on the accounting system of the Hudson's Bay Company in the 17th century to a Complete Philosophical and Moral Account of the Universe (one of its most famous denizens was Karl Marx), is a kind of intellectual cyclotron. There are people, especially those with an interest in the building of the proposed new ziggurat capable of housing *all* books, instead of many having to be fetched from some 14 other storage places, who would stoutly deny that all human knowledge worth having is obtainable here. But one look at this magic circle, 140 feet in diameter, 106 feet high, alive with silent concentration, like some celestial examination room where God is the invigilator, would convince the chance visitor (and they will let you in at intervals for a stereotyped lecture) that it is.

Obviously it is the nodal point of the Museum itself, with its amazing and unique treasures: the Rosetta Stone, from which via the Frenchman Champollion the entire foundations of Egyptology were laid, since it contains an inscription both in Greek and in the previously indecipherable hieroglyphics; the Elgin Marbles from the Parthenon, treasures from Assyrian reliefs, Carolingian ivories, entrancing books of hours and manuscripts, including an original *Magna Carta*, the famous treasure discovered in the Saxon burial ship at Sutton Hoo in Suffolk . . . it is very easy to get into the British Museum (FREE!) and very hard to go out of it.

North of it you are still in the intellectuals' area (Bloomsbury, in fact, and what could be more intellectual than that?) for now you come to London University. Before you find yourself enrolling for a course in Sanskrit or something, therefore, it is time to get back to New Oxford Street, probably not resisting very much the highly individual and exotic print, art and thing shops in this area (including one called Collector's Corner, for tracking down elusive LP records. If it is 78's you're after, they still have *them* at the Gramophone Exchange in Wardour Street, the end of which you will pass in a moment).

Over Tottenham Court Road and you are now in **Oxford Street**, probably London's most famous shopping street, with all that that entails. Lot of camera shops and open, Calcutta-type bazaars selling various garments of cheesecloth, and boots and such things, as well as department stores such as Bourne and Hollingsworth. Half-way up to Oxford Circus is the Academy Cinema, the only one in London where *every* film I have seen has been a good one. On your right in the first part of this progress is what you might call the decent extension of Soho, with **Charlotte Street**, particularly, offering the full international range of restaurants, at all prices.

Oxford Circus

Oxford Circus itself is Nodal Point 11. You won't want to go north from here up Regent Street past the Russian Tourist Office unless you're going to the BBC to take part in a studio discussion, or give a talk on your speciality, as everyone in England seems to sooner or later. You are now in the slightly posher section of Oxford Street, indeed you are in the West End. One shop ought to be mentioned before you go any farther, in this very shoppy area; **Liberty's**, a few yards into Regent Street on your left, has a reputation for taste in fabric design going back to good old Art Nouveau times, indeed further back still, since they had their centenary in 1975. There were connections with William Morris and, later, the Aesthetic Movement. For generations it has been a kind of instinct for anyone who, however vaguely, wanted to get away from the mass-produced, to say 'let's have a look round Liberty's'. (There actually was a man called Arthur Lasenby Liberty who founded it.) They have splendid leather animals—elephants, bulls, a splendid Eeyore—which are indestructible (ours having survived six children) and look as if they were made by Old Craftsmen in Hungary or somewhere but turn out to come from Hertfordshire. Just a little farther in, and off Regent Street, is Carnaby Street, now so famous that it has been pedestrianised.

Well, yes, Oxford Street. You go via John Lewis (lot of taste there too) to the crown of it all, the not-so-rich-as-all-that man's Harrods, **Selfridges**. I don't think they ever sold aircraft, but they've got pretty well everything else. Another good example of Shopping as Theatre. They've got seven restaurants there, too. Slightly before them, on the other side of the street, is the HMV shop, the Vatican of records.

Marble Arch

The best time to be at Nodal Point 12, Marble Arch, corner of Hyde Park, end of old road to North Wales, is Sunday afternoon, when the well-known **Speakers' Corner** is loud with very un-well-known but often interesting orators; some eccentric, some passionate, some sober, advocating everything from anarchy to totalitarianism.

Now the best way to get to the next nodal point is to go *back*, past Selfridges, and to go north not by Baker Street (which is just, well, a street) but by Marylebone High Street, reached by the short, Selfridge's-skirting James Street. Just off it, on the left, is the best place in London for knowing what it must have been like to be an English *milord* building up a collection.

Although it is now one of the accepted glories of London, the **Wallace Collection** in Hertford House, Manchester Square, only got here because Sir Richard Wallace, 'believed', says the catalogue, to be a son of that fourth Marquess of Hertford who brought that aristocratic family's collecting mania to its zenith, removed it to London from the family house in Paris during the Commune (1871).

The whole place (it somehow seems absurd to call it a museum) thus reflects a personal taste with a leaning towards the joyful, the opulent, even the frivolous. Indeed its most famous picture is *The Laughing Cavalier* of Frans Hals, but there is a lot of Watteau and Fragonard, including the lady on the swing; the wonderful solemn little boy on his little fat horse, *Don Baltasar Carlos in the Riding School* by Velasquez, the great Titian *Perseus and Andromeda*, lovely Boningtons . . . It has *the* collection of ceramics, and it was here that I discovered that Boulle was a man, not a material, even though they sometimes spell it *buhl-work*; for there is a marvellous cabinet by him here. And as for all those clocks . . .

A visit to this magnificent (FREE) show will delay your progress up **Marylebone High Street**, but this is not an area to rush through; lots of Italian and other restaurants, nice specialist shops, but at the same time a still quite discernible neighbourhood, almost a village feeling, something you don't find in the more metropolitan shopping areas. Not that you will find any simple villagers here. To live anywhere around Marylebone High Street you have to be Lord Hailsham (the Lord Chancellor) or Peter Ustinov, or at least a rich Arab-treating specialist from nearby Harley Street. All the same, you walk a few paces from a very grand antiquarian bookshop and there is a greengrocer's with one of those splendidly arranged displays of oranges and grapes and cauliflowers and apples, a cornucopia so artistically poured out that you wonder if there isn't some influence in the air from the Wallace Collection.

Marylebone Road

Nodal Point 13, at the top end of the second S, is where Marylebone High Street comes into Marylebone Road. Facing you is the Royal Academy of Music and York Gate, but before you go through here into the glories of Regent's Park you cannot fail to see, slightly more to your left on the far side of Marylebone Road, the Exhibition of **Madame Tussaud**.

Perhaps a word of warning. You have to *like* waxworks, and to be prepared to spend some time there, if only to get your money's worth (for this certainly isn't free). No, perhaps *like* is the wrong word. You have to feel the creepy attraction of this amazing verisimilitude (there's no need to go into the Chamber of Horrors, which really *is* rather horrible in its obsession with blood and death and murder and hanging and guillotining) when you enter the conservatory and there is Liza Minnelli or (an unlikely pair, I should have thought) André Previn apparently discussing a tricky point in a Shostakovich symphony, or something, with the late Paul Getty on the patio. If you've read about a personality often enough you'll be bound to find It here.

Madame has been there a long time, attracting more and more visitors. As a rhyme of 1884 put it:

> There was an old woman called Tussaud
> Who loved the grand folk in 'Who's Who' so
> That she made them in wax
> Both their front and their backs
> And asked no permission to do so.

As everybody knows, Madame T.'s, which either drops people when they have stopped being Personalities, or, if they go on being Personalities (as for instance the Royal Family inevitably must) makes new models of them from time to time as they get older (now there's a profound thought, which has exercised many philosophers; which is the real *you*? At 15, 25, 35, 45 . . .?) is very strong also on history. You can see all our kings, and quite a lot of foreign ones.

You often find Madame Tussaud's yielding to the instinct which possesses all of us when faced with puppets or waxworks: the better they are, the worse they are, in that you want to hear them speak or see them move. At the Battle of Trafalgar, and in the sequence 'Heroes' (who often turn out to be mere showbiz heroes, you don't have to be Nelson to get into this category) there are sound and light effects; and perhaps the ultimate is the Sleeping Beauty, who actually breathes. Any minute now she will . . .

But no, she will not. Madame T. is not God. Instead, she carries the aforesaid sound and light to their logical abstract conclusion. In the (separate entrance fee) **Laserium** you may see the only permanent example in Europe of light, in various shapes and forms, *dancing* in an extraordinary 3D pattern to the music of everyone from Emerson, Lake and Palmer to (you might have guessed!) John Sebastian Bach. And Holst, *The Planets*. Appropriate, since this is in the same building as the **Planetarium** (another separate entrance fee), where in 35 minutes you can learn about the universe (the Laserium show lasts an hour).

Well, that's one way to revive your sense of wonder. Another is to go on a few yards into **Regent's Park**, the biggest, best, most varied and beautiful in metropolitan London. In summer the undoubted glory of it is the magnificent Queen Mary's Rose Garden. You often see people going round with notebooks writing down the names of varieties, or you hear people mildly quarrelling. 'Of course it's not a *Gloire de Dijon*, that's a climber.' 'Oh, look, here's Dr Van Fleet, why doesn't ours grow like that?' Hardly anybody's roses grow the way they do here. Happy the commuter who can plan his way in to London to include the path where first tulips, then high-summer flowers, then truly breathtaking ranks of dahlias, and finally chrysanthemums bring a voluptuous passion of nature into the stone and brick of the city; and with none of the messy in-between bits of one's own garden.

When the dahlias come they come suddenly, as though they had been put there overnight. Can it really all have been done by these occasional young men, obviously vacation-job students, that you see doing a little desultory-looking weeding from time to time, here or in the Japanese water garden with its little bridges and tinkles of water, where the people suddenly look too big? It must be so.

There's a willow-fringed lake for rowing or sailing; the clunk of rowlocks, laughter heard across water, true summer sounds. There's the open-air theatre, now a rather more formalised arena than it was when we sat in deck chairs and I saw absolutely the most magical performance of (what else!) that most magical play, *A Midsummer Night's Dream*, that I ever hope to see. For once the aircraft had stopped their deafening descending sighs, Bottom emerged in the dusk with his normal human head and began that miraculously moving attempt to explain ecstasy. *I have had a dream, past the wit of man to say what dream it was* . . . Patrick Wymark, that unforgettable Shakespearean actor, God rest his soul, had us all in tears.

There's a rather good restaurant (a favourite venue for Sunday lunches). And on the north side of the park there is of course the **Zoo**. *The* Zoo. The *Zoo*. Surely going to any zoo, especially one so all-embracing as this, should make the most pragmatic person a bit philosophical. What an extraordinary creature one *might* have been instead of a human being, with all the worry and the glory of a mind! How splendid not to be a snake, or this sad-looking hornbill with that huge useless-looking two feet of beak clapped in front of its face. Might be fun to be an Australian bower bird, though (it makes a kind of 18th-century gazebo with twigs, bits of mirror, anything it can find, for its mate). Or the fish, where we all started. Ibis, Goby, Tompot Blenny . . . you can be Cousteau in the aquarium, without any of the risk.

The Inns of Court

Placed strategically across the area between the commerce of the City and the social and political life concentrated round the west end of central London are the Inns of Court. To saunter through these lush, quiet gardens, past these grand Georgian houses from which you catch the faint clicking of electric typewriters and a faint whiff of money, is to realise why going to law costs so much. Those lawyers have made for themselves a broad swathe of commodious and graceful living, a secret comfortable nest of gracious civilisation, shutting out the noises of the 20th century.

It is the old monastic dream of *thought* (though unmonastically, very highly-paid thought) going on round a quiet quadrangle of perfect lawn, which inspired Oxford and Cambridge in their building heyday, carried over into the outside world, into the adult career. It is unique to London.

Except for the grander parts of gardens 'reserved for members of the Inn', the public are allowed to savour these delights. Probably just as well. If they had been excluded from this secretly beautiful and private area Londoners might well have acted on the advice of Dick the Butcher to the rebel chief Jack Cade in *Henry VI Part 2*: 'the first thing we do, let's kill all the lawyers'.

You can walk over half a mile, starting at the northern end of **Gray's Inn**, hardly noticing the momentary interruption as you cross busy nondescript High Holborn and busy, far from nondescript Fleet Street, all the time in perfect gardens or squares, under arches, under great plane trees, by the sunny walls of old houses, along stone-flagged corridors, to within sight of the Thames.

Of course there are everywhere indications of a secret corporate life of which the outsider can know nothing; chapels that always seem to have just closed, great halls where lawyers, to be called to the bar, must have eaten a certain number of meals from their student days.

You will get the sketch straight away in Gray's Inn. Leaving the statue of Francis Bacon (seems only yesterday *he* was there) surrounded by perfect wallflowers, you come to a little arched passage into a High Holborn full of scurrying people most of whom have no idea of the amazing calm a few yards away, where there is a notice, white hand-painted letters on black, saying:

> The Servants of the Inn have orders to remove all hawkers, persons begging and disorderly people as well as children playing or making a disturbance. No perambulators are allowed nor are motor cars, motor tricycles or bicycles permitted except in the case of persons having business in the Inn. Non-residents must not bring dogs into the Inn. Any person committing a nuisance will be prosecuted and a reward of Twenty Shillings will be paid for any Information resulting in the convicting of the offender.

So be warned, and don't try to get your motor tricycle in there.

Just the other side of High Holborn is **Lincoln's Inn**, not only a marvellous group in itself, but contiguous with a beautiful public square, Lincoln's Inn Fields, which has tennis courts, a bandstand, a netball league where legal and other gents may be seen eyeing the teams of office girls leaping up and down in winter in their short skirts, or where you may see two young men taking the afternoon off with some hard, no-nonsense tennis singles. And everywhere these great noble trees.

Most of all, in **Lincoln's Inn Fields** (London's largest square, by the way), at No. 13, there is a house-turned-into-museum which is the most rewarding and atmospheric of any I have seen (and *I* have seen the House of the Cretan Woman in Cairo). This is **Sir John Soane's Museum**. The famous architect (1753–1837, who designed the Bank of England) lived here, in the house he designed to hold his marvellous antiquities and paintings. If I were an antique dealer visiting it I should either go away and commit suicide or organise an amazing, Great-Train-Robbery-Style night attack on it. It is *perfect*.

Sir John Soane's Museum: the library.

The Library, cunningly using glass to increase space, is a miracle of elegance, then you go along a corridor where there are not only classical marbles but a memorial to Soane's dog, saying ALAS POOR FANNY. In the Picture Room are the two famous Hogarth series, *The Rake's Progress* and *The Election* (supposed to be satirical, and so it is with all that boozing, pate-breaking etc., but it does look more fun than elections are now) and many other works crammed up to the ceiling. There's a gothick-fantasy Monk's Parlour, there is the Sepulchral Chamber containing the brilliantly-placed Sarcophagus of Seti (1303–1290 BC, as everyone knows) with its delicate drawing on the base of the goddess to whom the dead king was committed. There are wonderful architectural details: the Dome, the enchanting Break-fast Room, subtle niches and recesses. And *what* a magnificent Turner in the New Picture Room! *Admiral Tromp's Barge*; where had this picture been all my life? If you like the poetry of light (so well captured architecturally in this house) you will think the same when you see that glorious gold stern, the magic light in the sails over luminous water, the other shadowy ships on the dark sea background. What a picture! What a museum!

And yes, *it's* free too.

To get back to the Inns; just across Fleet Street, is the grandest, the **Temple**; or, to be more more precise, *are* the grandest, the Middle and Inner Temple. I was once a dinner guest at a moot in their great hall, which has the largest double hammer-beam roof in England. Before three distinguished Queen's Counsel the young gentlemen pursued the hypothetical case of Adam Neve, Appellant, and Walter Butler-Sawe, Respondent—in this case the police upon whose evidence concerning the comings and goings of women to his residential clinic for male impotence Dr Neve had been convicted of keeping a brothel, though he, as a qualified doctor and Member of the Institute of Psychiatry, maintained that the women 'volunteered' to act as 'sexual surrogates' and were therefore not prostitutes.

Coarse laughter? Not a bit of it. There was grave discussion about the appellant's claim that this was indeed 'a specialised form of nursing service', about the definition of prostitution; did the fact that the visits were determi-nate and not random count, was it simply enough that they *had* been paid (£25 a time, but Dr Neve did not touch this money, the 'patient' was charged)? There was much talk of law and fact, of *Winter* v. *Woolfe* (1931), *Calvert* v. *Mayes* (1975), *Regina* v. *Ansell* (1975 . . .

Bit of a change from the world which saw the nearby Temple Church, one of the hidden treasures of London, built; one of five surviving examples (the others are at Cambridge, Northampton Ludlow Castle and Little Maple-stead, Essex) of 'round churches'. It was built by the crusading order of Knights Templars who gave their name to the district. There's a quite extraordinary sense of telescoped history in this amazing little church—and it's almost as if you were at the wrong end of the telescope, for the round part, which you somehow expect from the outside to be the chancel or altar end, turns out to be where a nave would usually be.

What you feel here is the Gothic style being born. You go through the great, solid, round, Norman west porch, good thick solid stuff, and suddenly you see these slender arcade colums of polished Purbeck marble which surely must end in pointed arches—and they do, as if these had just been invented, as indeed they had (the church was consecrated on 10 February 1185; that makes you forget those lawyers' typewriters, doesn't it!). Rebecca West said 'it is a thankless task to be the perfect embodiment of a transition period'. But of course she was speaking of writers. In this Temple Church the architectural text-book word 'Transitional' suddenly becomes not an abstraction but a real, exciting thing.

There are stone seats all round, as though it were a chapter-house, with another arcade where the capitals have wonderful grotesque heads full of the wildest Gothic fantasy. The stalls, for those lawyers at prayer, are in the rectangular choir adjoining, now fully Early English (consecrated 1240). Ah, you wouldn't think the whole place was nearly destroyed by fire bombs on the night of 10 May 1941. Until you look at the new east window, where you will see in the stained glass pictures of the Blitz flames in the City, with St Paul's in the middle . . . You see what I mean about the telescope.

Admittedly it wasn't the Temple; but just after typing those lines I read that the debating society of Gray's Inn had voted, by a substantial majority, for the legalisation of cannabis. Ah, well.

City churches

I'm sorry—no I'm not, I'm *glad*, as anyone with a soul must surely be when faced with the ubiquitous, life-enhancing torrential genius of Wren, that this part of the book is full of churches. Some were pulled down, some were destroyed in the war, some have been restored. But enough of this extraordinary achievement—52 London churches including St Paul's (not to mention Chelsea and Greenwich Hospitals and various palaces)—remain for them to be the chief treasure of the City. Now they are often hidden away, dwarfed by nondescript glass slabs. You push through a brass-studded leathern door in some uncaring commercial street and you are back in that world-changing 17th century, so confident about the human race, especially the English, Protestant part of it, somehow combining sober mercantilism with gaiety. They are not Catholic, Real Presence churches. They are the church as holy meeting-place. They are jewels.

No wonder T. S. Eliot wrote, about the church which stands under the Monument itself, near London Bridge, a golden phoenix on a 202-foot Doric column,

> Beside a public bar in Lower Thames Street,
> The pleasant whining of a mandoline
> And a clatter and a chatter from within
> Where fishmen lounge at noon: where the walls
> Of Magnus Martyr hold
> Inexplicable splendour of Ionian white and gold.

Everyone knows the famous epitaph composed by his son for Sir Christopher; *Si monumentum requiris, circumspice.* If you would see his monument, look around you. It is inscribed over the north door in St Paul's, but it could apply all over the City.

The **Monument** (designed of course by Wren) is 202 feet high because that is supposed to be the distance of its site from the bakery in Pudding Lane where the Great Fire of 1666 began. 51 churches were rebuilt, cost borne by the Government (in so far as any Government can be said to bear a cost. What they actually did was put a tax of one shilling on every ton of coal coming into London, later raising it to three shillings when this turned out to be inadequate). The total cost was £263,786. Wren got 5%; about £13,000. There are detailed accounts, including some charming oddities, such as women craftsmen, if one may so express it nowadays: Sarah Freeman, plumber (St James Garlickhithe), Widow Pearce, painter (St Magnus), Widow Cleer, joiner

(All-Hallows, Lombard Street). And, in the accounts for St Stephen Wal-brook:

> Paid to ye Survaer Gennarall by order of Vestry for a gratuety to his Lady to incuridg and hast in ye rebuilding ye church twenty ginnes.

Lady Wren's twenty guineas were in a silk purse. But although he was always being given jolly dinners and hogsheads of claret and was never exactly poor (here the Mozart analogy ends), it is the sheer exuberance of his creativity that takes your breath away. There used to be (and therefore presumably still is) a song about him, to music by Victor Hely-Hutchinson, which went in part:

> Every day of the week was filled
> With a church to mend or a church to build
> And never an hour went by but when
> London needed Sir Christopher Wren:
> Bride's in Fleet Street lacks a spire,
> Mary-le-Bow a nave and choir,
> Please to send the plans complete
> For a new St Stephen's, Coleman Street . . .
> The Dome of St Paul's is not yet done,
> The Dean has been waiting since half past one . . .

Just to look at a page of drawings of the towers is to realise the infinite invention of the man. Plain towers, towers with parapets, urns, pineapples, obelisks; with bell-cages or turrets, with lanterns on domes, with elaborations of the bell-turret, with built-up spires, with true spires . . . A good built-up spire is **St Bride's**, hidden away in another sudden quiet just off Fleet Street. 'A madrigal in stone', Henley called it. This 'printers' cathedral' (it actually shares heating with the neighbouring Press Association) is a fascinating throwback to Wren. The spire was all that was left standing up among the calcined walls after the Blitz on 29 December 1940. When you stand in yet another quiet white-and-gold interior you are *closer* to Wren's original plan, since the architect, Godfrey Allen, a successor to Wren as Surveyor of St Paul's, did not replace the galleries which were added soon after the opening of Wren's church in 1675, destroying the beautiful line of the windows which you now see. All he had to do was follow Wren's plans.

Lot of American connections; Winslow's parents were married there. When lightning struck the steeple in 1764 George III thought the new conductor should have blunt ends, Benjamin Franklin said no, sharp. There were pamphlets about good blunt honest King George and those sharp-witted colonists . . .

Well, I did say it is very easy to get diverted if you stray a few yards in London. And there are other sudden quiets just on the other side of Fleet Street from St Bride's: Dr Johnson's house in Gough Square, the sanded-floor Cheshire Cheese where his portrait looks down on you (and *down* is the word). But to get back to Wren's City (which would have been much better if his plan for the layout of the whole place, never mind a few churches, had been adopted), its supreme glory is of course **St Paul's**. Of what comparable building in the world could one man say 'I designed all that'?

The dome is an airy miracle, whether you look at it from Fleet Street, climb to the outside gallery and observe the interesting part of London below you and the boring (except for the rest of the dome, rising to 363 feet) part above you, or try the Whispering Gallery, some distance from the next equally impressive acoustic miracle, which I take to be the theatre at Epidaurus,

Greece.

Everything about St Paul's is big and open and public and grand and impressive; big wrought-iron gates, even a big crypt, with the tombs of Wellington and Nelson. And then, if you are clever, you will look at the Grinling Gibbons choir stalls. And if you are lucky, you will hear the choir. The last time I was there was for the memorial service for Alfred Deller. All who had loved this supreme artist, who alone, untaught, re-discovered the counter-tenor voice and, as Norman Platt, Director of Kent Opera, said in his address, revolutionised our idea of how Purcell should be sung, were present. And out of nowhere (well, in fact from an adjoining chapel) came the heart-melting sound of the choir singing Tallis's *Salvator Mundi*. Alfred was once a Vicar-choral (lay singer) in that same choir. When Stravinsky was dying it is said that all he wanted to hear was Purcell sung by him. Alfred, with his sudden chortle. 'Once I was passing the choir school, and I heard this angry voice, shouting *"No no NO! I saw the one two three four, sitting upon the one two three four"*. . . .'

So there is also scope for the private, the individual, the intimate, in that vast building. But we bade Churchill farewell there too.

Needless to say there are plenty of books and pamphlets about Wren and his work. It would be a lifetime's job to know it all. But here is one thing worth doing if you are in the City (you might even have seen the splendid state rooms and Egyptian hall in the Lord Mayor's **Mansion House**, but only if you had *written* for permission and got it): just round the corner is **St Stephen's Walbrook**, and you will not be wrong in thinking it is like a tiny St Paul's, because Wren built its dome as a model for his masterpiece.

The South Bank

The words would not have meant anything before the war. Unless you actually *lived* south of the Thames (like about five million other people) the south bank was just a jumble of blank-faced warehouses. A lot of the river frontage still *is* a jumble of blank-faced warehouses, but since the war the section on the bend of the river as it flows past the City was bit by bit developed into the 20th century's answer to private enterprise in the arts: the publicly-funded and/or publicly-built complex. Although the idea of a National Theatre took root in the early 1900s (and a site was acquired in *Bloomsbury* in 1913) this was actually the last to be built. The South Bank began with the **Royal Festival Hall**, and *that* all began with the Festival of Britain, 1951's answer to 1851. A lot of that curiously dreamlike, *what's-happened-to-us, well-let's-smile-on-a-new-and-nice-vaguely-socialist-future* atmosphere of Britain in the fifties has gone. But the unfussy, functional, yet mysteriously welcoming Festival Hall is a permanent reminder of it. In some strange way that architect's-drawing quality, where you always have receding perspectives with casual human figures sketched in, has come alive. It really does welcome you. Because of the generous ancillary space at the entrance level, it is always a warming experience to see more and more people coming in, life intensifying, laughter at tables and bars, as the hour for the concert draws near.

There has been a certain amount of huffing and puffing among the food-and-drink boffins about the main restaurant. I tend myself to use the excellent and courteously-manned cafeteria. But if anybody offered me a meal up there, especially if I could have a seat by the window, as long and high as the room itself, overlooking the Thames and providing me with one of the most thrilling urban riverscapes in the world, Houses of Parliament to the left, St Paul's and the City to the right, I should accept with the greatest pleasure.

The Royal Festival Hall established itself immediately as the focal point of musical London—and nowadays that is pretty focal in the world; for London has four major symphony orchestras. The fact that they don't get between them as much subsidy as one orchestra in a provincial Dutch town is part of a crazy but on the whole exhilarating pattern (although it does impose a certain amount of safe crowd-pulling programming with composers like Mahler). But then, in an increasingly materialistic world music itself is crazy. Certainly the flawless (indeed some say clinical) acoustics of the RFH have welcomed the greatest orchestras, soloists and conductors (from Klemperer downwards) in the world. In fact it is to London's eternal credit (and especially to that of the late Walter Legge, founder of the Philharmonia Orchestra) that Klemperer was rescued from the curious obscurity of his late middle life for his glorious Indian summer. But whoever the artists, any concert at the Festival Hall is, simply because of the building, an occasion.

Outside, you go along the riverside terrace, up steps, past walls where the rough surface shows the grain of the timber frames into which the concrete was poured—the whole thing is in a curiously neutral style of the new civic brutalism outside, lushness within—and there are the two ancillary halls: the **Queen Elizabeth Hall**, where you tend to get chamber orchestras, and soloists known more to the cognoscenti, and the **Purcell Room**, where I have heard many a recital of the kind of intimate and eloquent music which the very name of that composer somehow suggests.

Next you come to the **National Film Theatre**, the country's focus for serious study of the cinema. It organises events centred round the films of particular countries or directors or stars, issues a monthly bulletin, runs a library, and in general attempts to open people's eyes to the fact that there is more to the cinema than *Secrets of a Danish Dentist* or *Penelope's Lustful Body* (and you mustn't think I have just invented those, they are genuine) at your friendly local fleapit. Membership costs £7 a year, but for visitors there are considerably lower rates, for short periods.

Passing the **Hayward Gallery** with averted eyes you now come to the other side of Waterloo Bridge and the biggest complex of the lot, the **National Theatre**.

It has taken the people who produced the greatest playwright in the world quite a time to produce this extraordinarily living focus of the theatre (in the literal sense; *focus* is Latin for 'hearth'). Never mind 1900, people were beginning to talk about a National Theatre a hundred years ago.

That was in the heyday of the period when 'the theatre' meant the proscenium arch, the red plush curtain rising on the always heart-stopping silence when the house lights go down, the darkened audience of *individuals* each responding in his own way to the magical, godlike, brilliantly-lit statements being made to him from Up There (or Down There, if you were in the circle or the gallery). I am old enough to feel a certain nostalgia for this, and for part of me to feel that the modern theatre only achieves, for all its avowals of communal feeling with the audience, that same godlike, removed feeling of *otherness* from us ordinary playgoers because it can now use technical resources of lighting, electronic sound, etc. which were beyond the range of the Victorians.

I am also young enough, at least in spirit, to respond to this classical statement, or restatement really, that the theatre is a communal experience. The National's first director, Sir Peter Hall, maintains that the proscenium theatre, from 1700 till now, was 'a historical hiccup'; it was not so from the Greeks to the Elizabethans. But the period was not entirely barren of great dramatists.

Denys Lasdun, the National's practical, brilliant architect, told the actors that this was his first theatre, and was quite prepared to learn what their ideal requirement would be. In the end it seemed that what they wanted was a square room, with the stage in one corner of it and the seats curving up round in the L-shaped space left, in such a way that there was direct eye-and-ear communication with every person in the audience of 1,150. And the Olivier, the biggest of the three theatres, for all its expensive gadgets (a revolving drum can drop 40 feet with half the stage and be fitted with another set, there are computerised lifts and hoists) is essentially just this. From a 'point of command' up stage an actor can, in fact, see everyone within an angle of 120 degrees, which is the angle of a man's vision; and that embraces the whole audience, in such a way that no member of it is looking across the stage at another member.

The Olivier is the one for classics and most new plays. The 890-seat Lyttelton is a proscenium theatre, though of the most modern kind, and is equipped with simultaneous translation booths connected to every seat, so that London's tradition of hospitality to world theatre may become even stronger. The Cottesloe, which can hold up to 400, is the barest, and the most fluid and experimental.

All these are part of a complex which is also practically a factory, with metalwork and carpentry and of course tailors' and other shops (they claim to make everything except boots and shoes). If you go on a conducted tour you can look down on windows round a central well and see people typing, working at sewing machines, driving lorries laden with papier-maché dragons, working at desks. Where are the actors? you wonder, and then you pass seven rehearsal rooms.

This is the inside, as are the 8 bars, the foyers with their free pre-performance entertainments, the restaurant. But the National Theatre was also conceived in its relationship to the noble bend of the river (called King's Reach) which it dominates. The verticals of the fly towers are answered by the horizontals of the terraces from which life seems to be flowing in and out at all levels. Lasdun's words are interesting.

> It's going to weather. It's going to streak, and the streaks will have white patches, which they're already getting and which I think will be beautiful. It isn't only stone that streaks! I want the concrete to weather so that in the end lichen grows on it and it becomes part of the riverscape. I want the feeling that the audience—like the tides of the river—flow into the auditoria and become a community within them. Then the tide ebbs and they come out into the creeks of the small spaces that are made by all those terraces; because they're not vast terraces, they are very small, human, little places for people to go.

It isn't free, yet. But its ticket prices are said to be lower than those of the unsubsidised theatre (which not unnaturally causes a certain amount of heartburning and mine in fact was £5.50) and there is a policy of always having some tickets on offer, however successful the production, on the day of performance. Pity the last thing I saw there was a bored, semi-audible Ibsen *Wild Duck* played with about as much passion as a branch meeting of chartered accountants in Beaconsfield. Others give golden reports.

The River
The Thames still offers the best, and perhaps the least tiring way of getting a

quick impression of the essential London, and there is a curious detached pleasure in cruising along it, hearing its traffic and seeing its metropolitan sights, yet being reminded, by gulls and the movement of tides (which reach as far as Teddington, indeed that is what the word means, tiding-town) that you are on water which reaches to Amsterdam, Bombay, New York.

If you have only half a day to spare it is better to go, from the piers at Charing Cross, *down* the river. It takes pretty well an hour and a half to get even to Kew up-river, from Westminster pier. You may well see MPs having tea on the terrace of the Houses of Parliament, and shortly after pass the **Tate Gallery** (ah, always forgotten, because it is simply not near any nodal point, you just have to go along the Embankment and there, surrounded by a lot of nothing-offices and flats, is our finest collection of Impressionists and Post-Impressionists, including the Van Gogh *Sunflowers* and the Seurat *Baignade*, plus the Whistler *Nocturne*, a lot of Manet, British art of all periods . . .). But after that, beyond a few oddities, such as some rather jolly figures on Vauxhall Bridge, only visible from the river, of allegorical ladies who turn out to be things like Art, Literature, Science, Agriculture and such, by (who would have thought it) Lady Scott, wife of the Antarctic explorer—and wisps of straw traditionally hanging from any bridge under repair, as a warning of something or other to bargemen, presumably not to come with too-high loads of hay—and a suspiciously sewage-like smell by Mortlake, all you see is a lot of old warehouses till you get to Kew, after this nearly an hour and a half.

(No, stay, I see from the map there is a Main Drainage Works at Mortlake, maybe that's where the smell comes from. I *knew* I had read that anti-pollution measures have been so successful on the Thames that there are salmon in it again.)

Kew Gardens, as everyone calls the Royal Botanical Gardens, are of course one of the glories of London, where the pleasures offered range from that which anyone can feel at the sight of glorious seasonal displays, a landscaped park containing the famous pagoda, woodland, river views, a royal palace (it was here that Pope wrote the well-known couplet for the collar of the Prince of Wales's dog: 'I am His Highness' dog at Kew; Pray tell me, sir, whose dog are you?') to the most rarefied intellectual joy of the true botanist, for it is a world centre for plant identification and classification. And there's the very elegant hothouse by Decimus Burton, reflecting that marvellous first Victorian excitement of the possibilities of cast iron and glass. There's the sheet of ornamental water by which I heard one of my favourite Overheard Remarks. *1st Woman to 2nd Woman, after long silence watching the squawking comings and goings of mallards*: 'H'm. Very bird-like, aren't they?' There's the Queen's Garden, laid out in formal 17th-century style, full of rare herbs.

In fact the river is beginning to get interesting now. Across the river from you is **Syon House**, more great gardens, in fact designed by Capability Brown, surrounding a house designed by Robert Adam; the nearest place to the centre of London where you can see a major collaboration between these two supreme exponents of that remarkable urge of the turbulent, violent 18th century to tame nature without killing it, to develop a classical architecture which although tuned to the kind of harmonious mathematics that only the mind of *man* can appreciate, yet somehow is anything but dead, cold, merely a cold exercise in the classic. Oh, there was a seething mass of brutality and struggle behind it all, as the no doubt correctly egalitarian lumpen-intellectual boys are always telling us (in our own sublimely peaceful and non-brutal century). Nevertheless it was Yeats who wrote (in a poem which in fact goes on to recall a highly apocryphal tale about an obstreperous tenant farmer's ear being brought in to his no doubt English landlady, Mrs French, on a little silver dish):

> Surely among a rich man's flowering lawns
> Amid the rustle of his planted hills
> Life overflows without ambitious pains
> And rains down life until the basin spills.

It's a matter of having a dream of what life could be, in an ideal world, for you, on this earth, if you had the money and the land and the architect and the landscape gardener and all the other craftsmen of your choice. That is the appeal of great houses. Come to think of it, that is the appeal of Kew Gardens as well.

As a matter of fact as you go up the Thames you are doing on a larger scale what I described on p. 32, getting from one rurality to another, mysteriously by-passing urban stone and brick. Only instead of merely (*merely?*) getting from Bayswater to Westminster you are getting large, ample hints of the broad meadows of the Thames valley, of Berkshire, even Oxfordshire, while you are in places which to reach by road means many a dismal suburban or cross-town traffic jam. Because the next thing you come to after graceful **Richmond Bridge** (1777, painted by Turner when he lived in Twickenham, and the best one over the Thames) is **Richmond Park**: 2,358 acres, the largest urban park in Britain, a real tame wilderness with rides and trees and woods and slopes and lakes and wild deer; wonderful at any time, but perhaps especially on fine golden autumn days, when it somehow seems even more in tune with the Georgian calm of the town of Richmond, for all its modern interpenetration by new housing for people whose incomes start at £10,000 a year.

And so, if you do not stay too long at one of the marvellous riverside pubs, such as the London Apprentice of Isleworth, which I see I have myself unaccountably passed (it was just beyond Syon Park) you come to unquestionably the greatest treasure of the river: **Hampton Court**.

Everyone knows about the Maze, which actually only dates from the reign of Queen Anne, 1702–1714. Curious reign, that. Anglican, daughter of Catholic James II, knowing that the Act of Settlement ruled out Papists and that the throne would go through the female line to George, Elector of Hanover, because he was the son of Sophia, the only Protestant granddaughter of James I (really we ought to say the Sophian rather than the Georgian Age), Anne determined that her brother James the Old Pretender should succeed, but on her death German George, coming over all the same, couldn't have ruled even if he had been much better at it since he and his ministers literally didn't speak the same language, hence Robert Walpole, the first Prime Minister . . . well, it's no good resisting these digressions, history is in the air at Hampton Court. What I meant to say earlier on is that the place itself is a maze, of glories in which you could get lost.

Really it is two palaces. When you stand in the south-east corner of the heavenly semicircular Fountain garden, with its blazing formal beds and paths and formally conical yew trees (very pre-Capability Brown!), it overlaps the southern, riverward end of the classical east façade of the part which Wren built for William and Mary (1689–1702), with its white stone parapets over a front with its perpendicular rows of three windows—tall, surmounted by round, then the cornice, then square—in their confident red-brick setting. But stretching away from you to the west you see the wonderfully organic, 'they-just-growed' lines of the original Tudor palace, made of those much darker and smaller, burnt-red, unattainably mellow bricks.

This, with its fantastical chimneys and turrets and stairways and courts, with names like Fish Court, Chapel Court, Master Carpenter's Court, was the palace of Cardinal Wolsey, which he gave to that monster Henry VIII in 1529 in a vain attempt to avoid downfall, inevitable if he couldn't wangle a divorce from Catherine of Aragon. In the Clock Court there is a kind of Elizabethan computer, the Astronomical Clock by Nicholas Oursian (1540) which shows not only the hour, the day, the month, the number of days since 1 January and the phases of the moon, but the times of high water at London Bridge.

One side of this court is the Great Hall, which has the kind of roof (like the one at the Temple, and in several Suffolk churches I know, which convince you that some man-made objects reach a kind of perfection from which subsequent ages can only decline. The railway, and probably the postal service, in Britain, reached a peak in 1913; the old black public phone, 2d in the box which you could get back if not connected, reached perfection of service and design in the 1950s; the digital watch is a sad decline from the instantly clear round-faced one . . . well, the hammer-beam roof is an unsurpassable peak in the conception of a roof where the timbers, while demonstrating principles of mechanics and weight-bearing as nakedly as a text-book diagram, are simultaneously majestic and joyous works of art. It is like keeping the rain out with a symphony.

Hammer-beam, though not perhaps in the class of, say *narthex* (it only means a covered porch) or *astragal* (a small moulding of circular section), does have the kind of technical-term sound that frightens laymen away. But to appreciate the soaring, fantasticated splendour of the roof of the Great Hall at Hampton Court all you need to know is that a hammer is T-shaped. The vertical part of the T, resting on a *corbel* (but never mind) supports a horizontal, half of which you don't see, since it goes out into the great thick wall. The part you see projecting inside supports an *arched brace* flying across to meet the hammer-beam on the other side. Above the arched brace there is a horizontal *collar-beam*, from the centre of which the *king-post* goes up to the peak (sorry, the *ridge*) of the roof. . . but oh, the carvings and in-fillings, the development of the bosses like marvellous hanging wooden stalactites; the triumph of it!

I once heard a Purcell masque and an Elizabethan jig (really a ballad opera) in this heavenly room; all the pleasures of being a king without the awfulness of being someone like Henry VIII. What an evening!

Of course there are books about Hampton Court too, but now we shall have to rush round the rest of it: the paintings in the Royal Apartments (in the Wren part)—Correggio, Tintoretto, wonderful Veronese of the *Marriage of St Catherine*, the famous *Young Man* of Bellini; the view of the gardens and their avenues from the Queen's Drawing-room; the fountains (both inside the Fountain Court and outside in the gardens); the real (i.e. *royal*) tennis court, where that infinitely complicated game is played involving bouncing the ball off a kind of bicycle shed at the side; the vine, the riverside walk, the superb wrought-iron gates—and, good heavens, nearly omitted, the roof of the Chapel, where you can see that the transition has really been made from the medieval roof to the Renaissance ceiling; almost, for paintings and stars now appear on such surfaces as are not occupied by the exuberant vaulting, and the stalactite bosses are delicious works of art of their own, with gilded angels playing musical instruments.

And so to Windsor, last and greatest of the royal castles by the Thames, still an official residence of the Sovereign; but not here, for Windsor is outside London, and we shall come to it on p. 66. And in any case the logical counterpoise, as a Thames-side glory, to Hampton Court is at the other end of the metropolitan Thames. **Greenwich** was the site of a royal palace for centuries, a favourite place of Henry VII (1457–1509), for instance (the one who, as Richmond, defeated Richard III, ended the medieval-type Wars of the Roses, married Elizabeth of York and let England settle down to some good old solid peaceful development, ready for the fantastic Elizabethan age). The present building, which for a short period was a palace for William of Orange, was by, guess who, Wren. But William did not use it much, and it became the Royal Naval Hospital, and, in 1873, the Royal Naval College. It is the finest piece of architecture to be seen from the river (which enhances it marvellously, and is a great argument, if you are pressed for time for a river trip, for taking it *downstream*).

In the old days (i.e. the Fifties) when the *Observer* was a smaller, more intimate and, dare one say it, *jollier* paper than it is now I once organised the annual outing. Two really not very large boats, perfectly capable of holding the entire staff, from Ivor Brown, ex-Editor, Shakespeare scholar, etymologist and theatre critic, to the boys from the front office, went from Blackfriars Bridge to Southend, where we got on to the longest pier in Britain, over the muddy estuary, enjoyed shrieking fun-fairs, ate whelks and jellied eels, then had a very convivial dinner on the evening return voyage.

We had disembarked for a brief stop at Greenwich in the morning. Truly a magnificent sight over the sparkling water; two noble classical pedimented wings, with an open parade ground between them, and at the rear centre the even more elegant Queen's House, designed by Inigo Jones, flanked by two splendid domed Wren turrets. In my party was Johnny Minton, for my money the best of that temporarily-forgotten school of British romantic artists of the Forties. No one could have guessed, from his ebullient conversation that day, that we were only a few months from his tragic suicide. There was a slight thump from the bowels of the boat. 'Oh dear,' he said, 'I do hope there hasn't been some sort of marine *disaster*.' Then, surveying the great empty parade ground as we drew alongside, 'I do think they should have been drawn up in some kind of military formation to welcome us, perhaps even fired a volley of *muskets*.' Ah, an artist different from those solemn blokes that get half-hour TV documentaries to themselves these days.

We saw the main things, the mainest of all being the chapel and the famous painted ceiling of the great hall. On a shorter, evening trip years later, this time with the staff of *Punch* (writers are always drinking on boats), I passed moored in the river the little *Gipsy Moth IV*, recently sailed single-handed round the world by the man who was to become *Sir* Francis Chichester later that very week. Today you can still see it at Greenwich, near the splendid old clipper *Cutty Sark*; a glorious but slightly sad sight, since this lovely, valiant creature of the waves is now set solidly in concrete. But she is one of the many sights worth seeing in Greenwich, with its park, its Royal Observatory (now with a Planetarium) and of course that Meridian. In fact, since Greenwich was also the first place to build itself one of the new arena-type theatres (and very comfortable it is too), which has got quite a reputation for being the place to see good new plays before they move to the expensive West End, a very good way to spend the second half of a day would be to sail to Greenwich, disembark and explore it, go to the theatre and come back by train (you're only four miles from central London).

On the river trip you will still see quite a lot of grotty-looking warehouses;

and you will not see the dockside activity below Tower Bridge which before the war made London the greatest port in the world. Containerisation (a word as unlovely as the process it describes is visually unromantic, particularly on the narrow inland roads choked by its giant cubic trucks) and incessant labour troubles have meant that the old **docks** are now either filled in, or inland lakes about which half-hearted claims are periodically made that they are going to be jolly residential and amenity areas. But you will also see (if you have started from Charing Cross) the historic although now commercialised southern shoreline. That huge tower you see by London Bridge is the new Guy's Hospital; but half-buried by viaducts just near it is **Southwark Cathedral**, and near *that* is the site of the Globe Theatre, of which Shakespeare in 1599 was one of the builders. Then Tower Bridge, through the Pool of London, the Thames twisting through an area where every other name reflects the growth of this misty riverside into the greatest and first *entrepôt* of the modern (i.e. 19th-century) world: Jamaica Road, Odessa Point, Canada Dock, Greenland Dock, West India Dock, East India Dock, Deptford (where Peter the Great came to learn shipbuilding, foreseeing no doubt a time when Russia would *have* a navy), and so to Greenwich. No more bridges. A sense of opening out, sails filling, history starting with voyages, London's huge part in creating the modern world. To quote T. S. Eliot again:

> The river sweats
> Oil and tar
> The barges drift
> With the turning tide
> Red sails
> Wide
> To leeward, swing on the heavy spar.
> The barges wash
> Drifting logs
> Down Greenwich reach
> Past the Isle of Dogs. . . .

Hampstead

It is often said that London is a collection of villages, and before we leave it—before *anyone* leaves it—it would be a pity to miss Hampstead. It has been tarted up, expensivised, and filled with rather awful boutiques since my wife and I moved into our first married home, at the end of a little cul-de-sac called Prospect Place, as well it might be, since we could see out over the cemetery where the painter Constable was buried, over London, to the blue heights of Surrey. Just below us, the handsome 18th-century parish church, at the end of grand Georgian Church Row. Just above us, on Holly Hill, a wonderful little road which was even more withdrawn till the late Hugh Gaitskell MP sold off some land for private building opening on to it, the most beautiful little Catholic church in London, St Mary's, with its little Brazilian-mission-type bell and Madonna in niche, its quiet blue-and-white interior. Long pre-dating the re-establishment of the Catholic hierarchy in England, it is more than old enough for people like Dickens (attending the requiem for a Catholic friend) to have been there.

When we lived in Hampstead (in 1956 we moved from the place where Constable was buried to East Bergholt, Suffolk, the place where he was born) there were still old-established grocers with coffee-grinding machines with those curved-spoke, cast-iron, primitive, Victorian-looking flywheels going round and blowing magic coffee roast smells into the street; and wonderful

St. John's, Hampstead.

ironmongers with floor-to-ceiling drawers containing various kinds of nail and screw. It was here that, having learned that a door hinge where the cut slopes so that the door rises a little over the carpet as you open it is called a *rising hinge*, I went in and asked for a pair with an understandable pride. 'Certainly sir,' said the ironmonger, 'left-hand or right-hand?' There were little non-ethnic restaurants, and not a Fash'n-Pash'n boutique in sight.

But Hampstead is still *the* classic reminder that all Englishmen, Londoners included, have a feeling for the country. If you climb all those steps to the equivalent height in Paris, Montmartre, all you come to is the Sacré Coeur and a lot more buildings. But the climb up narrow Heath Street offers a promise of open sky and space that is not denied when you get to the great space of Hampstead Heath, London's own wilderness of open space, sandy lanes, sudden grassy skylines, trees, ponds, views over London or to blue western and northern horizons. Two splendid famous pubs for summer outdoor drinking, Jack Straw's Castle and The Spaniards. Down at one end of the tidemark of brick, Keats's House, now a museum devoted to the poet. At the other end of the Heath, one of the treasures of London, the delightful **Kenwood**.

The whole thing is a notable example of the English skill in finding answers to that profound problem so succinctly expressed by Dr Opimian in Thomas Love Peacock's *Headlong Hall*:

> 'I distinguish the picturesque and the beautiful, and I add to them, in the laying out of grounds, a third and distinct character, which I call *unexpectedness*.'
> 'Pray, sir,' said Mr Milestone, 'by what name do you distinguish this character, when a person walks round the grounds for a second time?'

(Come to think of it, that's the problem of life itself, not just landscape gardening; how to avoid sameness, staleness, boredom . . .) Well, Kenwood somehow is always a rewarding surprise. You come out of the wildest part of the Heath to a vista of well-kept, sloping lawn at the foot of which is a lake, backed by huge trees, and crossed by an elegant-looking classical bridge at one end. On closer inspection this turns out to be a dummy wooden façade, a characteristically 18th-century human landscape joke by the man for whom Robert Adam built the great house at the top of the lawn: the first Earl of Mansfield, a great Lord Chief Justice (from 1756 till 1788). He made the famous judgment compelling a man who had brought a black slave back to England to release him. *Fiat justitia ruat coelum*, he said; let justice be done though the heavens fall. As we all know, the heavens stayed where they were, and quite right too; but he was a great man all the same, and not only because of that charming bridge, now seen by thousands on summer nights when the big London symphony orchestras make this natural arena London's nearest approach to the Hollywood Bowl.

The house itself is a constant delight. The last time we were there we had its rooms practically to ourselves on a glorious sunshiny January day. Yes, there was the sublime Rembrandt self-portrait (best of them all, who would have thought an old man could paint that turban affair on his head with such a sense of joy, let alone portray such a depthless, self-knowing, all-knowing gaze?); there the great calm Cuyp *View of Dordrecht*, my favourite marine painting with that wonderful pink sunset light beginning to spread over everything, the towers, the water, the noble sails and rigging, the clouds, from somewhere off to the right of the picture; there the library with its perfect proportions, Corinthian pillars, a room, Adam says, 'intended both for a Library and for receiving company'. There too the great works by

Reynolds, Gainsborough, Turner (magnificent, all stormy green and grey, *Fishermen Upon a Lee Shore in Squally Weather*), Raeburn, Lawrence . . . and of course we must go and see that Vermeer light-miracle, *The Guitar Player*, that girl in the yellow dress and the ermine-fringed jacket plunking gently away in the window of that unattainably peaceful, perfect, happy interior. And all the time as we wandered yet again (FREE!) through this treasure-house we were aware of an actual twingling and twangling of guitars and rather unsteady open-string violin notes and recorder tunes. When we got to the room which contains the Vermeer (and now I look at my notes, the Rembrandt as well, so it's poetic licence to suggest we had already seen it that day; but everything else here, everything else in this *book*, is true), we found a lot of children, up to about age 12, with these instruments, and their teachers, one of whom was dressed in an exact replica of the Vermeer, and was playing the guitar. All part of a little extra-mural scheme laid on by local schools. I just hope it changed one or two young lives. *I* shan't forget it. As we went out another teacher was saying to another group, in front of an elegant carved wooden pedestal in the hall, 'now when you think of the man who spent hours and days and weeks doing that beautiful carving, it's not very nice for him to think of you rushing past without even looking at it, is it?' Ah, Hampstead!

Windsor

There is so much to see at Windsor, so many actual buildings, so much history, so much art (and if you happen to be there on the right day so much pageantry—is it real or is it just dressing-up in the age of the micro-chip?) that you can go there many times and still only (*only?*) have a great jumble of impressions, odd contrasts, still feel you haven't found out much more than a first-time tourist who has reported to the Tourist Information Office (in the station) and been taken round on one of the excellently informative, roughly two-hour trips. (But fee, now without State Apartments, £3.) Most people with any romance in them (and breathes there a man with soul so dead?) must come away with a kind of shorthand notes in their heads. Thus:

Turn off M4, great whizzing howling daren't-turn-your-head motorway escape route from London to relaxed romantic orcharded west, suddenly, instantly, there it is, why never even noticed before, immense towered crenellated outline on low crest, and heavens, that's Eton down there on the left. Round one-way typical English small-town system into car-park, easy, but then this a wet October morning, must be hell in season. Can already see grassy bank, round great brooding Curfew Tower, stop to read tablet in wall

ROBERT KEAYNE 1595–1626
A MEMBER OF THE HONORABLE ARTILLERY COMPANY OF LONDON, A DISTING-UISHED MEMBER OF THE ANCIENT AND HONORABLE ARTILLERY COMPANY OF MASSACHUSETTS, THE OLDEST MILITARY ORGANISATION IN AMERICA, 1638. A WISE AND PUBLIC-SPIRITED CITIZEN, A LIBERAL PATRON OF EDUCATION. A GENEROUS CONTRIBUTOR TO THE FOUNDATION OF HARVARD COLLEGE, CAMBRIDGE, MAS-SACHUSETTS, 1636. ERECTED BY THE ANCIENT AND HONORABLE COMPANY OF MASSACHUSETTS, U.S.A., 1912.

No, come on, a thousand years or so to get through yet. But good heavens, look, this is a town as well as a monument-cum-jewel-casket, people live here. Here is a snug-looking repertory theatre. The posters outside it are for a play called *Jet Set*, the photographs show a lot of Home-Counties-looking actors and actresses involved in some sort of massage. What would the Old

Queen have thought of *that*? Next-door, a very English-looking Tea Room, with bentwood chairs, tables with cloths, but it's called Don Pepino's.

Turn left, up-hill, southwards from river, round massive Curfew Tower, main street, smart pubs, touristy wool, leather, etc. shops. Before entrance to Castle at top of hill, turn off right to station, whole road has glass roof, greeny light, faintly holiday resort, no-tradesmen-or-commerce feeling about station. Notice on wall says '2 million visitors last year. HELP to keep Windsor tidy'. The '2' is on a new piece of board obviously placed over the original '1', and HELP is in red.

Go to Tourist Information Office here, book accompanied tour, they say come back 3 p.m. (while I am waiting they phone round and fix up nice cheap but good bed-and-breakfast for young couple with rucksacks in front of me). Pass open wide stone-and-cobble space on left in front of now all-dominating castle, at top of hill is jolly Guildhall by (was the man *everywhere*?) Wren (well, he was certainly here, his father was a Dean here, though nobody quite knows where he was during the Commonwealth, 1649–1660). It has pillared portico reaching out over space with seats where tourists, school parties, eat sandwiches. Outside pillars are weight-bearing, city council insisted that inner ones should also be, but Wren actually made them stop short about 2 inches from ceiling, just to show them.

Niche contains statue of Queen Anne, rather cross-looking lady with sceptre, it says ARTE TVA SCVLPTOR NON EST IMITABILIS ANNA, Anne cannot be imitated by your art, sculptor. Could be taken two ways, that.

Behind Guildhall, round narrow cobbled short streets like film set, huddle of smart pubs, King's Head has facsimile of warrant for execution of Charles I above door, Ye Olde Nell Gwynne's House full of clocks and antique silver. Windsor Chocolate House, Viennese Patisserie, Edinburgh Woollen Mills. By now aware that Windsor must be in direct line of planes landing at Heathrow, centuries of time but a few miles in space away, every two minutes huge sighing wheel-down monsters dip over, at what looks like 600 feet, can see people at windows, just hope there aren't other-wind days when they're climbing, at full power . . .

Yet in mad way, every curse has blessing, lovely when it stops etc. Come out on to south front of Castle, look down vast walk that stretches to horizon, it ends at Copper Horse, statue of George III, but that is still only in middle of enormous Windsor Great Park, which contains Village, mysterious farms Closed To The Public, trees, vistas, the Savill Garden, the Obelisk, more shut-off bits, Smith's Lawn where the grandees play polo, the Valley Gardens, and farthest off, Virginia Water, tree-fringed lake, London opening out to bosky south . . .

And over all this, huge aircraft sighing down every two minutes.

A splendid notice: VISITORS ON HORSEBACK ARE REQUESTED TO KEEP OFF THE VERGES OR ANY MOWN GRASS. Should like to be a visitor on horseback but too late now. Another notice, Aerosol-sprayed on old wall, says WINDSOR WHITES KILL DATCHET REDS.

Well, accompanied tour, guide knows his stuff, it's all in guide book but somehow you take it in more and anyway it's quicker. Castle is huge curved oblong. Circular Middle Ward contains Round Tower (perfectly magnificent picture of George IV by Lawrence, whose exuberant paint makes you see that, as King he could wear ceremonial clothes as well as he had worn fashionable ones as Prince Regent–it's in Garter Throne Room in State Apartments, a few paragraphs off yet–is of the man who had apartments of Upper Ward extended and made more comfortable. He cheerfully added 38

The Thames at Windsor.

feet to this Norman [1170] feature so that it shouldn't lose its dominance).

At bottom, westward, townside end of Lower Ward is Curfew Tower and slightly above, Horseshoe Cloisters, like elegant Tudor block of flats, now homes of lucky old priest-vicars and choir. Organist lives in house of well-known composer John Marbeck (d.1585, wrote first Anglican chants). Here also Chapter Library, and from Library Terrace marvellous northward view down to curving Thames, you can see why William the Conqueror chose this as strategic site. Enemy visible from miles off, now you see spreading London, tower blocks, newer kinds of factories, electr brrrraaaaaaaaaaaa AAAAAAAAAAAAAAaaaaaa (sorry, another aircraft) of modern times.

Yet here we still are, here Queen still lives (in April, and bits of March, May, June, December), here headquarters of greatest, oldest chivalric body in world. Order of Garter, founded by Edward III in 1348, perhaps inspired by legend of King Arthur. Hands up who doesn't know origin of its motto, *Honi soit qui mal y pense*, uttered by king who noticed smirks of courtiers when he picked up blue velvet garter of his dancing partner, Countess of Salisbury; 'shame on anyone who thinks ill of it', which can be generalised into 'if you've got a nasty mind you'll do nasty things'.

Still, tourist or not, you can't help thinking on large themes such as the passage of time, mortality, etc. even while the Nikons and Pentaxes are clicking. How very appropriate that the poet Gray is also closely associated with this area.

> The boast of heraldry, the pomp of power,
> And all that beauty, all that wealth e'er gave,
> Awaits alike the inevitable hour:—
> The paths of glory lead but to the grave.

They do indeed, but meanwhile how splendid to be alive, capturing this delicious holiday moment with a Nikon (or, in my case, an old Rolleicord, poor man's version of Rolleiflex). And look again, just down below you, easily reachable by a pedestrians-only bridge, is **Eton**, of which T. Gray wrote gloomily:

> Alas! regardless of their doom
> The little victims play;
> No sense have they of ills to come,
> Nor care beyond today

in a gloomy poem, all about how awful life is going to be, even for Eton boys, and ending with lines which I have always thought particularly appropriate to several of the admittedly not many Old Etonians I have actually met:

> No more;—where ignorance is bliss
> 'Tis folly to be wise.

You can see his tomb in the churchyard, *the* Country Churchyard in which he wrote the *Elegy* from which of course everyone knows that first quotation comes, five miles up the road at **Stoke Poges**. Meanwhile, down below, you can see the beautiful Perpendicular Chapel of **Eton**, built by Henry VI, like a kind of echo of the miracle now about to be entered, **St George's Chapel**.

People argue about whether this is the most beautiful Perpendicular chapel in England (and therefore the world, since by that time on the Continent they were well into Renaissance domes and such) or whether the palm goes to King's College Chapel at Cambridge (see p. 112). In the end, for my money, the latter wins because less clutter (after all, *they* didn't have to find room for all those royal tombs) and for the same reason that people get the gold at ice-skating competitions: a marginally greater elegance.

But St George's Chapel has the same pillarless, box-of-light, effortlessly sophisticated fan-vaulted roof and other heart-lifting qualities the moment you enter, *plus* the sense that Henry Ford was talking out of his radiator cap, history is *not* bunk, it is real, it is here, it is *us*, this *happened*. And, perhaps most of all, this *grew*.

It was built between 1477 and 1528. Even before you enter you must crane your neck to see the 'King's Beasts', heraldic stone animals perched against the sky; the antelope of Henry V, the swan of Henry IV, the Lion of England, and, coming down a notch, the Yale of Beaufort (pretty grand family though; earls and dukes of Somerset. The *yale*, who would have thought it, is in the *Oxford English Dictionary*: 'a fabulous beast with horns and tusks'). Some of them are 1920s replacements, like some of the stones in the roof. But do not worry. People as early as (here he comes again) Sir C. W. were worried about cracks appearing in so vast a building on such not very deep foundations. But essentially it is what it has always been: an original Perpendicular miracle.

Go in by south porch (i.e. bottom right hand as you face altar, in east as always, it isn't only Moslems who have this compass sense of where God *is*), perhaps eye drawn straight away to marvellously post-medieval, indeed Romantic monument, since it is by Matthew Wyatt to Princess Charlotte, only daughter of George IV, who died in childbirth in 1817; she lies under shroud under which her face is moulded, angels are escorting her soul away, very dramatic, upward-moving composition. Nice idea for newspaper or art competition, Design Your Own Tomb. Here obviously somebody royal or grand in every available chapel. George VI has simple black marble slab saying George VI, Edward VII has effigy with his dog Caesar (George V last effigy to have animal, a lion). Tomb of Edward IV has simply the most marvellous iron grille work that can ever have been made, in 1482 or any other time. On other side of chancel, huge sword of Edward I, no wonder he clobbered the Welsh and was called the Hammer of the Scots, it is about seven feet long. Delicious little chantry, like kind of holy doll's house full of gold paint and tiny paintings of martyrdom of St Stephen, it is like being inside an illuminated missal. Bigger, grander, more commercially boastful, chantry of Sir Reginald Bray, who like many textile men of those days, and unlike those of ours, gave a lot of money to the church, and in his chantry (place where priests are supposed to say Mass for soul of the deceased for ever, pity so many of them were built such a little time before the Reformation) has his device of the hemp-bray (looks like a kind of comb) repeated 175 times. All this and much more in the great high-roofed, green-lighted, high, holy stone hall, shuffle-murmur of tourists replacing the sound of prayer. But there, history there, right there . . .

And of course the centre, the heart, the dark oak stalls of the choir, where there is one for each Knight of the Garter. Above each stall a helmet and crest, a mantle and a banner. The one for Emperor Hirohito has banner surprisingly reminiscent of the Tudor Rose. Last time I was there, Lord Mountbatten's shield had been taken away. There was a wreath there.

The pomp of heraldry. No safer than anything else from some oaf with a bit of plastic explosive and a closed mind. But still there.

Behind the chapel some delightful cloisters, and reminder that one of the things that disappeared at the Reformation was celibacy of the clergy, since there are holes in the cloister seats made for the old children's game of nine-men's morris. Unless the adult and now married clergy played it, of course; but this seems unlikely.

This brings you out towards the Middle Ward, go past Round Tower to State Apartments. Enter through Grand Staircase into Grand Vestibule, nice Gothick-fancy vaulting and lantern roof, walls lined with weapons arranged in symmetrical patterns as if in superior ironmongers's, then showcases of pistols etc., and the actual bullet that killed Nelson. After that it's a matter of your personal taste how many of the pictures in this incredible sumptuous setting of one gilt, chandeliered room after another you remember.

I found it more concentrated, more interesting towards the end (worth remembering that you don't *have* to be in a party or move on, at least not during the off-season occasions when I was there). I've already mentioned the wonderful Lawrence of George IV (in the Garter Throne Room, to see which you will already have been through the Waterloo Chamber, *full* of Lawrences of all kinds of foreign grandees like Marshal Blücher, Cardinal Gonsalvi, splendid red robes and curtains, classical buildings in distance), but these are rather high up and far away. It's only when you get to smaller rooms with names like the King's Dressing Room, King's Dining Room, etc. (reminder that in old days king ate, went to bed publicly, or at least for privileged spectators, often before retiring to *real* bedroom, with real mistress etc.) that you can get close.

But do not, even if you have to turn back, to displeasure of attendants, miss marvellous Van Dycks (Queen's Drawing Room), especially of Five Youngest Children of Charles I—two girls, young James in crimson satin looking straight at camera, huge St Bernard-type dog, smaller girl and baby; the famous Van Dyck also of Charles I, full-face and two profiles, in particularly rich little King's Dressing Room, with the Vermeer *Lady at the Virginals*, the Rembrandt *Noli Me Tangere* . . . oh, and then you get to the *Queen's* Audience Chamber, with one of those tumultuous painted ceilings by Verrio, showing one of them, Charles II's Queen Catherine, being drawn by swans to the Temple of Virtue. Poor dear, not much Virtue around there. She brought us Bombay among other things in her dowry, but went back to Portugal in the end.

Marvellous ceiling, though.

So you leave Windsor, glad that it was built, glad that all those kings and queens were there, glad *you* are not a king or queen and can drive off and see some more England; glad the—good heavens, it's all gone quiet, ah yes, no more aircraft—glad the wind has changed.

The South-East

It is very curious how an area which is passed over in ten minutes or a quarter of an hour between that sudden change in the aircraft engine noise, the stewardesses' scramble to clear the last cups and glasses to the galley, the final no-smoking and fasten seat-belts bit, and landing at Heathrow, can remind you, even when you are merely driving a car about in it, of infinitely greater scales of time and space.

There is a long ridge of high land west of **Guildford** (good, fat, rich, traffic-bound county town of Surrey, steep main street with enormous gilded clock projecting over pavement, post-Reformation Anglican (1936) cathedral on rather isolated hill other side of by-pass), which reaches eastward through hilly chalk London subtopia, makes one of its several dramatic view-affording drops to let the Medway flow northwards into the Thames, of which it is the largest tributary (now it's *really* an estuary, no accident that Chatham, prime naval base in the great old days, is there) and sweeps round the north coast of Kent to end at the South Foreland, which is only four miles north-east of Dover, nearest point to France; here the coast has already turned south from the North Foreland, at the top right-hand corner of Kent. This ridge is the **North Downs**.

If you follow the curve of the coast westwards, through Hythe and Rye (p. 74) you come to Hastings 6 miles from Battle, where the Abbey of St Martin stands on the historic site of the last successful invasion of England. Then you come to **Beachy Head**, at Eastbourne (quintessentially genteel English watering place, although for a perfect, preserved-in-aspic example of this, worth a visit in itself, I would recommend the beautifully isolated Sidmouth, p. 147, a long way further west in Devon). Beachy Head attracts lovers of exhilarating cliff-top walks or seascapes including the famous lighthouse, and, unfortunately, suicides.

And it is the beginning of the **South Downs** (as the people in these parts perversely call their noble rolling uplands). Technically these end in the broken high land above Southampton, in one of the valleys of which lies Winchester (p. 107). A glance at a relief map will show that north of this lie the Hampshire Downs, north of *them* the Berkshire Downs—a whole joyful summer day's landscape of blue views, wooded hills, snug stream-side villages, bare grass skylines, wonderful pubs, *this* is an industrial country?—then once you have crossed the Thames at Goring Gap you instantly rise to the Chilterns which run north-eastward round London finally to fizzle out by Newmarket in what *my* relief map optimistically calls 'The East Anglian Heights'; and there you have the whole system.

But for our purposes 'the South-East' means the area between the North Downs and the South Downs, and particularly that area, embracing most of Kent and Sussex, called the **Weald**, where you always seem to be coming upon fresh vistas with three folded horizons before you, seen across vistas of farmland, oast-houses (once used by individual hop-driers, now inhabited by stockbrokers), houses with a lot of hung tiles and white-painted clapboard.

Rightly called 'the Garden of England' and certainly the most rewardingly lush and characteristic countryside within easy reach of London.

But first, in every sense, comes—

Canterbury

Before you go into the premier cathedral of England you should go a little way (well, only half a mile outside the city walls, quite a lot of which remain) along the road to Ashford, and there you will find the tiny little church of St Martin. Of course it's utter bosh to say that England is a Christian country now, but it was *formed* by Christianity, you can see layers and layers of that medieval tumult ossified into stone; and nowhere is there a more dramatic dialogue than that between St Martin's and the splendid acme of church building in the high age, its impossible creamy bulk topped by the great Bell Harry Tower, occupying the sky, visible across the roofs from this small porch.

In AD 560 Ethelbert, King of the East Saxons, entered into alliance with Charibert, King of Paris and a dissolute character even though he was a Christian. But his daughter Bertha, whom Ethelbert married, was a devout Christian, and the Venerable Bede, father of English history, says 'there was on the east side of the city a church dedicated to St Martin which had been used by the Roman Christians in Britain. To this church the Queen, accompanied by Bishop Luidhard, came to worship.'

Roman Christians. Silver spoons bearing the old Christian CHI-RHO symbol (first two letters of the Greek name of Christ) found in Canterbury go back even further to a Christian community in Canterbury in AD 400, before the departure of the Legions. Certainly this is the oldest parish church in England that has been in continuous use since the 6th century. The west wall, incorporating Roman tiles, may be the oldest church wall in England: by comparison the Saxon doorway set into a chancel wall is quite modern. The church also has a marvellous, strong, primitive, round Saxon font in which the tradition is that Ethelbert was baptised, after he had agreed on the epoch-making visit of St Augustine in which, as the church's little booklet charmingly puts it, 'the King granted him freedom in a typically English way— "to preach his religion provided he used no compulsion or force in making converts" . . . the Queen must have been greatly touched to see the little church she had worshipped in so long in loneliness transformed into the hub and centre of a mission that was to sweep through England and effect the conversion of the people of this country in a very short space of time'.

Now you can appreciate all the more the overwhelming splendour of the cathedral: superb round-arched Norman crypt, the finest in England. That wonderful tower at the crossing is perhaps your first evidence that cathedral building was an art imported from France, and although we later caught up and developed differences, we have always preferred to put our height into towers rather than nave roofs. From the floor to the vaulted ceiling (inside the tower, of course) is 130 feet, and marvellously lofty it looks; but Rheims *nave* has a height of 125 feet, and Beauvais goes to an incredible 154 feet.

But you get more contrast with towers. And as in all cathedrals, a kind of stone text-book of changes in technique. After a fire in 1174 most of the church eastwards (i.e. towards the altar and choir) was rebuilt, and Canterbury has *two* lots of transepts. So you have first, westernmost transepts and Early English (i.e. the first pure Gothic arches) choir, even though they are not what you would expect since they stand on, of all things, Corinthian pillars; then the next transepts; then the famous Trinity Chapel, with the best glass in England; and of course the famous shrine of St Thomas à Becket, the troublesome priest got rid of on the altar by Henry II's too-zealous knights in 1170, canonised two years later, and buried in a shrine of which Erasmus 'who saw it in 1512', says Alec Clifton-Taylor in one of the 129 books that are required reading about churches, 'recorded that gold was the meanest thing to be seen there'.

His much-visited shrine was the chief (and, among other things, but only *among*), wealth-attracting feature of Canterbury. The Pilgrim's Way, which can still be followed on foot, is not, strictly speaking, that followed from London, via Rochester, by the immortal characters in Chaucer's *Canterbury Tales*. It starts, in fact, at another great cathedral, Winchester, goes over the high land to Alton, then follows the line of the North Downs the whole way.

They came, really, from richer, softer country. For all the smooth cathedral-city comfort of Canterbury, its comfortable geranium-hung pubs with visitors from all over the world sitting out drinking beer in the sunlight, its post-war pedestrians-only shopping precincts (now there's another miracle: there was bomb destruction during the last war all round that amazingly unharmed cathedral)—for all that, you are in East Kent, among the Jutes.

The people east (roughly speaking) of the Medway are called Men of Kent, as opposed to Kentish Men west of it. A bit farther down there are coalfields, that reach out under the sea. There is a kind of sandy, windy, open, no-nonsense feeling about this end of Kent. The business-like hovercraft, like a kind of marine bus, goes to France from Pegwell Bay, below Ramsgate. **Sandwich** is a nice little old atmospheric town, one of the **Cinque Ports**, those France-facing towns with special defence responsibilities (and privileges) going back to Norman times. It is one of the *original* ones, the others being Dover, Hastings, Romney and Hythe. Others, like Winchelsea and Rye, were added later, but they never changed the name to the Six Ports or the Sept Ports. At Chartwell (p. 85) you may see the full dress of the Lord Warden of the Cinque Ports, another favourite outfit of Churchill's. Like Rye and Hythe, Sandwich is not now even on the sea. It has a splendid gateway, the Barbican, ramparts, lovely houses, three fine churches and even more golf courses, one of which is the famous Royal St George.

Depending on the traffic (it's all right once you get on to the M2) you would usually be doing well to make Canterbury from central London in two hours, and even if you rushed round the cathedral and town (not recommended) you would have a very full day if you went on to Sandwich before returning. Certainly Hythe (still very much part of this open East Kent) would have to be part of another trip, or of a continuous tour.

But it is an extraordinary thing to have got this far in a book about Britain without getting to one of the things that sharply differentiates it from any other country. It is true that we have already passed Canterbury, where, near the gardens which contain a monument to Christopher Marlowe (local new theatre named, naturally, after him also), stands the engine *Invicta*, which was used on one of the first passenger railway lines in the world, from Canterbury to Whitstable, in 1830. It is therefore high time, before we look at any more of the South-East, or anywhere else, to consider—

The Steam Enthusiasts

Strictly speaking, the **Romney, Hythe and Dymchurch Railway** is not a classic example of the extraordinary steam-preservation enthusiasm which has given us, already, over three hundred steam depots (sometimes with only a few yards of actual line), actual lines, and locomotive-owning individuals or syndicates; hardly a county now where you can't, at weekends, smell that unmistakable smell compounded of steam, smoke and engine oil, or at the very least see four men in overalls, who turn out to be a dentist, an insurance man, a garage mechanic and a, yes, a retired engine driver, busily scraping rust from the boiler tubes of some huge locomotive, rescued just in time from the scrapyard in Wales, and brought here at enormous expense on a low-loader. By road, that is.

The R. H. & D. is a purpose-built line unique in the world; since its thirteen miles are 15-inch gauge, it has specially-built locomotives standing about as high as a man's chest. In fact everything is scaled down to a third of normal size. Neither of its termini, Hythe or New Romney, let alone the intermediate Dymchurch, would ever claim to be places of any particular importance, even though during the war their absurd and delightful little railway was 'taken over by the military', it says in one of the railway books. How absurd to think of soldiers trundling along the bleak evacuated shore, within range of large guns put on the French coast by Hitler and fired at this coast, used to invaders since Caesar; on what unimaginable errands or exercises could they have trundled along, at 20 m.p.h., which as the book points out is like 60 m.p.h. at that size?

It was built by two racing motorists, Captain Howey and Count Zborowski (lovely Twenties names!). You look *up*, from your seat in the tiny carriage, at cows and indeed people, elderly men hoeing the gardens, often shaped like small slices of pie, which is all that greedy real-estate land-carving has allotted to their close-packed bungalows. Level-crossing gates are closed, and real cars, at which again you are looking *up*, wait as the train chuffs past with tiny importance.

Now and then an unspoilt, pure vista of the waving grassy marsh (from which a famous breed of sheep took their name), or of beach and sea, gives an idea of what it was like when this splendid toy line, with its four-feet-high locomotives, was built.

It was rescued from economic trouble after the war by a new management consortium, packed with steam enthusiasts, the managing director being John Snell, ex-barrister. 'Suddenly I saw a great light and knew what I must do', he said. He was also ex-British Rail, like the driver of our train. 'Used to work in steam from Colchester.'

Was the money as good?

'I don't look at it like that. If you've got to work it might as well be at something you enjoy.'

That's the secret of it, of course. They, like their colleagues with full-size lines, do it because they love it. No doubt there is a certain element of nostalgia; it really was *Great* Britain that gave the world its railways. But mainly it is some kind of deep ancestral pride not only in steam and the purely engineering side of it, but, if they get half a chance, in creating the whole atmosphere and *service* of railways in the good old days.

No British Rail employee has ever looked anywhere near as smart as the uniformed Assistant Stationmaster, called John Frodsham (a progress chaser by trade), on his last week before being promoted to Operating Superintendent, whom I met at Bridgnorth, northern terminus of the **Severn Valley Line**. It runs 6½ miles through beautiful woods and meadows alongside the river to Highley. They began with raffles, 'steam week-ends', endless fund-raising activities, merely leasing Bridgnorth station. When later they formed

The Flying Scotsman.

a Holding Company with the ultimate intention of extending the line 13 miles to Kidderminster, crossing the river on a magnificent 100-year-old wooden bridge emerging from the high wooded banks, 60,000 £1 shares were taken up in a few weeks, and another £50,000 were shortly issued. They now have over 30 locomotives.

Of course, it's not intended to come back as a permanent railway (although if by some miracle it could, nothing would give them greater pleasure). It is open at week-ends, for tourists, families with children, and people who love steam trains—and on a summer Sunday it is easy to believe that this takes in most of the human race. The lines are technically inspected and not allowed to carry passengers unless they are passed to the same standards as those applied to British Rail. The difference is that they are run with enthusiasm as well as steam. A graffito in the men's lavatory at Bridgnorth says *Not everyone packs up at 5.30.*

They are all over the country. At Wakes Colne in Essex the **Stour Valley Railway** has eight locomotives at the moment crammed on to about a quarter of a mile of line. But they are on the branch line from Marks Tey, on the main London–Norwich line, to Sudbury in Suffolk, which is threatened with closure, and their ultimate ambition is to take it over and run it.

So far the only enthusiasts' society which has achieved such an ambition is the **Dart Valley Railway**. They made such a success of their line from Buckfastleigh, Devon (where there is a famous modern Benedictine Abbey) along the beautiful valley of the river Dart (six trains a day in the summer season), that they were allowed to take over, with good old Great Western Railway engines (of happy pre-nationalisation memory, with the still-remembered copper bands round their funnels) the marvellously picturesque route, *over British Rail lines*, from Paignton, next to Torquay, Britain's palm-treed, grand-white-villa-and-hotel answer to Nice, to Kingswear, of which more in the next paragraph but two.

The day I was on the Dart Valley line (which includes the Royal Mile, where royal trains used to be put for the night; nice quiet place for a night's sleep) they were getting ready for the evening Champagne Special, on which 40 executives (not *theirs*—paying passengers) were going to dine very well on the beautiful ex-GWR super-saloons, *King George* and *Duchess of York*, built for the old Plymouth boat trains. They would stop where they felt like it, dance in the dancing coach (evidently it wasn't going to be just executives) and come back when they felt like it. I was reminded of the splendid story in Churchill's *My Early Life* of his vewy gwand Commanding Officer who saw his London train disappearing round the curve at Aldershot. 'I'm afraid it's gone, Colonel', said the porter. 'Gone? Bwing me another.'

Their managing director (you see that sometimes the thing does blossom out from amateur part-time enthusiasm into professional whole-time enterprise, with all kinds of fusions of the two) came to them after they went public in 1969. It seems typical of England that when, after protracted negotiations, the first train ran on the line, they asked Lord Beeching, architect, if that is the word, of the brutal cuts of uneconomic British Rail lines in the sixties, to perform the opening ceremony. Not surprisingly, he said, 'If I had not closed this line, I should not have been able to open it now'.

They never looked back. They carried 200,000 passengers in the year. When they were allowed to take over the Paignton–Kingswear line it became, and still is, the only year-round scheduled steam rail service in Britain. It goes along the beautiful Goodrington Sands, climbs inland to Churston and descends through a quarter-mile tunnel to run along a southern bank of the Dart estuary, a sudden vision of climbing white houses on green hills across the yacht-crowded water and the Royal Naval College; five magical miles.

Returning from Kingswear on the first train, at 8.5 a.m., I found it full of many children going to the grammar school at Churston. It seemed an incredibly romantic journey to me; ferry across the bright water from Dartmouth, and here was this GWR locomotive, copper band round chimney and all, ready to puff away. What a way to go to school!

But they ambled up the platform. 'They just stroll up—never hurry in the morning', said the guard (who had worked for years on the GWR, including the Torbay Express). In the walk-through, slightly fusty carriages, the schoolkids were just schoolkids. Tough twelve-year-old long-hairs playing cards and smoking, but an equally tough-looking lot arguing about linear motors over a copy of the *New Scientist*, a studious girl carefully finishing off her homework.

Did steam mean anything to them? 'Well, I did notice the day we went over to steam it took ten minutes longer', said one girl (the Light Railway Order restricts them to 25 m.p.h.). Later in the day, when the train was crowded with holiday-makers, I heard one man repeat exactly what I had heard a man say on the Severn Valley: 'ah, the smell of it, I'd forgotten the smell!' At the station it was men of all ages who went up the platform to look at the engine. The kids did not seem particularly excited. Yesterday a jet, the Concorde, today a steam train, it's all one, their eyes seemed to say.

At **Quainton**, in an idyllic part of Buckinghamshire, they have only two-thirds of a mile of line for their weekend rides, but that doesn't stop them working happily away with thirty locomotives, and in one of their coaches, a wonderful 1901 LNWR (London and North-Western, before my time) diner there was a smell of furniture polish as a young woman rubbed at the carved walnut cornices, the *silver*-plated Art Nouveau curlicued brackets. 'This carriage is my baby, I'm not all that keen on the engines', she said as she showed me the spotless kitchen range and the wine cupboard.

The **Main Line Steam Trust** at **Loughborough**, Leicestershire, has ambitious plans to re-open 10 miles of the former Great Central line to Leicester. And predictably there is plenty of it about in the north of England, where after all the whole thing started. At Steamtown Carnforth, in Lancashire but only just (it is on the edge of the Lake District) they have twenty acres of workshops, five miles of line and the biggest heavy repair facilities in the country. In the Lake District itself they have another enchanting miniature railway where you sit in open carriages (although they have saloons as well) to be carried up from seaside Ravenglass seven miles into the beauties of **Eskdale** on a line once used for carrying ore. The full-size **Lakeside Railway** takes you 3½ miles to the shore of Windermere.

Shades of Wordsworth! The poem most often quoted in this context is the sonnet entitled 'On the projected Kendal and Windermere Railway' which begins

> Is then no nook of English ground secure
> From rash assault

and goes on in the same furious way, ending

> Speak, passing winds; ye torrents, with your strong
> And constant voice, protest against the wrong.

It's curious to reflect that nowadays so many people welcome back steam trains not only as something old but almost as something *natural*! As a matter of fact, there's a less-known sonnet, called 'Steamboats, Viaducts and Railways' which seems to say the opposite:

Motions and Means, on land and sea at war
With old poetic feeling, not for this,
Shall ye, by Poets even, be judged amiss!
Nor shall your presence, howsoe'er it mar
The loveliness of Nature, prove a bar
To the Mind's gaining that prophetic sense
Of future change, that point of vision, whence
May be discovered what in soul ye are.
In spite of all that beauty may disown
In your harsh features, Nature doth embrace
Her lawful offspring in Man's art; and Time,
Pleased with your triumphs o'er his brother Space,
Accepts from your bold hands the proffered crown
Of hope, and smiles on you with cheer sublime.

Many of the steam lines certainly run through poetically famous country. When you go down the incredibly steep hill from the moorland village of Haworth long made world-famous by the Brontës, at the bottom you may see a lovely old steam train of the **Worth Valley Railway** (*it* has thirty locomotives too) which runs from Keighley to Oxenhope Moor, about five miles, weekends and Wednesdays in July. Poor Branwell Brontë, outdistanced by his brilliant sisters, worked as a booking clerk on the London and Manchester Railway before he drank himself into oblivion. This little line was used in the filming of *Dombey and Son* for BBC Television. In *that* there is the most famous of many Dickens passages about railways:

Away, with a shriek and a roar, and a rattle, from the town, burrowing among the dwellings of men and making the streets hum, flashing out into the meadows for a moment, mining in through the damp earth, booming on in darkness and heavy air, bursting out again into the sunny day so bright and wide; away, with a shriek, and a roar, and a rattle, through the fields, through the woods, through the corn, through the hay, through the chalk, through the mould, through the clay, through the rock, among objects close at hand and almost in the grasp, ever flying from the traveller and a deceitful distance ever moving slowly within him; like as in the track of the remorseless monster, Death!

The very rhythm of the wheels is in those short phrases. No wonder the British were and still are poetic about steam; and it always seems most poetic of all on moors and high places. The longest line of all, 18 miles, runs over the airy, heathery, far-horizoned country between Grosmont and Pickering and is operated by the **North Yorkshire Moors Railway** (although, alas, only the northern four miles of it offer steam, the remainder as yet being mere diesel).

The Beeching cuts left Scotland with only one railway north of Inverness, and the steam enthusiasts don't seem to be so numerous there, either. However, their main operation is bang in the heart of an area you can hardly miss in a tour of the Highlands. The **Strathspey Railway** runs five romantic miles between its splendidly named HQ at Boat of Garten to Aviemore (p. 197).

By contrast, Wales can claim not only a considerable number but a kind of historical primacy. The whole fantastic movement developed when others saw the success of the **Tal-y-llyn Railway**, the first to be saved (1951) by a specially formed preservation society, of which that excellent writer on canals, railways and such subjects, the late L. T. C. Rolt, was the inspiration. It goes from a beautiful long lake, where you can float and look at the splendid height of Cader Idris, down through unspoilt hill woods to the coast at Tywyn. It is narrow gauge (2ft 3 in); and its neighbour some twenty miles to the north, which goes from the resounding Blaenau Ffestiniog to Porthmadog, as Portmadoc is now confusingly spelt, is even narrower (1ft 11½in). Both began their existence as carriers of stone and ore.

There are several other steam-preservation lines in Wales, but the most famous steam line of all has never needed preserving, having been in continuous use since it was opened in 1896. The **Snowdon Mountain Railway** earns the scorn of all mountaineers and the gratitude of everyone who enjoys superb mountain scenery without being as athletic as that, by taking people to the summit of the highest mountain in Wales. It is the only rack-and-pinion railway in Britain.

The pioneer line south of London was the very aptly-named **Bluebell Railway**—or at any rate aptly named in spring and early summer, when it runs through classic rural scenery between Uckfield, in Sussex, and Horsted Keynes; a year-round venture, week-ends in winter, daily in summer. And then there is the **Kent and East Sussex** (equally beautiful, three miles, planning to extend to ten, following the valley of the river Rother, already tackling, with some of its twenty locomotives, some of the steepest gradients in southern England). It runs to Rolvenden from Tenterden, a beautiful and characteristic small Kentish town—which brings us nicely back to the rest of—

The South-East (cont.)

At **Tenterden** you begin to get the real snug feeling of the Weald. To saunter down its beautiful wide main street, lined by Georgian and white-weatherboarded houses and excellent shops, you might perhaps think 'ah, tourist prices; rich-looking place!' Here you would be wrong. I seem to have bought all my shoes and trousers there for the past ten years, even though it is more than a hundred miles from where I live, and I just may not be one of their typical customers. But we are always passing through Tenterden, on a not really recommended journey which involves much frustrating queueing to get through the easternmost tunnel under the Thames (Dartford–Tilbury) to visit Norman Hackforth, Noel Coward's accompanist, inventor of the Tennis Elbow Foot Game, the best panel game in the world (and therefore thought to be too quick and frivolous by the BBC, who only really like people that talk v-e-r-y slow-ly; not that Norman himself gabbles—on the contrary, he achieved an enviable national fame in the days when there was only radio by being the Mystery Voice which said, in tones of truly oracular profundity *'and the next object is . . .'* in the long-running 'Twenty Questions'). Norman and his wife live in a magic cottage in a magic field overlooking Romney Marsh, and somehow the nearer I get there the more this feeling comes over me that I need new trousers, or new shoes . . .

Well, you would never think that the origin of this luxurious-looking place, *-den* meaning 'a woodland pasture for pigs', was 'the swine pasture of the people of Thanet'. Thanet is the name for the extreme eastern part of Kent, so you see that for all its snugness and smartness it is really only just in the Weald by courtesy. But it is here, coming from the east, that you suddenly find a great number of places ending in *-den*, *-field*, *-hurst* (knoll or copse) and *-ley* (forest, wood, glade) which are all reminders that this was all once a densely wooded area. The biggest paradox of all, of course, is that whereas it is now, quite rightly, regarded as a kind of vast park, which happens to grow a lot of fruit and do some farming but is really a kind of terrestrial heaven for the wealthier kind of antique dealer, retired person or commuter, the Weald was England's chief source of wood for the old heart-of-oak ships of the navy that Ruled the Waves. The purple heathery ridges of the beautiful Ashdown Forest once had far more trees than the Shepherd drawings of it in the *Winnie the Pooh* books today. But not only wood—it was also, until the Industrial Revolution, our chief source of iron, right back *to* the Iron Age.

Today almost any of the places ending in *-hurst* could justifiably be recommended as rewarding to visit; as rewarding as **Smarden**, also in this area, which some claim to be the most beautiful village in Kent (there is, or was, a Smarden Club in Oslo, Norway. This goes back to the days when Women's Institute ladies were making jam while the sky above them was full of Battle of Britain vapour trails, and later there were Free Norwegian troops in the area). Full of marvellous houses, a tremendous 14th-century church known as the Barn of Kent; and, like all such places, having a wealth of history in its field names—*Shatter Oak, Tainted, Gallows, Little Wild Carrots, Oyster Shell, Hawk's Eyes, Germany, Snail Thorne, Good Water, North America, Crooked Tom, Oven, Snug Horn, Fight Field*, this last commemorating a prize fight which took place there in 1859 between the champion Tom Sayers and Bill Benjamin. A thousand spectators came from London by train to where the new Dover Railway ended at that time.

Obviously nobody could write at that length about every village, and nobody would read him if he did. But I give it as an example, a few small particulars of something that is simply in general *there* in the air, in the feel of the place. Every one of these marvellously atmospheric places is atmospheric because of the centuries of change.

To get back to the *-hursts*, **Goudhurst** is one example of many (the *Goud* incidentally is pronounced to rhyme with *loud*, not *good*). You come up the wooded hill and there is this perfect rich village with its inviting pubs, its church from the tower of which you can see from Hastings to Rochester, the whole of Thanet; and the sense of being on a boundary which you always get on such hilltop villages, for a couple of miles south of you is the National Pinetum, and a couple of miles west is Scotney Castle in its lake setting, and—

—and more of these lakes. You can see whole chains of them from the high ground at the eastern Ashdown edge, called St Leonard's Forest. The streams were dammed to provide water power for the hammer mills of the old ironmasters. According to Sir William Addison in an invaluable little paperback called *Understanding English Place-names*, '*-hurst* seems to mean something more precise than wood—perhaps the wood from which timber was taken. Certainly Staplehurst must mean wood from which staples or posts were cut, and the hursts of Kent and Sussex were the woods from which timber was taken to feed the furnaces . . . we know that at Huggett's Furnace at Buxted on the edge of Ashdown Forest iron was worked at least as early as Vespasian'.

The iron masters built some of the finest homes in Sussex, including Bateman's in Burwash, the home of Rudyard Kipling. The more you look at this lush countryside of rolling forest, heath and snug village, the more extraordinary it is to think that this was once our chief industrial area. It would be nice to think that in a thousand years' time it will be possible for visitors, whether archaeologists or not, to get the same impression of romantic beauty from Manchester.

As a matter of fact the *-hurst* in this area most likely to be visited, and rightly so, is—

Sissinghurst

Like all the villages in this area, it is very pretty in itself. But its great glory is Sissinghurst Castle—or to be more precise, the gardens of Sissinghurst Castle. Not so much of a castle really; it is the pleasantly, age-tinted Tudor brick gatehouse, all that remains of the original manor. It is the entrancing, leading-you-on gardens on the land that slopes down to the lake that people go to see, some several times a year, to get the glory of each month. How glad I am that I went in July. The enthusiasts were walking through the first garden into the next one (I'll explain that in a minute) to see the roses, as well they might; but they hardly noticed on their way a bed, backed by one of those mellow brick walls, of columbines of a richness and purity that simply took my breath away.

There must be a first time for everything, and as it happens the first time I saw (or, to be more precise perhaps, noticed the name of) a magnificent climbing yellow rose called Lawrence Johnston was at Sissinghurst. Now Major Lawrence Johnston was the creator of a famous garden at Hidcote Manor, in Gloucestershire. It was (and still is, of course) divided into a number of 'rooms', and Vita Sackville-West, the creator of Sissinghurst, admitted drawing many of her ideas from his work. Not that she did not have many equally good ones of her own. She had a great respect for the self-sown seedling, feeling very rightly that Nature knows what it is doing, yet somehow she combined this with an amazing personal creativity. One of the best-known 'rooms' at Sissinghurst is white: blossom, spring and summer flowers, they are all white there. Others carry on her marvellous colour sense. People who knew her say how they would often find her wandering from one 'room' to another with a plant, making up her mind what clashed and what agreed.

The marvellous thing about Sissinghurst is this. Usually the very notion of a great garden carries with it the idea of age, maturity, tradition—consider Hampton Court (p. 60) or Kew (p. 59), or the greatest of them all, Stourhead (p. 97). But in 1928 Sissinghurst was, as Nigel Nicolson (son of Vita Sackville-West and Harold Nicolson) recalls, on sale as a Victorian farm of which the 'picturesque ruins' were a derelict part of an area littered 'with old bedsteads, matted wire and broken-down earth closets'. All the planting and laying out was achieved in the time between its purchase by the Nicolsons in 1930 and the outbreak of the war. It is worth while quoting her own words:

> The site of Sissinghurst was not a new one: it went back to the reign of Henry VIII. This was an advantage in many ways. It meant that some of the Tudor buildings remained as a background and as the anatomy of the garden-to-be, and that two stretches of a much older moat remained to provide a black mirror of quiet water in the distance. It meant also that the soil had been cultivated for at least four hundred years . . .
> But I must also draw attention to the disadvantages. The major nuisance was the truly appalling mess of rubbish to be cleared away before we could undertake any planting at all. The place had been in the market for several years since the death of the last owner, a farmer, who had naturally not regarded the surroundings of the old castle as a garden, but merely as a convenient dump for his rusty iron, or as allotments for his labourers, or as runs for their chickens . . .
> Yet the place, when I first saw it on a spring day in 1930, caught instantly at my

heart and my imagination. I fell in love; love at first sight. I saw what might be made of it. It was Sleeping Beauty's Castle; but a castle running away into sordidness and squalor; a garden crying out for rescue. It was easy to foresee, even then, what a struggle we should have to redeem it.

With today's labour costs (even though she did a great deal of it with her own hands—but there must have been, for instance, transport hired to take the stuff away) such a feat would have been impossible, even though it is not necessary to visit such a magical creation as this to realise that the English are the most garden-loving people in the world. Some Frenchmen are peasants, but all Englishmen are gardeners, allotment-diggers, makers of quirky villages, constructors of mazes, buriers of surprises among lost woods reached by side-roads over hump-backed bridges. And it's the same with new housing estates. One year, building rubble and huge sodden lumps of clay, all round the stark little thing with its green roof; and, almost it seems the next time you pass that way, a lawn and a blaze of aubretia, or rustic arches with hundreds of roses spilling over, or mature-looking gladioli in the autumn.

Surely nowhere else is the proportion of neglected gardens so low. And that goes for all classes. Before I was married I once shared a mews flat with a journalist colleague, in the days when such places were within the range of mere journalists. It looked out on to an estate of 'prefabs', long since demolished and built over: those standard-design, slab-sided bungalows, quickly erected, which mushroomed to supply the immediate post-war demand for housing caused by bombing and the return of the demobilised. One day there was a murmuring of crowds outside, there were children with Union Jacks, and presently a large Daimler bearing the royal pennant arrived, and out of it stepped HM the Queen Mother to present the award in the London Gardens Competition to a Mr Penny. He certainly deserved it. It was high summer, dahlia time. I have never seen, before or since, such a blaze of colour, and grading of flower heights, and relationship to what there was of lawn and path, as he got into that tiny space.

All writers hate people who say to them that they have always thought they would write a novel but hadn't got the time. But I'm sure Miss Sackville-West, no mean writer herself, would not have minded a bit if she had met Mr Penny and he had said he'd always wanted to make a garden like Sissinghurst but never had the time *or* the money. We all would, given the chance. Well, *most* of us would.

Sissinghurst is now owned and operated by a uniquely British institution—

The National Trust

This body, which owns and preserves more than 200 historic buildings, 100 gardens, 400 miles of the best unspoilt coastline, 94,000 acres of fell, dale, lake and forest in the Lake District alone, prehistoric and Roman antiquities ranging from Hadrian's Wall to the Cerne Giant [p. 100] in Dorset . . . lengths of inland waterway, even eighteen whole villages', to quote its handbook, was in fact a uniquely *English* (and Welsh and Northern Irish) institution from 1895, when it was founded, to 1931, when the National Trust for Scotland was founded.

It is not a government department. It is a registered charity, as well it might be (all this means basically is that it can reclaim tax on certain forms of donation, so that in effect it receives more money than the donor himself actually parts with). Each new property acquisition is assessed on merit, but usually the Trust is only able to take on one where there is an endowment

Little Moreton Hall, Cheshire, a famous example of the 'black and white' Tudor style, and one of many historic houses maintained by the National Trust

from the family owning it, who have usually come to the end of an often centuries-old ability to maintain it independently. Here again there may be certain tax advantages that make this the only possible course, and very often the family remain in a small part of the great house retained as private.

But the Trust now owns and administers the property (obviously including any productive side such as farming and forestry if it can). There is a membership approaching 900,000, who pay an annual subscription, at the time of writing, of £7 (family membership £14. These are shortly going up probably to £10 and £20 respectively). This carries entitlement to free entry to any National Trust property. Non-members are charged on admission to these calm, grand, peaceful, lovingly-preserved houses where 'the walking sticks in the hall, the flowers, silver-framed photographs, books and papers in the rooms are signs that the house is still loved and lived in and that visitors are welcomed as private individuals just as much as tourists'.

As a matter of fact, if you were in the fortunate position of making your first trip in the South-East, it is more than likely that your first visit would be to a fairly recent acquisition of the National Trust, but without doubt one of its most famous—

Chartwell

The home of Winston Churchill.

He was, as all the world knows, born prematurely in a small room on the ground floor at Blenheim Palace (p. 127), where his parents were staying with his grandfather, the 7th Duke of Marlborough; and he is buried in the little churchyard at Bladon nearby. But Chartwell, which he bought in 1922, is the place—well, not exactly where he was formed, since this is not a word applicable to a man who had already taken part in the last great cavalry charge, at the Battle of Omdurman, been President of the Board of Trade, Home Secretary (1910) and First Lord of the Admiralty for two years in World War I. But it was here, in this house, in this magical secret valley, during his out-of-office years, that he wrote books which included *The World Crisis, Great Contemporaries*, and the great four volumes of *Marlborough*; here that he brought up his family; and here, above all, that he became the natural figure around whom gathered those who saw the menace to the world's peace of Hitlerism. He also saw, rather more clearly than the Roosevelt who inevitably was to overshadow even him, not indeed as a personality but simply as the head of a super-power, the menace of Russian expansionism . . .

The place could hardly be more symbolic. When you get to Westerham, that pleasant little Kentish village, you are barely out of London sub-topia—indeed you are barely 25 miles from Charing Cross. You turn off a little road climbing steeply up the south side of the North Downs ridge. Nice little green on your left, rather posh-looking Victorian buildings, boys larking about, can this be a posh private school? Not at all. Church of England Controlled Primary School for Boys, it says. Lucky boys. The road levels off in beautiful, thick, bird-loud woods. Then, on your left, a modest gateway: Chartwell.

You can see at once why it appealed to him. You are in a secluded private valley, closed at its north end. The lakes, artificially added to by Churchill, are bordered by pasture sloping up to a crown of woods on the eastern side of the valley, which opens out at its southern end into a tremendous promise of distance. The best place to appreciate this is past the house; you should stand on the terrace at its south-western end. The whole glorious panorama of the

Weald, its ridges going from green to blue to purple, lies before you, that extraordinary combination of cultivation, snug farmsteads, with a hint of forest wildness. There is a superb magnolia tree (very Churchillian, somehow, its great, fat, lush petals figure in his paintings quite often; he wasn't one for niminy-piminy flowers). He had a new wing built on at this end, with his study—and his bedroom with the best view of all—at the top; 'my promontory', he called it.

You would have to be very dull, or very Marxist, or possibly both, not to appreciate what kind of spirit was being forged in that room up there, in calm weather or when Atlantic wind and rain from the prevailing south-west beat on it. It is too early yet to say whether the West was saved; but this place is redolent of the man who certainly gave it a breathing space.

Inside the house, the atmosphere of life as it was lived there in the thirties. In the dining room, a table set for tea, complete with a cake with white icing and cherries stuck in it. In the drawing room, patterned carpet, brown settee, lemon and pale green cushions, table laid with cards for bezique, Churchill's favourite game, splendid Lalique glass cockerel turns out to be gift from De Gaulle, of all people. Library, comfortable square room, relief map of Mulberry Harbour. Upstairs, Lady Churchill's bedroom, blue and white effect, Dresden figures of Napoleonic War officers; museum rooms with every uniform from robes of Order of the Garter to the famous siren suit, photographs, memorabilia, including marvellously awful (good workmanship allied to non-existent taste) gifts from Stalin, kind of crystal bowls turned into boats with elaborate silver poop and fo'csle, one has a bear scrambling in over the side (h'm). And of course the study, family photographs, state-occasion photographs, the desk where he worked standing up.

On the road side of the house, and screening it (though it is not in any case a road carrying much traffic), are trees, some gigantic including a magnificent cedar and other splendours, as well as rhododendrons. The garden has developed comfortably round the stream which supplies the lakes. There is a lawn with two huge lime trees. There are paths and vistas. In the orchard there is Churchill's studio, with his easel and paintbox and painting chair . . .

Chartwell was hardly in use during the war; and it was after the war that a group of friends bought it for the National Trust, with the obvious condition that Churchill should live there undisturbed for the rest of his life. He did in fact use it for another twenty years.

A recent addition to the garden is an avenue of golden roses planted to celebrate the golden wedding of Sir Winston and Lady Churchill. It was a present from Randolph and the other children. Randolph, realising that the roses would not be in place and blooming for the actual day, had the characteristically Randolphian notion of a collection of each of the 28 varieties painted in water-colour by a different artist, made into a sumptuous book, bound in a whole vellum by Maltby's of Oxford.

I have never seen my cantankerous, hospitable, infuriating, unpredictable and now sadly-missed East Bergholt neighbour happier than when he was organising this work, which took four weeks from inception to finish. Famous artists, sent a dozen of whatever species they had opted for, were incessantly telephoned. 'How are you getting along, dear?' said the familiar voice on the phone, 'I've sent you a dozen *Speks Yellow*.'

'Randolph, they only came an hour ago', said my wife (who once taught art at Willesden Grammar School; she studied at the Central, and had a mural in the funfair at the Festival of Britain), raising her eyebrows at me in the familiar it's-old-Randolph-again expression.

'Well, don't let them fade, will you. But let me know if they do, and I'll send some more.' This was the Randolph who, when she was expecting our fourth child, said 'I mean to send you every daffodil on the estate'. There would have been about a ton of them if he had.

She finished her painting in four days. She was in some great company: Matthew Smith, Ivon Hitchens (*All Gold*), Cecil Beaton (*Phyllis Gold*), John Nash (*Lydia*), Duncan Grant (*Fantasia*), Oliver Messel, Augustus John (*Golden Emblem*, in tempestuously swirling blue vase); and people who were famous, but not for painting, like R. A. Butler, who incurred Randolph's wrath by disobeying orders and doing it in oils; and many assorted friends.

This beautiful object is kept in a glass case at Chartwell, in the dining room, so obviously you only get the chance to see whatever page it is opened at. The day I was there it showed John Nash's *Lydia*. They did very kindly open it for me, and I had a good look at it, right through; the first time I had seen it since the summer of 1958 when they were done. You will perhaps guess which painting I asked them to leave it open at until the next time it should be changed. And it wasn't the title page, decorated with the loving skill of a medieval monk by my friend Denzil Reeves, of Colchester Art School. Nor was it even the page, decorated by Churchill's nephew, John Spencer Churchill, on which Denzil had copied out the little verse I took up to Randolph that summer morning:

Once golden words transmuted leaden doom
And fired all England to a golden age:
Now golden roses for you two shall bloom
Whose golden peace turns one more private page.

It is possible, especially in England, to have a surfeit of superb and famous old houses and gardens. You might only have come from London specially to see Chartwell and gone straight back, as many Londoners and others do. You might go straight on down the hill and have a look, for instance, at **Tunbridge Wells**. There are chalybeate springs here, and in the 18th century the place became a fashionable spa, Kent's answer to Bath (and conveniently a great deal nearer to London). Although it had nothing like Bath's Assembly Rooms it has many elegant houses, and you can still drink the waters in the renowned Pantiles, with their arcade pillars supporting the subtly varying frontages of buildings, jutting out over their ground floors, which are as attractive as they were in the days when Beau Nash was the ruler of taste here, and a classic example of how to use *trees* in an urban context, something we seem to have forgotten entirely. There are plenty of Englishmen who have driven straight down the hill through Tunbridge Wells, been vaguely aware of airy commons and greens on all sides, and never actually got out to look at the place, perhaps unconsciously dismissing it as the ultimate bourgeois nest, since they think of the legendary writer of apoplectic right-wing letters, now almost as famous a figure as Colonel Blimp, as 'Disgusted, Tunbridge Wells'. But really, a walk round it comes more as a *cure* for apoplexy.

Supposing, however, that even in this favoured area, because of its accessibility to London containing the biggest concentration of house-and-garden splendour (the National Trust alone has 14 in Kent and 12 in Sussex, as against, for instance, 7 in Shakespeare's Warwickshire), you are not yet sated, it would be a pity on your way from Chartwell to Tunbridge Wells not to stop (for at least three hours!) at **Penshurst**.

You need to be more than just good at figures to keep a 600-year-old property in the family; and it may be just a coincidence that the present owner of Penshurst, not the National Trust but the fifth Lord De l'Isle, who won the VC after the Anzio landing, whose first wife was the daughter of another VC (Lord Gort), and who was Governor-General of Australia from 1961 to 1965, should actually have qualified as a chartered accountant when he left Cambridge.

He is descended from the Shelley family to whom the property came by marriage from the Sidney family, but it is the earlier of the two poets, the famous Sir Philip Sidney, soldier, courtier, poet (*With how sad steps, O Moon, thou climb'st the skies!/How silently, and with how wan a face . . .* what a sonnet!) who seems to be the presiding genius of the place.

Even so, when he died of wounds received in the battle of Zutphen, in 1586, the magnificent Great Hall (another of those marvellous roofs!) was already 200 years old. Various additions were made up until the 18th century. The result is a marvel.

Although it is actually hidden from the village as you approach it from the north, you know from the dignified stone sameness of the houses, the air, not exactly touristy but somehow expecting visitors from all over, of the comfortable-looking ivy-covered hotel, the Leicester Arms, or for that matter the Quaintways Tea House, (as a matter of fact, most of the village was built in the 19th century) that there is something special here. And so you instantly discover when, having parked your car on the grass outside the Tudor walls, you go through and see the opulent herbaceous borders (on the other side you will find more formal, pre-romantic, knot garden, box hedge, yew hedge arrangements, and there is a Nut Garden, more of an orchard really). Inside the house, after the breathtaking Great Hall, one state room after another; the state dining room, set as if for a banquet for ten very distinguished people indeed; Queen Elizabeth's room, of which the furniture contains a gorgeous folding screen which reminds you how even the greatest were not immune from draughts; and the famous long gallery, built in the 17th century, with its elegant plastered ceiling and Sidney family portraits.

Brighton

The largest town in Sussex is a curious place. What with all the jokes about dirty week-ends (in itself now a phrase with an old-fashioned ring to it; who now would use that adjective or indeed bother to pay for a hotel?), and Graham Greene's *Brighton Rock*, and the rest of the jolly old vulgar mystique, what it still makes you wonder is what the hell they all *do*. There is still, somewhere in the British consciousness, a feeling of surprise at these huge seaside towns with their thousands of windows in great solid hotels and blocks of flats staring from low cliff-tops at the sea, their roaring buses and department stores full of ladies' coats, their carefully tended ornamental parks near or by the sea, the humbler recreational parks at the back of the town, their grammar schools, their confident assumption that they have just as much right to municipal status as a historic city like York or a manufacturing city like Manchester. Of course there are a lot of retired people, and a lot of commuters (Brighton is only 55 minutes by train from London), and naturally there is the tourist-service 'industry', although that only starts doubtfully in the cold winds of Easter and goes into hibernation in September.

One minute, a few fishermen's huts; then a few Regency houses, then the railway—and suddenly, Seasideopolis. The thing about Brighton, as everyone knows, is that here is Ur-Seasideopolis. This is where it all started, and you can see the historical strata.

Of course there is a tremendous new marina, and there is an establishment called an Engineerium which contains not only old locomotives and boats but an enormous 1876 beam engine, in steam every weekend; and there is, of course, a new (1977) Brighton Centre, with a 5,000 auditorium which can accommodate everything from an ice-show or one of those international star shows (Bing Crosby was there) to a conference; in fact the last time I was there there were big signs everywhere saying, mysteriously, INTERNETCOM CONFERENCE. But it is the amazing amount of surviving Regency architecture that still makes the place.

In fact a good case could be made out for saying that Brighton is *the* place for Regency architecture, and not only because of its close association with the Prince Regent. In most people's minds the term *Regency* suggests something both more eclectic and more frivolous than the strict, symmetrical, formal Georgian (see, for instance, 10 Downing Street) from which it evolved. It's a very confusing term, because what you have to remember is that poor old George IV, who only got to *be* George IV in 1820, had been Prince of Wales since 1762, five days after his birth, but only got to be Prince Regent in 1811.

That was after one attempt to get him made Regent, in 1788, had come to nothing because his father, George III (with whom, like all the Hanoverian sons, he did not get on) temporarily recovered from insanity. He wasn't allowed to serve with the army or indeed *do* anything, so it is not surprising that his life degenerated into a serious pursuit of frivolity, to put it mildly. He first came to Brighton in 1783, the year he came of age. The place had been growing ever since Dr Richard Russell arrived in 1754 and made sea-bathing a fashionable cure. There is a plaque to him in the wall of the Royal Albion Hotel, at the seaward end of the central space with its voluptuous fountained garden entirely surrounded by traffic, Old Steine, which borrows Wren's famous epitaph, only in English: 'if you seek his monument, look around you'.

George fell in love with the place, and shortly afterwards fell in love with his beautiful widow, Mrs Fitzherbert; a Catholic, apart from anything else. They were married by a C of E clergyman in 1785, and until the thing collapsed ten years later she often came to Brighton. Certainly it was he who was responsible for one of the maddest, jolliest buildings in England: the Royal Pavilion. From the outside it looks like a cross between the Taj Mahal and St Basil's Cathedral, Moscow, all onion domes and minarets (all right, so minarets are Moslem. Doesn't really matter, what they wanted was a generalised eastern effect, in Regency's last fling before Victorian solemnity).

The exterior is John Nash's rebuilding, between 1815 and 1822, of the building originally commissioned from Henry Holland by the Prince. But the interior is still full of that mad European notion of Chinese decor that always seems so much more fun than Chinese decor itself: chandeliers in the shape of water-lilies, exotic mythological figures, a table laid for a Regency dinner, with superb china and silver, mirrors, gilt, delightful furniture . . . anything that Kubla Khan could do we could do better in those days. The last time but one I was there I was drinking municipal sherry and eating municipal canapés with the Lord Mayor of Brighton and being filmed talking to Victor Korchnoi, the Old Pretender to the world chess title, concerning whom I was the presenter of a BBC TV film (on the principle that since most viewers don't know what a knight *is*, let alone which way it moves, the best man to tell them would be a complete chess ignoramus like me. A good principle. Can't think why they don't ask me more often, there are lots of other things I'm an ignoramus about).

The last time, I was there to get some more stuff for this book. It was late autumn, and I sat on a bench outside watching an extraordinary sight. Two men were going about the gardens with loud-hailers which emitted a terrible screeching noise, which everyone assured me was the magnified sound of frightened starlings. This was supposed to frighten the hundreds of thousands of real starlings that were wheeping and flittering in the twilight.

A woman on the next bench said indignantly 'it's a shame! The poor things have got to sleep somewhere. How would those men like it if they were going to bed and people came and made a noise like that outside *their* bedrooms?' Actually all that happened was that the starlings did indeed rise screeching from whatever tree the men were under, fly around a bit, and return. After the two men had solemnly gone round the gardens twice, they *all* returned. As far as I could count.

I went to have a look at the Theatre Royal and its arcade, very much of Brighton's Second Period, the Victorian, lots of plush and brass. Nice comfortable play they were doing, too, *Filumena*, by Eduardo de Filippo, good old bourgeois proscenium theatre tear-jerker, none of this modern in-the-round stuff. Then just up the road to the Dome, once, so you read in every authority, the Prince Regent's stables. He must have had a lot of very big horses, since it is now a concert hall (in which, come to think of it, I have been in a performance of the Bach *Magnificat* with the Philharmonia Chorus, under Daniel Barenboim. We recorded it too. Sorry to go on about things that have happened to me in Brighton, but it's such a memorable background, you never forget anything that happens there).

This night, however, there seemed to be a lot of people loading tables and lamps and chairs and commodes into vans or estate wagons or even the boots of ordinary cars. It was the antique dealers (a sizeable part of the population) removing their wares after one of the huge regular exhibition-cum-sales. A notice in the window of the closed box-office announced that the following Tuesday there would be an all-star variety programme, including the Foden Motor Works Band. There was also all-in wrestling. Mind you, this was the end of the season.

The place where everyone goes to look for antiques in Brighton is of course The Lanes: an admitted tourist trap, but undoubtedly a pleasant and atmospheric complex of little squares, and indeed lanes, lined with shops (although—one might have guessed—*lane* doesn't mean 'lane': it is derived from the medieval measure of land in Sussex, the *laine*. What the hell, they are certainly lanes now). Actually if some of the signs there are to be taken seriously, you could do worse than take a few things down to sell to *them*. *We buy Gold, Jewellery, Diamonds, Emeralds, Precious Stones, Watches, Coins. Weapons Wanted. Dolls Wanted . . .*

There's a Japanese Shop, a Persian Shop, there's Chez Monique—and very enjoyable it is to stroll through them, perhaps past the elegant pilastered Elim Church (one of 15 'other denomination' churches listed. For a place with such a raffish reputation, Brighton is surprisingly well supplied with places of worship: 59 C of E, no less than 4 of which are called St Andrew's, 14 Catholic, 13 Baptist, 10 Methodist, 3 Jewish . . .), or into the pretty little triangle, with inviting-looking pubs, of Market Street.

Once you get away from its roaring thoroughfares Brighton has several districts where the relaxed and colourful Regency-cum-seaside architecture gives pleasure at every turn, particularly in some parts of the eastern side where the ground rises from Old Steine. But for total contemplation of the mysteries of creation, a desire for which is apt to come upon you when there is so much humanity about, let me recommend the Aquarium.

Of course any self-respecting zoo has an aquarium, but the one at Brighton is something special. It is the only aquarium in the world that looks like the crypt of a Victorian Gothic cathedral, all cast-iron arches and mysterious, salty, gloomy green light; just the place to see extraordinary creatures, imaginable only by God, like Tiger Barbs, Black Mollies, Humbugs, Dominoes, Tomato Clowns. Piranha, surprisingly small, faces like angry old men with protruding lower lips, endlessly opening and shutting their mouths. Lobsters with that terrible creepy sideways walk, like marine spiders, you wonder if they aren't all saying, in their illuminated tanks, *for God's sake switch that light off*. The salty smell comes from the ones that have sea water. Something sad about the slippery streamlined smoothness of seals thwarted by concrete walls. On the other hand surely these dolphins thrashing up and down their dolphinarium and generally enjoying themselves are born showfish, exchanging jokes about the dullness of the audience at matinées early in the week.

There are two piers, although one of them, the West Pier, is closed for the time being. There is, needless to say, a West Pier Preservation Society, trying to get enough money to open it again. The Palace Pier offers the usual pier attractions: mainly souvenir shops and the chance to look over the edge at green water going up and down, and survey the thickly populated coastline of pleasure.

Behind all this tumultuous life, and perhaps all the more enjoyable when you are up there on the uncrowded, windswept, sea-breezy short turf, are the magnificent bare Downs, sweeping on to their culmination at Eastbourne. About four miles north of Brighton is the famous Devil's Dyke, a dramatic cleft in the Downs. But it is perfectly possible, with a little effort, to find wonderful solitudes, with nothing but harebells, sheep, and marvellous views.

Rather more refined, not to say aristocratic, tastes are catered for inland. Just up the road from **Lewes**, the county town (splendid Georgian high street and many others) is **Glyndebourne**, perhaps still unique in the world, for opera—which after all did begin as a sophisticated entertainment for Italian dukes and such, and only indeed got from the Nobs to the People in this century—performed in the most beautiful, far-from-the-madding-crowds setting possible; in this case a marvellous manor house on to which a theatre holding 820 people was added. From its inception in 1934, Glyndebourne, particularly under the producer Carl Ebert, set and maintained a policy of attracting world stars for performances with plenty of rehearsal (and the orchestra is the London Philharmonic). With the right weather, and the leisurely 75-minute supper interval with the chance to stroll about smooth lawns past wonderful herbaceous beds and yew hedges and under great trees, to look across the ha-ha at cattle grazing in idyllic pasture a million miles away from it all, Glyndebourne can be a supreme experience.

It was the brain-child of the house's owner, the late John Christie, who had once been a science master at (where else!) Eton, but, with an ancestral home like that, never exactly had to borrow money on next month's cheque. There are many stories about him, of which my favourite concerns the late W. H. Auden, who had written the libretto for an opera composed by the fairly far-out composer Henze, called *Elegy for Young Lovers*. It happened to be raining that night, and as the cars and buses were leaving Auden found himself, sheltering under an arch, standing next to Christie. They had never met, so he thought he would introduce himself.

'Good evening, Mr Christie. May I introduce myself? My name is Auden.'

'H'm?' Christie was rather deaf, by then.

'Auden. W. H. Auden.'

'What?'

'AUDEN. W. H. AUDEN. I WROTE THE LIBRETTO.'

'H'm. You shouldn't have.'

There cannot be a better setting for opera than Glyndebourne. In an ideal world the audiences would be as good as the performers. But, with ticket prices ranging from £10 to £21.50 throughout the May–August season, it obviously isn't the kind of place that your average opera fan can go to on the spur of the moment. Very often there is, except on first nights when at least there are some critics who haven't paid for their seats, a strong whiff of money, either company expense account or just real. Still, it was probably just the same with those Italian dukes. It's still marvellous. It makes me wish, more than any other place in England, that *I* was on somebody's expense account.

The South

Wiltshire

In terms of mere propinquity Wiltshire is in the area which has Bath–Bristol as its nodal point, not London. Yet the moment you are in it it's obvious that, in the combination of stark, noble sweeps of land with snug stone towns and sudden richnesses of trees which it shares with neighbouring Dorset, it doesn't actually look to anywhere but itself. Even if you are going to Bath–Bristol on the mere M4, the moment you go down hill from the first service station, unmemorably named Membury (unless you think of it, as I do, as Unremembury), you are aware of a totally new countryside folding away there on your left. (A better idea, in fact, would be to turn off before, at Exit 14, and go through the tremendous beech and oak splendours of Savernake Forest, to the sumptuous town of **Marlborough**, with one of the widest high streets in England; mainly a Georgian effect now, but it's a great deal older than that, in fact it is one of the several places in which Merlin is said to be buried—in this case he will be surprised if he ever does come back as the prophecy says, for he will find himself in the grounds of a rather smart English public (i.e. private) school.)

E. M. Forster wrote in his second novel, *The Longest Journey*, 'Here is the heart of our island: the Chilterns, the North Downs, the South Downs radiate hence. The fibres of England unite in Wiltshire, and did we condescend to worship her, here we should erect our national shrine.'

It is itself a nodal point. And we did indeed erect a national shrine.

Stonehenge

Good time ago now; lot of Celts, Romans, Saxons, Danes, Normans, all sorts of foreigners been coming in since we started it around 2750 BC. For this, according to Professor Piggott quoted in the Department of the Environment Official Handbook, is when Stonehenge I was erected; at the end of our Neolithic Period. That is probably the date, they say, of the Heelstone, or Sunstone. This is the solitary stone, standing alone, away from that extraordinary, awesome circle and 256 feet away from its centre, over which the sun rises if you are standing at that centre, at the summer solstice, 21 June.

It is much more awesome when you are there than when you are approaching it. You have been conditioned by atmospheric photographs to think of these gigantic slabs towering above you into the sky. They *do* tower when you are close enough, being about 17 feet high, add another four feet or so for the lintels, the huge flat stones laid across the top (only nine of these still in position). But your first sight of Stonehenge from almost any direction is from *above* it. 'Oh, is that all?' you mistakenly think from half a mile or so away.

When you are there, having paid your 30p to the lady dressed like a kind of civilian policewoman and gone past the ice-cream, postcard, poster, Stonehenge tea-cloth, souvenir and book shop, tunnel under the road, ladies' and gentlemen's lavatories, and come up on to the site (don't step over the ropes to the interior, keep to the rubber matting which has been there so long to protect the grass from tourists' feet that grass is springing up through it)—*that's* when you have the double-take, that's when you not only see it against the sky but realise that it is on the crown of a little low hill in a bowl of *higher* hills; as seen from the centre, it is the *top* of the Heelstone that is level with the horizon. The click of cameras, the voices of couriers doing their spiel to coach parties in half a dozen languages, the cows across the road and the suburbs of Amesbury spilling down the hill half a mile away, are trivialities that vanish as you try to think what the full glory of Stonehenge III about 2000 BC was like when the great Sarsen trilithons were put up.

In its final form Stonehenge consisted of an outer circle of Sarsen stones (the word simply comes from *Saracen*, i.e. foreign, as these great boulders of sandstone are to the Wiltshire chalk in which they were found—not *here*, but it is thought between Marlborough and Newbury), enclosing a smaller circle of Bluestones; inside this a horseshoe of Sarsen trilithons, inside which is another horseshoe (open ends facing the Heelstone) and the Altar Stone.

And the longer you stand surveying these enormous lichen-covered stones, in spite of the ruins and removals of over four thousand years still making this human-artefact *shape* on the bare hill, relating man to the great solemn motions of the sun and the stars in the void, the more awesome it seems. And just as much of an achievement. If those unknown men with their unknown language and their unknown thoughts had only managed to shape and get the Sarsen stones from twenty or thirty miles away, that would be cause for wonder. But the Bluestones came from the Prescelly Mountains in the extreme south-west of Wales; 170 miles or so even if you cross the Severn at its lowest crossable point today, much farther by the way they must have crossed it.

Stonehenge is of course *the* Ancient Monument of Britain, let alone Wiltshire. But you are here in an area rich in similar, if lesser constructions: **Silbury Hill**, the greatest artificial mound in Europe, not far from **Avebury** (about 20 miles north of Stonehenge, and actually a larger site), **Winterton Bassett** (another stone circle) . . . no wonder current interest in astrology and Druidism leads to all kinds of theorising about *what* the exact 'religious' significance was. Stonehenge in a planetary system, as Saturn; at Marden, in the Vale of Pewsey, Mars; the beehive of Silbury, the earth; Winterton Bassett, the female circle of Venus.

The official booklet, right at the beginning, is pretty scornful about Druids. 'The average visitor', it says, 'will in all likelihood have been taught that Stonehenge was built by the Druids. You can clear your mind of this statement'; and, later on, 'the ancient Druids had no connection with Stonehenge or any other monument of the Bronze Age or indeed of any earlier period in the British Isles. No doubt they pretended they had, or even that they built it. They were a class of people who no doubt had a good deal of knowledge; they came to Britain during the early Iron Age invasions in about the third century before Christ.'

'A class of people'; that puts *them* in their place. But of course this is the natural idiom of scholars, whose large knowledge makes them realise how little they know, when dealing with popularisers whose little knowledge makes them think how much they know.

Stonehenge.

But it is a holy place, even if we don't know the religion.

It is pleasant to think of some kind of silent dialogue, which one day we shall understand, being carried on across a few miles of soft Wiltshire air between Stonehenge and the other great religious building of the county—

Salisbury Cathedral

—a supreme expression of a religion of which the details are very well known indeed.

I suppose it *is* possible to be there without even noticing the cathedral—indeed I now know it is, for I have just been reading a news story, entitled *Maggie douce-dure*, 'Soft-hard Maggie', i.e. Mrs Thatcher, in a French weekly called *L'Express*, in which the lady journalist, following Mrs T. on a speech-making trip, wrote: '*Il n'existe pas de palace à Salisbury, petite ville industrielle à 200 km au sud-ouest de Londres. Seulement un simple hotel provincial le White Hart. Clientèle de représentants en semaine et, le week-end, de gens aisés entre deux âges, qui se promènent dans le cher vieux pays.*' There does not exist a palace at Salisbury, a small industrial town 200 kilometres south-west of London. Only a simple provincial hotel, the White Hart. Clientele of commercial travellers during the week and, at the week-end, leisured people between two ages who promenade themselves in the dear old country.

Well, yes. I don't know about simple; the White Hart, like the Rose and Crown, has three stars in the Automobile Association handbook, for which the definition is 'well-appointed hotels with more spacious accommodation and some private bathrooms/showers; full meal facilities for residents and non-residents, including chance callers, on every day of the week'. (And none of those giant's-footstep lavatories either, I'll warrant.) Maybe there isn't a palace. But I'm willing to bet 100 new francs that what those people between two ages had come for was not to promenade themselves in the dear old country but the dear old town, before and after looking at the dear old cathedral.

There seems to be a lot about cathedrals in this book (but then it *is* called *Britain*, and there are a lot of cathedrals in Britain, all marvellously different), so perhaps you will forgive me if I rush through this most peaceful, water-meadow-set, Constable-famous cathedral in a breathless Mr Jingle style. Early English, all built in one go, starting 1220, harmonious, very. Spire added next century, tallest in England, 404 feet, seems to echo niches of west front, windows of transepts. Perfect from outside, inside lot of 18th-century tablets, mourning nymphs, memorials, along both aisle sides, tick tock, wrought-iron cog-wheels, in frame on ground, oldest clock in England, interesting, very. Chapter house, vaults flower out from single pillar, effect of purity, calm, Gad sir, wish was one of those old canons, lovely cloister too, huge tree in middle, even though they not monks . . .

As a matter of fact the Close, where the canons lived, wasn't always so peaceful as it looks now, lined as it is with some of the most beautiful houses in England, including Mompesson House (1701), belonging to the National Trust (but don't try on Thursdays and Fridays), wonderful baroque plaster-work and (so much has a kind of 18th-century patina overlaid Salisbury's earlier history) great collection of 18th-century drinking glasses; and the Walton canonry, so named after Izaak, so well known as a fisherman, not so well known as having a son who was a canon of Salisbury. It was at the Walton canonry that Constable stayed when he was doing the famous paintings. The connection was Archdeacon Fisher, Constable's great friend (and the man who performed his marriage), whose uncle was Bishop of Salisbury. Once the Archdeacon asked Constable how he had enjoyed his sermon. 'Very much,' said Constable, 'I have always enjoyed that sermon.' *That's* the kind of friends they were.

Marvellous town to walk about in. From a large square (always easy to park unless it's market day, with colourful stalls), lot of trees about. It is fringed with pleasant pubs, Blue Boar, New Market Inn. Claire's bakery, nice little coffee places, 15th-century market cross like a huge stone crown. One road leading off is splendidly named Endless Street. Comfortable jumble of architectural styles. Must be some Wren here. Yes, Bishop Seth Ward's College of Matrons (well, 'possibly', they say cautiously. It has the right symmetrical elegance. Home for twelve clergy widows). Close has gate-house, used to be locked, indeed fortified, in old days. In delightful street approaching it, lovely book etc. shops, one called D. M. Beech has huge bulging oversail, obviously is never going to fall down after all these years. Handel said to have given his first concert in England in the room over the gateway, obviously to *very* select audience.

One reason why this medievally wool-rich town (what a lot England seems to owe to wool!) is yet so open, indeed spacious, to move about in is that the building of the cathedral was the key point in a move of the whole community from a much older site (Iron Age, Roman, Saxon, Norman) on the ditch-protected fortified hill site just north of the modern town: Old Sarum, where you can see the perfect cruciform ground-plan of *another*, earlier, great Norman cathedral. Dear old country, indeed. You could spend a week exploring Salisbury, never mind a week-end.

Wiltshire is dotted with mysterious military signs, you have to look out for tanks in some places. *Logistic Executive, M.O.D. Army* says one notice. *Thruxton Circuit*, says another, mysteriously. Ignore them all, get back on to the A303 by the A36 (oh, but you *must* stop to see **Wilton** on the way; now *there's* a *petite ville industrielle*, although you wouldn't think so to see this dreamy Georgian townlet with clear water running under classical façades, let alone famous Wilton House, by Inigo Jones, with the 'cube room' 30 feet in each dimension, and many other glories, for here also is the Royal Wilton Factory, also visitable; probably the first, and certainly still one of the best, places in England to make carpet. Someone should write—maybe someone *has* written—a thesis that you pass from the rude peasant-warrior stage to the civilisation stage when you have *carpets*. Especially Wilton Carpets) . . .

. . . Yes, along the A303 till you come to Mere, then look out for the signs to—

Stourhead

There you will find the most marvellous garden in England, which as you will know by now is saying something.

Most people who have ever looked at any book or tourist literature or calendar or whatever about Beautiful Britain will at some time have seen a photograph of the famous Palladian Bridge, the kind of bridge Adam and Eve would have idled on, many a perfect summer afternoon, across an arm of the kind of lake there would have been in another year or two if there hadn't been all that business with the serpent. Is it just me, or can it be true that the bankers of today are not what they were? You don't seem to get people like Henry Hoare I (1677–1725), known as Henry the Good, because he was, and his son Henry Hoare II (1705–1785), very rightly known as Henry the Magnificent,

Stourhead, Wiltshire.

since it was he who build the classical Palladian house (architect Colen Campbell) and laid out that paradisal garden.

Richard Hoare, Henry the Good's father, admittedly started the family fortunes as a goldsmith, which comes nearer to aesthetics than banking (though not *much* nearer). Be that as it may, when he got the place from the original Stourton family it was already one of those snug, hidden Wiltshire valleys, with the river Stour, which rises here, forming a chain of natural ponds in Six Wells Bottom.

What Hoare did was create a lake which, when you look at it on the map, bears a curious resemblance in shape to that of England and Wales, especially if you, so to speak, took Cornwall in one hand and East Kent in the other and pulled a bit. The result is a roughly triangular shape which, as you walk round it, offers a different view practically every twenty yards. There are a few flower beds just after the magical entrance, but this whole place is not so much a garden as an ideal, a dream landscape. Always when you look across the water you see some perfect classical building, perfectly placed; the Temple of Flora, the Pantheon, the Temple of Apollo on its hill.

People who could think of Wren's style as having 'too much of the Gothick', as Lord Shaftesbury did, clearly wanted something pretty pure and severe, all that we associate with the word *Palladian*, and in fact Colen Campbell was deputy to Wren's successor as Surveyor General, William Benson (who was Henry the Good's brother-in-law); a foretaste of the 18th-century Whig dominance. But of course the effect is profoundly romantic. There is no such thing as Palladian *mist*, and there is that in the air on the brightest summer day in England, and in the soft outlines of the wooded hills, that imparts a soft, vaporous magic to these prospects, and incorporates shapes designed for hard, bright Italian sunlight into something mystically western, Atlantic. The best of both worlds.

You go through a grass-both-sides-of-road model village, quiet church with low, Early English arches of green sandstone, with typed information sheets stuck on things like wooden hand-mirrors, shop-cum-post-office like Victorian doll's house and—what is this? very un-Palladian, soaring Gothic needle (1373), with niches for saints, angels etc., of Bristol Cross, brought here so that from other side of lake (Pantheon) you would have idealised view of English Village. *That's* how Magnificent Henry was.

Admire vista of Pantheon, and, at this starting end leaving that Bridge on your left (you can walk over it, it is turf) across arm of lake about where Cornwall starts (if you remember my analogy). Retrace steps, turn right, up east coast, great rhododendron walks and trees, trees. You can get a map giving details of hundreds of them; *Abies nobilis*, Noble Fir, and it certainly is, wonderful hanging-branch Turkish Oak, Sitka Spruce, Lawson's Cypress which always meant a hedge to me till I saw this 65-foot splendour (no wonder cutting my hedge is such a job each year), tallest pine in Britain, Liriodendron see Tulip Tree, Thuja see Cedar, Ghost Tree see Handkerchief Tree, Gingko (which apparently you can also spell as Ginkgo)—and each one set in the one right spot. Temple of Flora, pillars and pediment, 4 huge wooden thrones inside, perhaps a god or so would come in for shelter if it rained. It says over entrance *procul, o procul este profani*, from Virgil, 'keep away from here, if you haven't got good taste'—well, it's more democratic than Horace who said *Odi profanum vulgus et arceo*, 'I hate the vulgar mob and ward it off', and anyway you're secure in the feeling that only people who love gardens, the chosen of the earth, bother to come to such a remote place.

Murmured conversations and laughter float across the water (*risus ab angulo*; thank you, Horace), you notice little gap of about six inches where grass, etc. stops and there's a little rim of dark roots etc. between it and the water, like tiny tide mark. Up east coast, wonderful wooded bank opposite, cross England with calm lily pond, Diana's Basin (= Scotland) above, tinkling water sound, down south-west, now it's the Grotto, dark tunnel, emerge into magic cave, light from circular opening, greenish, on to concentric-pebble-circle pavement, statue of reclining nymph over gushing spring of Stour. An opening on to lake frames view of Stourton village, *now* you see it. Climb past Rustic Cottage, then Temple of Apollo. Well-known statue of Hercules was not there when I was, it being repaired. From here you get highest viewpoint, you can see people coming in and out of Temple of Flora like little weather-vane figures. And . . .

. . . and of course there's the house; hall, another of those 30-foot cubes, they're mad about this in Wiltshire, Music Room, Library, Italian Room, Picture Gallery, Cabinet Room, Saloon, lots of gorgeous Chippendale and other furniture.

Dr Johnson said, as is well known, 'if I had no duties, and no reference to futurity, I would spend my life in driving briskly in a post-chaise with a pretty woman'. In Wiltshire would be the best. And they could stop at the pub at Stourton, very snug. £15 bed-and-breakfast it was when I was there. You can't just drop in, though.

Well, must tear ourselves away from divine Wiltshire to Cosmic Dorset; known to all Hardy readers as the core of 'Wessex'.

Dorset

Dorset is like Wiltshire only more so. Its wildness is wilder and its snugness is snugger; and in addition it has the sea. It has the most euphonious collection of place-names in England: Sturminster Newton, Cerne Abbas (where the Giant is cut into the hillside), Droop, Fifehead Magdalen, Gussage All Saints, Winterbourne Whitechurch, Turner's Puddle. Toller Porcorum, Piddletrenthide, **Blandford Forum**, **Wimborne Minster** (two towns as beautiful as they sound, one that was lucky enough to have *its* Great Fire 65 years after London's, in 1731, so that it could be rebuilt as a kind of Georgian dream; the other with a splendid, all-periods-from-Norman Minster dominating the town in a way churches no longer dominate in larger places. Dickens borrowed the names Snodgrass and Wardle from tombs). The North Dorset and South Dorset Downs.

At the eastern end, **Lyme Regis**,

> the principal street almost hurrying into the water, the walk to the Cobb, skirting round the pleasant little bay, which, in the season, is animated with bathing machines and company; the Cobb itself, its old wonders and new improvements, with the very beautiful line of cliffs stretching out to the east of the town, are what the stranger's eye will seek; and a very strange stranger it must be, who does not see charms in the neighbourhood of Lyme, to make him wish to know it better. The scenes in its neighbourhood, Charmouth, with its high grounds and extensive sweeps of country, and still more, its sweet, retired bay, backed by dark cliffs, where fragments of low rock among the sands make it the happiest spot for watching the flow of the tide, for sitting in unwearied contemplation; the wooded varieties of the cheerful village of Up Lyme; and, above all, Pinny, with its green chasms between romantic rocks, where the scattered forest trees and orchards of luxurious growth declare that many a generation must have passed away since the first partial falling of the cliff prepared the ground for such a state, where a scene so wonderful and lovely is exhibited, as may more than equal any of the scenes of the far-famed Isle of Wight.

Take that, knockers of guide-book writers. No wonder 'the young people were all wild to see Lyme' in Jane Austen's *Persuasion*, even though Louisa Musgrove was to have her dramatic accident there.

It is the southern strip of Dorset which has the true Hardy expanse of bare horizons with that strange primeval feeling which he captured so well, from Dorchester (where he is well commemorated) and nearby **Maiden Castle** (not actually a castle but a grass-covered Ancient British hill fortress, haunted by a Roman slaughter there in AD 43) to Corfe Castle (marvellous everybody's-idea-of-romantic-ruin, haunted by King John), and, away from the grinding holiday roar of holiday traffic up the village street from which you have escaped to it, Nine Barrow Down, Ballard Down, Studland Bay (unspoilt, dunes, seaweedy bathing last time I was there, but that was some time ago, I couldn't go *everywhere* to write this book). The oldest known settlements in England were here, going back to Mesolithic times.

From here you look across Poole Harbour to the most un-Hardyish town in the world, with the possible exceptions of Birmingham and Chicago. Not that **Bournemouth** is anything but agreeable, with Britain's only municipally–financed symphony orchestra (and very good too), theatres, casinos, ice shows, water shows, night clubs, Winter Gardens and Pavilion, piers (one at adjoining Boscombe), 50,000 beds (that's just for visitors), the famous Chines (cleft cliffs with many of the well over 2 million pine trees in the area), and, ah yes, of course, beaches; but it is essentially a place to stay at, not just to visit.

Just across the county border, in Hampshire, and in fact now joined to it by Bournemouth suburbia, is something truly magnificent, one of my favourite buildings both for itself and for its symbolic situation—

Christchurch Priory

Even if you only turn off from the could-be-anywhere ring road traffic up through the busy high street and go straight to the landing-stage and hire a little puttering motor-boat to go up the widening confluence-estuary of, good heavens, the Stour, all the way from the grotto in that magic garden well over 30 miles away, and the Avon (not the Stratford Avon, not the Bristol Avon, this country is full of Avons, Celtic word for river; it is the East Avon, rises above Salisbury Plain) you can look back over the blue water and see how this great building stands up, as a ship, as a fortress, as a huge statement against the sky. And of course it has been doing so since long before Bournemouth existed.

The place was originally called Twynham, 'between the waters'. When they were building there seemed to be an extra workman that no one knew, and one day a beam was cut a foot short by mistake, and the next day it was miraculously long enough and in its place; the workman was Christ himself; that's how *this* place got its name. But it would be a terrible mistake not to have seen the inside before you took the boat. It has everything; immense solid round-arched Norman nave and transepts, Perpendicular Quire (as they like to spell it here) and Lady Chapel, with examples of intervening styles; and all those life-loving Gothic jokes in the misericords carved under choir, sorry, quire stalls—a jester, a salmon, a bagpiper and harpist, the latter turning away from the sound made by his colleague . . .

I said 'symbolic situation' because, at my first sight of those colossal, confident, strong Norman pillars I knew I was reminded of something—of course, Durham (p. 162), at the other end of England. Then I bought the booklet, and what did I find? The first Dean was Flambard, under whom the work of building went on till he became Bishop of Durham in 1099.

Dorset, again

We have left Dorset for the moment, and we haven't finished with Hampshire yet, but there is no such thing as a totally cold-blooded, logical way to explore England, in fact the *ideal* holiday would be to wander about from one marvel to another in such a way that your actual route, drawn on the map, would look like one of those drawings that people did blindfold at parties in the days when parties were, I dunno, less, well, *sophisticated* than they are now. All of which is another way of saying 'to get back to Dorset'.

To get back to Dorset; an absolutely basic Dorset town is **Shaftesbury**, Hardy's 'Shaston', indeed not only Hardy's: this was an old name for it. The last time I was there it was not long after the famous 'white-out', the great blizzard which covered south-west England with snow, not one flake of which was seen in East Anglia. Shaftesbury is a crossroads town on high land which sweeps south-westwards down to Dorchester and Lyme; the eastern slopes of this are the rolling, open, beechwood-studded vistas of Cranborne Chase, ancient royal hunting country. A lady who lived in a bungalow told how she had woken to find an elegant little dune of snow stopping just short of her bed, having been blown under the door by the horizontal wind.

But already the early spring sun was shining, the cobbled, cottage-lined Gold Hill falling down to green country looked as wonderful as ever. I went and looked at the amazing sideboard in the Grosvenor Hotel, in which the battle of Chevy Chase, with horses, soldiers, spears, is carved in tumultuous detail in one huge oak panel; how splendid to see such a thing not in a museum.

I had a drink in the Mitre pub with Stanley Mansbridge, local poet—

Sometimes I have such flights of mind,
That leave my body far behind

—and Town Crier, not only of Shaftesbury, but of St Louis, Missouri, where he goes from time to time, bell and all. As we drank our beer looking out over that marvellous view he told me of the Byzant, which in June is ceremonially carried down the hill, in a procession with the Mayor, and clergy, and the Pomegranate Ladies, and they give two penny loaves, a gallon of beer, a pair of white gloves, down at the Fountain pub, Endmore Green, to the Lord of the Manor, for water to take back to their cisterns. Well, they've had it laid on for some time now actually, but they still have the procession, dating from the days when, not surprisingly, the only water was at the bottom of the hill.

'Well, what *is* the Byzant?' I asked.

'Well, it's a kind of *thing*, a kind of Arcadian *thing*.'

'A kind of bowl, then?'

'No. Well, more like a well top, I suppose. Made of wood and plaster. You can see it in the Museum. 'Course we take a fibre-glass replica in the procession. Calf's head is fibre-glass too. Ah, good ol' time we have. Lot of drinking afterwards; well, come you now with me, I'll show you a fine view from Park Walk, over to Melbury Beacon . . .'

We'll come back to Dorset later, as everyone does who has ever been there. But this seems to be the place for a bit about Britain's—

Old Customs

We may not have as many saint's days, liberation anniversaries and the rest of it as they do on the Continent, but there's no one to touch us for Old Customs. We go on creating them, too, as if we hadn't enough already. In every town in December there is bound to be some church having a Christmas Fayre—a completely phony word which someone invented after the war and which has now acquired a spurious reality. And I myself have seen a poster announcing a Monster Old-Tyme Traction Engine Rallye.

Most of the hundreds, indeed thousands of Old Customs, however, have quite as genuine historical roots as the one at Shaftesbury (which isn't even on the British Tourist Authority's official list). At Hocktide, after Easter, in **Hungerford**, Berkshire, the crier sounds a horn and the tutti-men, carrying tutti-poles decked with ribbons, nosegays and an orange, go round demanding a kiss or a coin (with a ladder to reach upstairs windows), accompanied by an orange scrambler carrying a sack of oranges.

St Ives, Cornwall, celebrates Feast Day in early February by Hurling the Silver Ball. The mayor tosses it to the crowd, no player retaining it for a moment longer than necessary—unlike the players of the **Haxey Hood Game** on 6 January in Lincolnshire, when the Lord of the Hood, attended by the Chief Boggan (in hunting pink but with fantastic tall hat) and the Fool, throws the leather-covered Sway Hood on to the muddy field where eleven other Boggans scramble furiously for it, sometimes breaking limbs (said to date from the 13th century when thirteen peasants chased the silk hood of Lady de Mowbray who was out riding when it blew off, and they were rewarded with grants of land).

In spring and summer one Derbyshire village after another has **Well Dressing**, where Biblical pictures painstakingly made from thousands of flower petals pressed into clay in a frame adorn well heads; Tissington on Maundy Thursday, Wirkworth on Whit Sunday, Youlgreave nearest Saturday to feast of St John Baptist (2 June), Eyam last week in August . . .

Before the **Helston Furry Dance** (it's in Cornwall, next door to Culdrose, one of the most modern naval helicopter stations in the world, you mustn't think we live entirely in the past; come to that, some of the well-dressers work for Rolls-Royce in Derby), on 8 May, people bring in green branches and sing that they have brought the summer. It's not furry at all (they wear evening dress): it comes from the Latin *feria*, a holiday. In the old pre-Vatican II days, in the Latin *Ordo* which told every priest what feast day it was and whether it was Double with Octave, Double, Semi-double or whatever, *Feria* meant that there *wasn't* a feast, I've forgotten why now. But then everyone has forgotten the *Ordo*, haven't they?

And you needn't think it's only England. At **Lanark Cross**, 1st of March, they have Whuppity Scoorie; children race round church as bells ring whirling 'maces' of tightly wrapped paper at end of string. Said to date from English refugee from Wallace shouting 'Sanctuary!' (*scoorie*) as he tried to get into church, while pursuers shouted 'up at ye!' (*whuppity*). Or something.

Hallaton (Leicestershire) Bottle-kicking and Hare-pie Scrambling, Easter Monday. St Ives (*Huntingdon*, this is another one, Cromwell's county) Digging for Bibles. Bit of a let-down, they only dice for them now. Third Saturday in July, at **Stroud**, Gloucestershire, Brick and Rolling Pin Throwing. Ah, but there are *four* Strouds, the others being in Ontario, New South Wales and Oklahoma. The men throw the bricks, the women throw the rolling pins; results are exchanged by cable, and the winning town takes the trophy for a year. You see what I mean. Deep down, *everyone* loves an Old Custom.

Dorset and Hampshire (cont.)

Well, to get back to Dorset *again*, the last time but one I was there I arrived in a 1905 Rolls-Royce Silver Ghost.

I hope you didn't miss that. *I arrived in a 1905 Rolls-Royce Silver Ghost.* Actually I was on one of those jolly assignments that writers get from time to time, in this case to do a piece for the *Telegraph Magazine* about the difference between driving a brand-new Corniche (then £15,000) and a Silver Ghost (then £35,000; I dare say you could treble both figures now). The Silver Ghost came from Lord Montagu's Motor Museum, the best-known, and certainly the most beautifully situated, in the country, since it is deep in the—

New Forest

This, as I have pointed out, means very much the Old Forest—indeed it was here, as every schoolboy knows (thank you, Macaulay) that William Rufus, son of William the Conqueror, was killed by an arrow while hunting. It is another magic place. Huge forest glades, sudden open heaths, cattle-bangs (grids in the road which make an alarming clank when you drive over them but serve to keep the wild New Forest ponies in the parts where they are supposed to be, since they can't walk across). From a local village scrapbook:

The only important common right nowadays is Common of Pasture, which is attached to a considerable amount of land in Bransgore. People who occupy these lands are New Forest Commoners. They have the right to pasture ponies, horses, cattle and donkeys on the Forest throughout the year, on payment of a small fee, collected by the Agisters, who mark the animals by clipping their tails by way of a receipt. As the beauty of the Forest is largely maintained by the grazing of cattle and ponies, and it tends, in the opinion of the Verderers and the Forestry Commissioners, to be under-grazed, non-commoners may put out animals on payment of a slightly larger fee. Although the 'marking fees' are low, there are offsetting drawbacks to running animals on the Forest. They are liable to injuries from tins and broken glass left out by picnickers, they may wander miles from where they are put out and take weeks or even months to find. If not enough pigs are put out at 'pannage' time ponies may be poisoned by eating too many acorns. Each of the Agisters has his own tail mark. Ray Stickland of Lynwood is responsible for animals in our part of the forest. His tail mark is 'one cut out of the offside' [of the tail] . . .

So there is, evidently, some kind of coherent life with mysterious ecological and historical roots going on all round you as you drive through this tree-mysterious landscape, where you feel as if at any moment you might come on knights riding through a clearing, or hear the far cry of hunting horns. (The actual towns that you come upon are rather an anti-climax, consisting of Edwardian-looking hotels of dark red brick with a lot of woodwork painted white, and houses much the same, as if everything had been built in the same month in 1910.) Rather bourgeois, in spite of those Agisters. Probably a few exclusive golf clubs dotted around, too.

But it is a richly symbolic, removed, *other* landscape; although if you do find yourself going from Beaulieu to Shaftesbury, with all the glories of Cranborne Chase before you as you climb from (true Dorset name!) Sixpenny Handley, I don't really recommend a Silver Ghost, with one of Lord Montagu's mechanics wincing every time you muff a double-declutch, and with no footbrake (removed because it acted directly on the transmission, which it tended to set on fire) so that all you have to stop two tons of £35,000 (£70,000?) worth of car when a Mini suddenly lurches out into the main street in Shaftesbury before you, is the handbrake.

Not the least advantage of Dorset, for the tourist anyway, is that it provides, in Lymington, also on the edge of the New Forest, the most beautiful departure point for Jane Austen's 'far-famed'—

Isle of Wight

There are of course several other ways of getting a car across; Sealink (nothing to do with seals or ink, they are British Rail) run from Portsmouth to Fishbourne (near Ryde) and from Southampton to Cowes. Red Funnel do this latter also, as well as a hydrofoil service for passengers only.

But you can't just get on, unless it's about October already. It's essential to book ahead. The Sealink numbers are Portsmouth (0705) 27744, Southampton (0703) 26211 and Lymington (0590) 73301 (and no rot about calling after 5 p.m., you're in England now; although the ferries themselves do run practically till midnight). For Red Funnel, Southampton 26211.

But the main street (and come to that, a few side streets) of Lymington are well worth having a look at. The thing is, most Georgian-architecture streets have an air of knowing it; but this is a kind of miracle, an *unselfconsciously* beautiful main street (perhaps because many of the grandest houses seem to be solicitors' offices), full of people chatting, as if they all knew one another.

'Been here all my life,' said the lady who came in to do the flowers in the church, which frames the end of the street in a most satisfying way. It's a marvellous jumble of styles, Gothic east window and strange Renaissance gallery. Book has list of people to be prayed for each day of month. On the 6th, work and services, commerce, industry, all engaged in building, factories, offices, shipyards, shops. 8th, the Far East. 15th, organists, choirs, the Parish Church and All Saints, bellringers. 16th, writers, artists, pressmen, broadcasters, arts, stage and film people . . . right on to 31st, the sacraments and those who use them and those who neglect to use them. One memorial, to Sir Matthew Blakiston, I wouldn't mind having for myself:

TO THOSE WHO KNEW HIM THE ENUMERATION OF HIS VIRTUES WOULD BE SUPER-FLUOUS. TO THOSE WHO KNEW HIM NOT IT MIGHT BE TEDIOUS.

Strangely, the Isle of Wight does not prompt the what-do-they-all-*do* feeling that Brighton (p. 88) and such places do. Interesting though the Solent, that uniquely double-high-tide stretch of water between it and the mainland, is to the visitor, with its shipping (though not so much as in the old Cunarder, pre-airline days) and yachts, obviously it is a fairly serious barrier to anyone who wants to set up an industry; and really nobody has, except in Cowes where they build yachts (of course, this being to yachting what Wimbledon is to tennis) and other boats—and hovercraft.

If you cannot be a widowed queen, like Victoria (Osborne House), or a great poet, like Tennyson (Farringford) or Keats (Shanklin), then what you do in the I.O.W. is be retired, have (if the right fairies were invited to your christening) a farm or, in the majority of cases, have something to do with holidays (unless of course you have the misfortune to be in Parkhurst Prison, maximum security, on the edge of Parkhurst Forest, the largest of half a dozen or so woods which are all the more noticeable in an island much of which is rolling downland).

This time, I went from Portsmouth to Fishbourne, where you drive off in a little creek just east of Ryde, a huge-beached resort. Resisting the temptation to go to nearby Havenstreet, where there is a steam railway, nearly two miles of it—for I was determined to see Osborne House after all these years since my first seaside holiday, at Sandown, in, God help us, 1934—I was already aware of the easier pace of driving, of life itself, even before I stopped at the first pub, the Ship Inn, children welcomed, terrace with landing stage, lots of small boats.

You can't say, somehow, that the place is *geared* to tourism, although it is, very efficiently indeed. At their tourist information office they not only shower on you exhaustive, detailed brochures listing every kind of accommodation, but sharpen the feeling you already have of wanting to explore this place on foot with their leaflets giving the carefully worked out routes of the Nunwell Trail, the Worsley Trail, the Hamstead Trail (saltings, wild life, tumuli), Coastal Path (60-mile views) . . . 'gearing' sounds too modern and pressurised. It's more natural here.

To get back to Osborne House. Ho. Ha. Hum. Yes. Well, it's in wonderful grounds and there are magnificent things in the house, including some rooms which show that High Victorian taste could sometimes have a cool elegance; grand rooms with grey centre panels, pink side panels, green medallions, blue parts of ceilings, all in what we would now think of as poster-paint colours, can give a very restful feeling (and part of it is, appropriately enough, a convalescent home for officers, of any service).

Perhaps *too* restful, perhaps we are still even now too close to the old lady and the extraordinary achievements of her age, the triumphalism so sadly balanced, for her, by the widowhood of which Osborne came to be more or less the symbol. It was, after all, designed by Thomas Cubitt very much to the Prince Consort's ideas. Of course, there *are* grand bits: drawing room with marvellous Calcutta carpet, Privy Council Room where Gladstone, Disraeli, Palmerston and Co. must have stood and walked a lot, since there is only one chair (for H. M., of course), then *really* triumphalist Durbar Room, all filigree thingumajigs, huge majolica vases, mantelpiece against which no one could ever have leant, since it's about 8 feet above fireplace, peacocks, Indian Corridor with photographs of people who made the carpet, Queen's hand-operated lift with damask seat, L-shaped drawing room so that Albert could discreetly play billiards round corner.

But it's the personal things which still give slight feeling that you ought not to be looking. Albert's bath filled from the bottom, it has three taps labelled Hot, Cold, Waste. Not only children's dining set with little table, chairs inlaid with names, *Alfred, Alice*, etc., but alabaster models of children's arms, hands. Figure of fubsy-looking dog, *Moira*, descendant of favourite *Noble* (it was taught to curtsey out of room, backwards). Queen's Bedroom, portrait of Albert always kept over his side of bed. Brass plate in floor, HERE IN PEACE QUEEN VICTORIA LAY IN STATE AWAITING BURIAL AT WINDSOR, FEBRUARY 1ST, 1901.

Ghastly month, February.

But out into smooth summer lawns, great trees, and to realisation that the whole island has somehow kept a Victorian spaciousness. It is diamond-shaped, 21 miles east to west, 12 north to south. Obviously the three favourite places are the practically adjoining, south-west-facing resorts of Sandown, Shanklin, Ventnor; piers, theatres, esplanades, electric lift to town level, self-catering flats, cliff paths, sands, Shanklin Old Village with Thatched Cottages, posh hotels, camping, Britain's record number of hours of sunshine . . . well, it's all there. But Victorian too.

After the highest downs behind and east of Ventnor (Do Not Miss Tropical Bird Park In Sub-tropical Climate Sheltered By Wooded Cliffs From North Wind), drive down open landscape with classic bay-and-chalk-cliff vista, and after Freshwater, park car where they have restaurant, The House of Popcorn, souvenir shop, etc., and go down 252 wooden steps to Alum Bay, I.O.W.'s famous geological freak, crumbly sand cliffs of sharply differentiated colours; maroon, ochre, white, pink, etc. In a corridor at Osborne House there is neat little picture of Georgian original house all done in this sand. Notice on beach: *Cliff Falls Can Be Dangerous And Without Warning*. And outside wooden cabin: *Fill Your Sand Tubes Here*.

There is view of Needles, famous rocks, lighthouse, yachtsmen's mark. You can get up again (or come down, for that matter) by chair-lift. But it is much more of a serious Victorian pleasure to walk up. Behind you, in fact, is one of the finest cliff walks in the country. It is the end of the Tennyson Trail, which, if you are up to walking 15 miles, actually starts near centre-of-island Newport, at splendid Roman-Saxon-Norman Carisbrooke Castle, which some visit because Charles I, imprisoned there, after failed escape attempts, was taken from it to his Whitehall execution; and some to see the donkey-operated treadmill which brings up water.

Tennyson's house, Farringford, is now a posh hotel; but the country behind it made me resolve to go back one day and do that trail, while I can still manage 15 miles.

But such a tide as moving seems asleep,
Too full for sound and foam,

When that which drew from out the boundless deep
Turns again home . . .

Freshwater, marvellous name when you come to think of it, seems to sum
the place up. I left from Yarmouth, a pleasant boaty little place (and incidentally there's another river Yar on the island, flowing eastwards to the sea at
Bembridge), to Lymington, Hampshire. And of course it is absurd to be in
Hampshire without seeing—

Winchester

All cathedrals are special, and you could spend your life trying to decide
which is the most special one in England. In many ways Winchester could
qualify (and here I will make an admission which may well qualify me for
inclusion in Pseuds' Corner in the satire magazine *Private Eye,* which has a
very British suspicion of emotion. I say, chaps, there's Jennings blubbing
over Keats, let's scrag him). Well, the first time I pushed open the leathery old
door—I was 21 and had been in the army three days—the exterior had in no
way prepared me for the truly breathtaking splendour of the nave; that men
should have made this! I simply stood there and found tears running down
my face.

In a way it is our capital cathedral. The statue of Alfred the Great in the
High Street reminds you, even before you enter this deeply moving building,
that not only the Wessex kings were crowned here, but William kept it as his
capital, and Richard I was crowned here. It is the longest church in England,
the second longest in Europe; but it is not exactly the size that overwhelms
you so much as the way it shows, most starkly of all of them, the contrast
between Norman and Gothic which are yet combined to make one supreme
whole. For the transepts are Norman. In fact the stone from which they were
built in 1079–93 came from the Isle of Wight. Then the famous William of
Wykeham, who also founded the adjoining Winchester College, began the
miraculous transformation of the Norman nave into that Gothic, with its airy
cross-vaulting, which was to culminate in Perpendicular—a style which
sometimes has arches so broad that they might better be called Horizontal;
but not here, all is aspiring, vertical, a prayer in stone.

People from St Swithun to Jane Austen are buried here. He was the apostle
of Wessex, although nobody is quite sure of the origin of the legend that if it
rains on his feast day (15 July) it will rain for the next forty days. There are
many other things to be seen in Winchester, a relaxing little town to walk
about in, notably the Great Hall; and, just outside the town at Holy Cross,
you can get the Wayfarer's Dole, free bread and beer, as wayfarers have been
doing since the 12th century. But that nave—and I hope you will agree
by now that this really means something—is the finest thing in the south
country.

East Anglia

Statistically speaking, if you are a tourist, especially a tourist from abroad, visiting East Anglia, you are likely to have done so from London. Certainly from the point of view of the schema of this book it is part of the area which has London as its nodal point.

Psychologically, however, the way to appreciate its hard, bright, sharp distinctness, its peculiarly *unblurred* quality, is to enter it from the Midlands, or better still from the blue-distanced, orcharded, rolling west. It really is time some qualified psychological boffin did a study in depth of the differences in character between wooded-hill people and plains people. If you come along the A45, from the Midlands, let alone if you come from, say, 'Leafy Buckinghamshire' (which thrusts a curious northern arm up into Northamptonshire), there is already a hint that you are leaving the Cavalier west for the Roundhead east. It is probably pushing things a bit to say that the statue in Northampton itself of Charles Bradlaugh, one of those determined pioneer Victorian atheists, is a sign that once you leave the comfortable, amiable, vague Tory High Church fug and go in for some kind of personal-illumination religion, the progress is from that to Protestant work-ethic, thence to secularism, a progress illustrated on a huge scale in America. But soon after Northampton you do come to Bedfordshire, the county of John Bunyan, and Huntingdon, the county of Oliver Cromwell, and his Eastern Association, and Puritanism.

The Civil War (1642–1646) and subsequent Commonwealth (to 1660) had economic and social causes about which historians will argue for ever. All the same, let me make a generalisation (the exceptions which prove the rule, the qualifications and contradictions coming later!): no war since that between Athens and Sparta was ever fought between two sides so clearly defined psychologically, or in a country where the terrain so matched, perhaps even produced, the two different types.

Although Charles I raised his standard at Nottingham in 1641 it was at Hull, that frontier city of Yorkshire facing all East Anglia down below the Humber, where the governor refused to admit him, that the thing began. Incidentally Yorkshire, and the north as a whole, was also Cavalier. That was pre-industrial Yorkshire. In fact a fascinating side-issue (which, like many such in this book, would make a book in itself) is that of the large numbers of East Anglians who later migrated north and helped to get the Industrial Revolution started when their own wool trade had declined from its medieval primacy. John Kay of Coggeshall in Essex, for instance, inventor in 1733 of the flying shuttle, moved to Lancashire when his workers refused to use it.

The King used Oxford ('home of lost causes') as his capital when he couldn't get into London. The whole Cromwellian drive, of course, came from East Anglia, and surely from a psychological mould that had been forming for centuries—certainly for generations; in Boston, for instance, where the magnificent spire of a noble church dominates the fens for miles, the 'Boston Stump', you may see the horrible tiny cells in which some of the Pilgrim Fathers were imprisoned before they all got to Plymouth for their famous voyage in 1620.

It is not an accident, either, that at one end of this scale you have the music of Elgar, most romantic and Cavalier of all English composers, redolent of the soft country where England fades into Wales, and at the other the spare, muscular, fundamentally Roundhead music of Benjamin Britten, for ever associated with Aldeburgh and the hard North Sea.

This brings us to—

Cambridge

Here again, it is no accident that Cambridge should be famous for its scientists and economists, from Newton to Keynes, all hard clear thought, and Oxford for, well, a certain frivolity, in spite obviously of great classicists and philosophers, from Duns Scotus onwards. Of *course* there are exceptions. What more Cavalier poet than old Lincolnshire Tennyson? If this theory were watertight the 17th-century Cambridge Platonists, those defenders of 'spirit' against the materialism of (Oxford's!) Hobbes, would have been the Oxford Platonists; and today's Oxford Logical Positivists, who say we can never know anything at all, we can know only what we say about anything, surely belong to Cambridge with the late Bertrand Russell, whom I once heard saying, in the first week of the BBC's Third Programme in the good old days when they used to argue about the existence of God, 'the only necessary proposition is an analytical one'. End of Jesuit opponent who said God was Necessary Being.

All I am really saying is that it is impossible to imagine either an Oxford E. M. Forster or a Cambridge Evelyn Waugh, let alone a Cambridge Oscar Wilde (or even more, come to think of it, a Cambridge John Betjeman). It is pleasant to imagine all the other universities in England being moved into one enormous long thin one, reaching all the way from Oxford to Cambridge, perhaps with the engineering and technological parts somewhere in the middle, astride the M1 motorway. Such a university would undoubtedly be Cavalier at its Oxford end and Roundhead at Cambridge.

It is characteristic of Cambridge that the calm splendour and beauty of its buildings should be more instantly visible. E. M. Forster described Cambridge as a lantern or lighthouse raised up, and there is something magnificent in the idea of these ultimate articulations in stone and warm brick and carved wood of civilisation, of thought and art and science, standing up for so many centuries as a kind of outpost against the lonely wastes of the fens. At Cambridge you still get in an English context the feeling that you get in a European one at that marvellously Italianate city of Cracow, where the radio time signal recalls the legend of the watchman's warning call interrupted by an arrow in his throat from the advancing Tartar hordes. It is a feeling marvellously expressed in a poem by Rose Macaulay:

> As I walked in Petty Cury on Trinity Day,
>   While the cuckoos in the fields did shout,
> Right through the city stole the breath of the may,
>   And the scarlet doctors all about

Lifted up their heads to snuff at the breeze,
  And forgot they were bound for great St Mary's
To listen to a sermon from the Master of Caius,
  And 'How balmy,' they said, 'the air is!'

And balmy it was; and the sweet bells rocking
  Shook it till it rent in two
And fell, a torn veil; and like maniacs mocking
  The wild things from without passed through.

Wild wet things that swam in King's Parade
  The days it was a marshy fen,
Through the rent veil they did sprawl and wade,
  Blind bog-beasts and Ugrian men.

And the city was not. (For cities are wrought
  Of the stuff of the world's live brain.
Cities are thin veils, woven of thought,
  And thought, breaking, rends them in twain.)

And the fens were not. (For fens are dreams
  Dreamt by a race long dead;
And the earth is naught, and the sun but seems:
  And so those who know have said.)

So veil beyond veil illimitably lifted:
  And I saw the world's naked face,
Before, reeling and baffled and blind, I drifted
  Back within the bounds of space.

I have forgot the unforgettable.
  All of honey and milk the air is.
God send I do forget . . . The merry winds swell
  In the scarlet gowns bound for St Mary's.

(You have to realise, in the second verse, that 'Caius' is pronounced *keys*).

Yes. Well. It is always said, with truth, that Oxford's peace and quiet was ruined by through traffic and the huge car factory at adjacent Cowley. Cambridge has always been more fortunate in this respect, although recently it too was threatened, by increasing traffic from the east coast container ports. Now it is happily by-passed, and most of the Cambridge traffic is again that of people who want to be *in* Cambridge.

There seem to be increasing numbers of them, so be warned; you can't always get even into the multi-storey car park; it just isn't multi enough. But somehow you have to walk about Cambridge, where you can go in and out of serene quadrangles, spy an arch leading to a more secret inner quad or chapel, or a statue, or a fountain, or a wrought-iron gate through which you see a blaze of flowers but which bears a notice PRIVATE. FELLOWS' GARDEN.

A Fellow is, of course, a don, and as such very different from a mere fellow, or chap. Until very recently Cambridge University, which like Oxford consists of independent colleges where resident members may indeed get some of their 'tutorials', armchair essay-discussions with a small group or sometimes just one student in the don's own room (although they also attend other 'public' lectures in the relevant 'schools'), was indeed restricted to fellows; girls had their own colleges, starting with Girton, which actually began in Hitchin, a safe thirty miles away, in 1869 and only got to Cambridge itself in 1873.

Now freshmen, and of course freshwomen, starting at Cambridge get a students' union booklet which rates each college in terms of what it has to

Cambridge: the Cam.

offer in—well, in everything that would have been strictly extra-mural in the old days. Still, obviously this doesn't show in the architecture, except presumably in the internal rearrangement of bedrooms and bathrooms. What you are looking at is a classical arrangement, unique in Europe and therefore the world, of the sub-monastic, quasi-cloister, quiet (until hi-fi got in) centres for thought and study from which the university ideal developed.

At Cambridge they are fortunate in two respects. Eight famous colleges lie between the road called in turn St John's Street, Trinity Street, King's Parade and Trumpington Street, and the river which has broad sweeps of lawn and garden and noble-tree'd avenues beyond. These are the famous Backs. Right in the centre is what many people take to be the supreme last fling of Gothic, miraculously airy, lofty, delicate-roofed, dark-wood-stalled, full of a kind of gentle awe, a polyphony in stone, sounding-box for the polyphony of its justly world-famous choir (even if they do tend to sing of the *lah—eet* that *shah—eeneth* in the darkness and to praise *Almah—eety* God). I never thought as much of D. H. Lawrence as Dr Leavis (a Cambridge man) did, and I thought even less when I read that King's College Chapel with its crocketed buttresses reminded him of an upturned sow. It was built by poor old religious, unstable (two notably un-Cambridge adjectives) Henry VI, or at any rate started by him in 1446, his eponymous college having been founded five years earlier; the full glory of that uniquely English style, Perpendicular. Wordsworth (who was at St John's, three colleges away), was nearer the mark in his famous sonnet:

> Tax not the royal Saint with vain expense,
> With ill-match'd aims the Architect who plann'd
> (Albeit labouring for a scanty band
> Of white-robed scholars only) this immense
> And glorious work of fine intelligence!—
> Give all thou can'st; high Heaven rejects the lore
> Of nicely-calculated less or more:—
> So deem'd the man who fashion'd for the sense
> These lofty pillars, spread that branching roof
> Self-poised, and scoop'd into ten thousand cells
> Where light and shade repose, where music dwells
> Lingering—and wandering on as loth to die;
> Like thoughts whose very sweetness yieldeth proof
> That they were born for immortality.

St John's, at the northern end of this amazing stretch, has a lot of warm Tudor brick as well as stone, three quads, or more properly Courts, and since it is the only one to straddle the river, two bridges. One of these, the Old Bridge, was built by one Grumbold to the designs of—here he is again, Sir Christopher Wren; there's quite a lot of Wren in Cambridge, notably the magnificent library of Trinity. The other is the well-known Bridge of Sighs, in fact a jolly Victorian-Gothic covered arcade.

After St John's comes the richest, biggest-of-all Trinity, to which we owe, among other famous men, Tennyson and Newton. It was on the bust of the latter in the ante-chapel that Wordsworth wrote the famous lines in the *Prelude*:

> The antechapel where the statue stood
> Of Newton with his prism and silent face,
> The marble index of a mind for ever
> Voyaging through strange seas of Thought, alone.

If it were not for the fact that you have to pass so many private, college-only landing stages where you can't get off to look round, a very good way to see the Famous Eight would be indeed to get a boat, which you can do at Bridge Street, just above St John's, and go upstream; St John's, Trinity, Clare, King's (splendid view across lawn), one beautiful bridge after another, including the one at Queen's, the wooden 'mathematical bridge' built in 1749 'with no nails' as they proudly tell you, although such a feat would have been child's play to the carpenters who built the incredible roofs of many churches in neighbouring Suffolk, such as Woolpit, Mildenhall, Needham Market . . .

Perhaps it *is* the best way to start in any case, because you can disembark near the end college, Peterhouse (it is also the oldest, having been founded by the Bishop of Ely—and wait till you see *Ely!*—in 1284), and then go back towards St John's, looking not only at what you have missed but at the ones on the other side of the road—Pembroke (Wren chapel!), Corpus Christi; and the ones farther into the city but mostly looking out on to even larger grassy spaces, wonderfully preserved within the city, with names like Jesus Green, for the college of that name, Midsummer Common, Christ's Piece (and Milton was at Christ's College), Parker's Piece just a block away from Emmanuel (and guess who designed the chapel? Right again), Downing.

Heaven knows what time it is already, but you simply cannot leave Cambridge without visiting the Fitzwilliam Museum, even if you do have to skip the Round Church of the Holy Sepulchre (like the one in the Temple, p. 53) on your way back to the nearby multi-storey. The Fitzwilliam, a few yards down the road back from Peterhouse, has behind that Victorian Greek façade a collection that is just the right size for a morning's or afternoon's visit. No, that's nonsense of course, you could spend a week, a month, a diploma course there. What I mean is that it is a nice comfortable size, for it has everything from the sarcophagus lid of Rameses III to Graham Sutherland and Paul Nash, taking in representative work of major national schools in between, including the well-known (for all that it dates from a time when the fire had begun to go out in Italy) *Ecce Homo* of Guido Reni.

Everybody remembers certain things in any museum, and goes back to stare at them the next time he is there instead of covering new ground. At least, I do. For me in the Fitzwilliam it is the endearingly primitive English salt glaze work, not just jugs and things but a splendid bear; and the Peter Brueghel *Village Fete*, with all those yokels' heads staring up at the promised excitements on the stage; and the Gainsborough *Heneage Lloyd and his Sister*, delicious elegantly-clothed youth and girl outside in a romantic landscape, a kind of classical introduction to the better-known *Mr and Mrs Andrews* in their famous Suffolk cornfield. And of course the Constables. View towards East Bergholt Rectory, 1808, when he was still finding his style; miraculously airy and atmospheric one of Hampstead Heath, 1820, when he had perfected it; and, in a way most moving of all, one of his rare portraits, in this case of his lifelong friend John Fisher, the man who performed his marriage, the man to whom he wrote the letter containing his most often-quoted words. 'Old rotten banks, slimy posts, & brickwork. I love such things . . . But I paint my own places best—painting is but another word for feeling. I associate my "careless boyhood" to all that lies on the banks of the Stour. They made me a painter . . .'

Which brings us, of course, to Suffolk. Well, not quite yet. It will bring us to Suffolk in a moment. First—

Ely

Many-splendoured though Cambridge is, if your time is limited it doesn't matter how many of its glories you miss—even if you just see King's College Chapel and then rush on—you simply cannot, must not be in this area for the first time, without seeing Ely, a mere 15 miles north.

You will remember that Peterhouse, the earliest Cambridge college, was founded from here. I know it is anachronistic, since the great cathedrals were built centuries after the various invasions from northern Europe; but there is something fortress-like, some suggestion as of a linked frontier-line of holy watch-towers, about the magnificent line of cathedrals up the eastern side of England: Waltham Abbey, Bury St Edmunds, Ely, Peterborough, South-well, York, Durham. And it doesn't need much imagination to see how hugely Ely must have stood up alone from the old undrained fens and marshes. It is not the only thing on that flat skyline now: it shares the honours with a sugar-beet factory.

But when you are there, *what* a building! None of your symmetrical west fronts. On your left as you face the west end, a tower, preceded by a two-storey Galilee porch; then, if you please, a *transept*, ending in two graceful smaller towers, all reminders that Norman finally got very graceful as well as strong before it was replaced by Gothic (of which there is an abundance at the eastern end of this extraordinary building). As Alec Clifton-Taylor remarks, 'never was the English love of blind arcading indulged to better advantage'. Well, you go up Norman nave, look up at painted wooden ceiling, and there, at the crossing with the transepts, in this miracle, the famous Octagon and Lantern, 'the only Gothic dome in existence'—certainly the only one on this scale.

When the original tower fell, as Norman towers were always doing, in 1322, one Alan of Walsingham conceived and carried out this breathtaking idea, which among other things involved getting eight oak beams 63 feet long and over 3 feet thick—altogether over 400 tons of material—by whatever means they had in those days, to make this amazing marriage of geometry and art in the sky. There are other glories: a beautiful Lady Chapel, almost a separate church, with the widest-spanning arches in England; lots of carving, even after the frightful iconoclastic Puritans to be expected in these parts had been let loose. But that Octagon is the thing you will remember.

Now we can go to—

Suffolk

What a county! Two charming stories from Constable's voluminous and fascinating correspondence illustrate its unique-to-itself atmosphere. Always homesick for it when he was in London, he was bringing his daughter Minna back for a stay in the Promised Land. 'Why, Papa,' said the child, looking out of the coach, 'it is only fields.'

Constable told his engraver Lucas a story which perfectly illustrates all Suffolk people's justifiable sense of its uniqueness. A farm labourer, crossing the Stour to the Essex bank in search of work, looked back and said 'Good-bye, old England, perhaps I may never see you more.'

Suffolk is a kind of ultimate paradox of landscape. It is dramatically undramatic, its understatement positively shouts at you. In fact it does fall roughly into three areas. 'High Suffolk' is the area above Ipswich, where you may find not only Framlingham with its castle, or such a delicious unspoilt small town as Eye, but some of its incredible number of fine medieval churches, five hundred of them, proportionately more than in any other county, and more merely numerically than all but the biggest; no wonder it was called *Silly* Suffolk, this word being derived from the German *selig*, 'blessed' (as all lovers of the Brahms *Requiem* know). Dennington, for instance, with its delicate light screen and its carved pew ends, saintly and grotesque, one of them being a skiapod, mythical man with a huge web foot which he can hold over his head as a parasol; or Fressingfield, or Woolpit with its famous angel roof.

The coastal strip is all sandy heath, pine woods, estuaries (by one of which was discovered the buried Saxon longship containing the glittering Sutton Hoo treasure now on display in the British Museum), commons, golf courses, shingly beaches, bird sanctuaries. Its natural culmination is **Aldeburgh**, a toughly beautiful little town of flint (that local material from which nearly all the churches are built, subtly catching the changing lights of Suffolk's wide skies) and Victorian red brick and seaside-white wood; surrounded by singing, herbal marsh and estuary, at the head of which is one of the most atmospheric concert-cum-opera halls in the world, the Snape Maltings, chief physical legacy of the Festival for ever associated with Aldeburgh's most distinguished resident, the late Benjamin Britten.

The third area, which might almost be termed Postcard Suffolk, extends from the river Stour to the south-western end of High Suffolk, into which indeed it blends imperceptibly at such places as Bildeston, yet another of those ravishing villages full of old timber-frame weavers' houses, where I once saw chalked on a wall the legend WE HATE BILDESTON FUZZ, presumably a country copper on a bicycle.

It includes not only the *real* Constable Country, i.e. those villages, for the most part along the quietly beautiful Stour valley which he could actually reach on foot or horseback for a day's painting, but what might be termed House Agents' Constable Country, which, if you were to believe their advertisements, stretches south of that county border river well into Essex and north to Hadleigh (lovely Guildhall, unspoilt wide High Street of which one half is more unspoilt, or less spoilt, than the other half, since it was the subject of an Electricity Board project for carrying power lines underground instead of messing up the wonderful roofscape with wirescape).

Nowadays the A12, the main road that takes you from London through all this to Yarmouth (though you would never suspect such marvels were within earshot of the thundering juggernauts) has become a semi-motorway, one village after another being by-passed over the years. Once it entered Suffolk at the Stour-side village of **Stratford St Mary**, and for once you really were conscious of a definite change. There was your first flint church. It has the letters of the alphabet let into the flint 'flushwork' of its buttresses. There seems to have been a period when no one knew (or, more strictly, it had been forgotten) what this was for, there being nothing else like it in England. Then a leaflet discovered in Strasbourg, of all places, produced the explanation. To a priest travelling between London and the important city of Norwich, this was roughly half-way; and he would not have time to recite his full daily office; but here, as evidently in Strasbourg or anywhere else, the 26 letters of the alphabet contain it all, potentially, so say it with a few short prayers. There is a little rhyme:

Per hoc alphabetum notum
Componitur Breviarium totum
Tempore Paschali; alleluia

'In this well-known alphabet is comprised the entire Breviary. (During Easter time; *alleluia*).'

You then went up the hill, on the other side of the Stour, and it was different. But to this day I cannot be sure whether the trees and landscape do have this special quality, which so to speak *had* to produce their Constable in much the same way as one feels that the moors above Keighley *had* to produce the Brontës, or whether it is the other way round, Constable imposing his marvellous animistic, breath-of-nature vision on all of us, for ever. Bit of both, probably.

Certainly, at the top of the hill, when you turn off the A12 and come into **East Bergholt**, a pleasant village but not in the postcard league, for all its unique bell-cage (the church having no tower) where the bells, mounted on axles and balanced by huge counterweights, are rung by men who swing them physically and directly, changes and all; an amazing sight and sound. It is when you walk about ten yards down the little lane that leads down to Flatford Mill (and you will have to walk; if you insist on driving, which don't, you'll have to go round the block, or round the fields, for the press of visitors has necessitated a one-way scheme) that England produces one of its round-the-corner marvels. There is the whole soft Vale of Dedham below you, with winding river and toy cows. There, down at the bottom, is Willy Lott's cottage. I once got out of an airport bus in Lisbon, with the Philharmonia Chorus, and there was a huge reproduction of the *Hay Wain* in a shop window right in front of us. A young man from the village, seeing another such in one of those last-gas-for-100 miles places in Arizona, when he finally persuaded them that he lived there, wasn't allowed to pay for anything.

To go along the valley to Sudbury, birthplace of East Anglia's other native genius Gainsborough (it must be the *light*), you pass through one postcard village after another. Stoke-by-Nayland, with the superb beige-pink-ochre-brown-grey-silver tower of its noble church dominating the ridge for miles round—a common Suffolk sight, paralleled in Kersey slightly to the north, most postcard of all with its steep street of executive and professional classes' cottages dipping down to the ford, with ducks. Slightly to the south, Bures, in a wonderful private valley of its own. Slightly more to the north, Lavenham, almost too good to be true, a Tudor film set (and absolutely classic Guildhall), with another of those ridge-dominating church towers. And after Sudbury, more and more of them, perhaps the finest of all (in Suffolk, I mean, and that means anywhere, of course), **Long Melford.**

What a street, bordered by excellent pubs and shops! What a marvellous Great House, Long Melford Hall, which shows what could be done with brick in the 16th century, delicious mad pepper pots all over the place; and above all, my God, what a noble, incredible, cathedral-like church at the top of that splendid huge triangular green! However rich those woolmen were, how did they get to build this—this cathedral in the middle of gentle fields, with its battlemented clerestory, its glass including the deep blue and white Lily Crucifixion? Lily Crucifixion? Well, yes. It's the Crucifixion, but it is also lilies. I can describe it no better. You'll just have to see it.

It was while sitting in an army truck, in 1952, when I was one of certain key troops involved in something called the Z Reserve Call-up, for a fortnight's training during some crisis or other—I do believe it was the Berlin Air-lift—that in this first-ever visit to East Anglia I saw bright September clouds, in a clear East Anglian blue, sailing over this divine, peace-exuding building and thought, I could happily live in this region. And so (though no way a Roundhead) I and my family have, since 1956.

Interval for boasting. I have sung in the Chorus in the Philharmonia recording of the *Missa Solemnis* under the Herr Doktor Klemperer, of immortal memory. But I have also (and so has my wife) been in the group of sixteen singers who did two Bach cantatas (and Janet Baker was one of the soloists, and George Malcolm was on the harpsichord) conducted by Benjamin Britten as part of an extension of the Aldeburgh Festival, on a later golden September Sunday afternoon, in Long Melford Church. No, not boasting really. Just rejoicing, and recalling good fortune, and communal happiness. And beauty.

By now, dear readers, you will have appreciated, I hope, not only the fun but the difficulties facing anyone writing a book called *Britain*. You can see for yourself, if you put a piece of paper in this page and shut the book, that we are well over half-way through it, and we haven't yet got to the Arthurian mysteries of the west country, the rainbow glories of the Lake District, the rich scenic and civic variety of Yorkshire, the ultimate English triumph of Durham: and Wales; and Scotland . . .

All the same we can't leave East Anglia yet (sorry, Scotland. Yet you shall presently see how I love you) without mentioning its beautiful capital—

Norwich

(*Mention*! They'll be furious I didn't start with Norwich and just mention everywhere else. It's a great place for local patriotism. NORWICH, A FINE CITY say placards on every approach road.)

There is a great deal to be proud about. Let a poet capture its essence, Louis MacNeice in *Autumn Sequel*:

> As one looks
> From the Maddermarket to Bishopsgate, a broth
> Of history garnished by ten thousand cooks
> Simmers around one; calamanco cloth,
> Cobbles, copper, pewter and blown glass,
> Serpents and bass recorders and the froth
> Of home-brewed ale, canaries, and church brass . . .

This medieval feeling is especially strong if you happen to be there on market day and can stand outside the elegant Theatre Royal (last time, I saw the Glyndebourne touring production of *Magic Flute* with neatly adventurous Hockney sets which somehow went very well with Norwich itself), and see noble St Peter Mancroft church (which would be a cathedral in any but this town of 33 medieval churches) on your right, colourful striped stalls down below, and really rather elegant, un-brutal modern City Hall on your left, in a tradition they have there of good *modern* architecture which culminates in the outlying new university of East Anglia.

It is also helped by the fact that Norwich pioneered pedestrianisation. This really is a city where you can walk about almost as if the car hadn't been invented. You therefore get a high medieval feeling, and when you see the Castle on its great hill in a bend of the river (the Wensum), you may recognise a classic defensive position found from Durham to Toledo. It now houses a museum, not unnaturally rich in works of the Norwich School—Crome, Cotman & Co.

But it is when you see the magnificent cathedral in all the pre-Gothic majesty of its Norman nave, for all that elegant lierne vaulting of the later roof, with its wonderful coloured story-telling bosses, matched by others in its perfect cloisters, that you realise just how many ages have left their mark on this fascinating, history-layered city which is yet, I repeat, so walkable, so exactly the right size.

In fact you've only got to look at the map to see that it is a nodal point in its own right. Nobody in his senses would visit Norwich from London for a day. He would be staying in or near Norwich, in which case he would have far more time than this book has to explore the whole county, notably the Broads, those reed-whispering, bird-haunted (and alas increasingly tourist-noisy, not to say pollution-risky) stretches of water, debouching into the rivers that enter the sea at Yarmouth, which have never been the same since cabin cruisers were invented (before my time, I hasten to add), but still provide the wonderfully heart-lifting sight of sails seen apparently moving through fields. And he would certainly visit the beautiful little town of King's Lynn, remembering ancient trade (and rows!) with Hanseatic League and other European ports, with its elegant Custom House and Markets.

Great houses

Perhaps because East Anglia is so open and, what was that word, ah yes, Roundhead, its great houses are the more strikingly aristocratic when you come upon them; from **Holkham Hall**, a tremendous statement of marble staircase, red carpet, state rooms, William Kent furniture, to the pale waters of the sea on Norfolk's north coast, to the equally magnificent **Audley End**, at the Essex town that with its superb church and wonderful houses so lives up to its beautiful name, Saffron Walden. Absurd to be in this region, too, without seeing **Euston Hall**, strategically placed in Suffolk where Newmarket-type heath, Thetford Warren-type forest, and pastoral High Suffolk seem to meet; Capability Brown vistas (well, two other geniuses were involved, John Evelyn and William Kent), pictures including glorious Stubbs. Or Ickworth (near Bury St Edmunds', you can't miss that either) with its incredible Rotunda, as though the Sheldonian Theatre, Oxford, had flown there in the night, becoming subtly Roundhead on the way. The splendid formal gardens come to an abrupt edge and you are looking at waving corn; you wouldn't be a bit surprised to see Gainsborough's Mr and Mrs Andrews *there,* either.

But one cannot for ever be going on about these dreamlike houses, which always leave you with a curious ambivalent feeling, glad that somebody at least had this dream, sorry that you can't live in it (or anybody else these days). Other great houses will just be sternly noted (otherwise we shall *never* get to Scotland); but not before we have had a look at **Burghley House**.

If you are going up to the north of England on the east side, and do not wish to use the boring, world-of-its-own motorway, in this case the M1 to Sheffield, outside which city you'll have to get via the M18 on to the Great North Road anyway, you might as well use it all the way. 'Great North Road' sounds more interesting than its other appellation, A1, although since it now by-passes pretty well every town through which the old coaches used to go *it* is now a pretty boring road too. You would never dream that you are whizzing past about half a mile west of not only Burghley House but the entirely delightful town of **Stamford** adjoining it.

You come to expect such dignified, mellow stone towns in the Cotswolds, but not here, somehow. Still there it is, simply full of enchanting buildings, even the Woolworth's seems to be in two Georgian houses. Needless to say it seems also to be full of churches, although one of them, St Michael's, was for sale when I was last there. 'I was the last one to get married there', said a lady I met in a nearby shop, pleasantly ready to talk as they all are in this magic

Burghley House.

town. 'They used to have big civic services there. Of course you know Malcolm Sargent came from here.' They are proud of their still-remembered conductor.

You can tell people have been living here a long time (in fact the Danes made it Capital of the Fens) by looking at a flat tombstone in the pavement in the churchyard of the lovely All Saints with its outside arcading; come the 19th century they only had room for initials. R. B. 1822, J. B. 1825, W. B. 1831, and seven more. Behind it is the office of the *Stamford Mercury*, the oldest provincial newspaper in Britain, founded 1695. Splendid Queen Anne and Georgian houses and inns suggest continuing prosperity; one elegant shop says *Davies: Optician, Silversmith, Jeweller, Watchmaker, Goldsmith, Gem-setter*. There are Affembly Rooms. The streets lead you gently down past St Martin's Church, where William Cecil, Queen Elizabeth's Lord High Chancellor, is buried, to the river Welland, beautiful almshouses, George Hotel, pleasant meadows, and a lane called Melancholy Walk . . .

And then, on the south side, Burghley Park, with its Capability Brown lake, and 'the largest and grandest house of the first Elizabethan age'. No wonder Sir Walter Scott said 'this is the finest scene between London and Edinburgh'.

They might as well have called the A1 Cecil Road, because down at the bottom end of it, or only just off it, is Hatfield House, also built by Cecil. To say that this palace, no less, has a more metropolitan grandeur about it (and indeed it is yet another place well worth the short trip from London, and you could do splendid **St Alban's** with its great solemn brick-and-flint cathedral and the vast Roman remains of Verulamium in the same day) is not to say that Burghley House is rustic. It's just that somehow, for all the 700 or more art treasures packed into its delightful rooms, this is still a country house—albeit on a majestic, a *celestial* scale.

I use this word advisedly, because the most famous feature of this enormous jewel-box of a house is the justly-named Heaven Room, one of several by Verrio here, but the only one painted right down to the floor in fantastic *trompe-l'oeil*. A riot of gods and goddesses everywhere (this is a sublimely heathen Heaven; Juno and Jupiter and the Zodiac on the ceiling, nymphs all over the place, somebody on horse, red cloak streaming behind him, flying down into the room past the classical pediments behind which is the sea, from which Neptune is also just stepping on to the Axminster. On one wall Verrio has painted himself as Dante watching Vulcan in his forge. The lady who took the group I went round with told me a classical story of the German passion for accuracy, for a German visitor said that the painting was not correct here, since the three heroic figures about to strike the anvil all have their hammers at the same height, no good if they are going to hit rhythmically one after another. I bet Mime and his assistants don't make a mistake like that in *Siegfried*.

But that is to start near the climactic end. You really start in the monastic-croft kitchen, huge copper vessels, spit turned by wind-operated fan in chimney; then the chapel, once you've got past things like the lovely Caravaggio Virgin and Child in the mere ante-chapel. The chapel itself, red carpet, gilt plaster swags, moulded ceiling, marvellous *fireplace* with jolly barley-sugar-twist columns, front two rows of chairs by Chippendale, Veronese over the communion table, makes you realise how very democratic God must be to listen to prayers, if any, from such a place as well as to those from a garret; then a billiard room in which surely nobody could be philistine enough to play billiards, stuffed as it is with Gainsboroughs, Knellers, Lelys, and a typically exuberant Lawrence of the 10th Earl and his wife Sarah, the 'Cottage Countess', the village maiden whom he married (wooing her disguised as a painter) but who died because it was all too much for her. It all prompted Tennyson to write *The Lord of Burleigh*:

> . . . Three fair children first she bore him,
> Then before her time she died
> Weeping, weeping late and early,
> Walking up and pacing down,
> Deeply mourned the Lord of Burleigh,
> Burleigh House by Stamford Town.
>
> And he came to look upon her,
> And he looked at her and said,
> 'Bring the dress and put it on her,
> That she wore when she was wed.'
>
> Then her people, softly treading,
> Bore to earth her body drest
> In the dress that she was wed in,
> That her spirit might have rest.

Well, then there are the Old Ball Room, the Brown Drawing Room, the Black and Yellow Bedchamber, the Green Damask Room, Queen Elizabeth's Bedroom with four-poster, canopy and tapestries to end them all, the Pagoda Room, the Purple Satin Bedroom; then you get into Verrioceiling country with the series of George Rooms, so called because they were prepared as a suite, with roughly the amazing array of pictures they have now, for a visit by the Prince Regent. The Heaven Room is in fact the fifth of these. Bit of an anti-climax to hear that Queen Victoria had *breakfast* in it. Well, Sydney Smith did say heaven was eating *pâté de foie gras* to the sound of trumpets . . . then the Grand Staircase, then the Great Hall. Largest wine cooler in the world, like huge silver bath.

Another great Overheard Remark as I was coming out in a daze from all this splendour. One woman said to another, 'It was better value than that brewery we went round, wasn't it?'

Well, not everybody gets to see Burghley House. But if you're going up the A1, don't miss it, even if it's the only Stately Home you see. You won't find a better.

The Thames Valley and Oxford

It is of course perfectly possible to drive all the way from London to Oxford looking neither to right nor to left, along a road which becomes dual carriage-way outside Madame Tussaud's and continues so, roaring on concrete stilts past the unfortunate bedroom windows of inner western suburbs, cleaving through the alternating subtopia and arcadia of the Chilterns, until you come to the big traffic island on the Oxford Ring Road. Indeed, if you are based in London and wish to see Oxford, as what right-minded person wouldn't, you may well have to do this. But be warned; once the A40 becomes the motorway M40 it is, as far as I know, the only motorway in the country without a single garage in its entire length—no, stay, there's nothing on the M11 either, and that goes from London to Cambridge, the Other University city. H'm.

No doubt petrol and other assistance are readily obtainable quite close to many of its junctions; but it does not give you this feeling, especially at night. It may be largely inhabited by the better class of commuter nowadays (and how odd to think of G. K. Chesterton, that great, essentially urban, indeed Fleet Street character, living at Beaconsfield, of all places!) but for all that there still remains something primeval about the **Chilterns**, with their great green hilltops and their rolling beech-clad slopes.

Because you are in the part above London where the basic road system is north–south, London-directed (in this case you are going north-west, but let's not quibble), you are crossing a much older route. Furious scholarly argument goes on about whether there is any etymological connection between the Iceni (Boadicea's tribe) and the Icknield Way, the long-before-the-Romans road that goes from the Wash, through the East Anglian corn-lands (from just about the days when corn had been discovered) and for scores of miles along the great highland (OK, Scotland, small h!) belt which goes via the Hampshire Downs right down to Dorset, being momentarily interrupted by the Thames at the Goring Gap.

The people up here, before those stockbrokers came, were a tough lot, who left the plains to the invaders. In fact they needed a special steward to control them, and that's how 'taking the Chiltern Hundreds', i.e. accepting a position of profit, which you eventually couldn't do if you were an MP, came to mean 'leaving the House of Commons'.

The A40, before the M40 days, descended a wooded escarpment from which you could see the blue plains of Oxfordshire laid out; this was clearly a natural frontier. Even the M40 is dramatic, as it drops down through a huge raw cutting in the chalk. You would need a fortnight, and a back-pack, and youthful fitness to walk the **Icknield Way** and its famous parallel route to the north, the **Ridge Way**, giving you marvellous views from the northern edge of the Berkshire Downs over the Vale of the White Horse, so nobly celebrated in Chesterton's long ballad:

The Chilterns.

Before the gods that made the gods
Had seen their sunrise pass,
The White Horse of the White Horse Vale
Was cut out of the grass . . .

For the White Horse knew England
When there was none to know;
He saw the first oar break or bend,
He saw heaven fall and the world end,
O God, how long ago . . .

But you can get a quick, motorist's-eye notion of the Icknield Way (if you have left for Oxford early enough) by turning off the M40 at Exit 6 and popping over to Bledlow, where you can find it as the bridle path it is for much of its length. Further east it goes through Wendover, close to one of the highest points of the Chilterns. John Hampden, not a village one as in Gray's *Elegy* but the real one, was MP for this place, and, as I have just this moment read in a piece by Elliott Viney, a fellow-contributor to the *Shell Book of English Villages*, so also from Buckinghamshire were at least a quarter of the 60 regicides who condemned Charles I. We haven't got to Cavalier Oxford yet. . . .

. . . and already we have passed West Wycombe, where there is a golden ball on the tower of the church (you can get inside it, nice little red plush dining room), part of the splendid eccentricities of Sir Francis Dashwood (great house nearby, needless to say), founder of the Hell Fire Club, the Mad Monks of Medmenham, exaggeratedly notorious for some certainly very un-Roundhead practices. West Wycombe Park is his great Adam-style house. Every house in the village is owned by the National Trust.

Medmenham itself, down close to the Thames, comes halfway between Marlow and Henley, at which point the river (as you go *up* it, if I may put this in so Irish a way) makes the terrible mistake of turning south to go through the northern outskirts of Reading. Marlow and Henley are pleasant enough places in their way, although **Marlow**, after you have crossed the river by the elegant pre-Victorian (1831) suspension bridge, does give the impression of being one rich Georgian High Street entirely filled with tiques, whether an- or bou-. It's all rather house-boaty, posh-hotelled and, on a summer day, touristy.

If you really want to enjoy being *on* the Thames, I can't think of a better way than starting upstream of Reading and taking a rowing-boat at **Pangbourne** (where there is still enough water for there to be a Nautical College, let alone rowing boats) and going up about six miles to a splendid pub called the Beetle and Wedge, at Moulsford (it's not what you think; this beetle is a kind of hammer), where you can have a delicious lawnside lunch and then go easily (i.e. downstream) back. A magic piece of river. Kenneth Grahame, author of *The Wind in the Willows*, lived at Pangbourne.

Oxford

Well, I have been to **Oxford** several times. Once I was speaking in the Oxford Union on one of those very serious motions, in this case 'This House believes that Blackpool is the last resort'. I've forgotten what I said now, but I remember very well what my opponent, Mr Malcolm Muggeridge, said. He simply didn't mention Blackpool at all. He had a copy of the British Standards Institution regulations about toilet paper from which he read extracts: '. . . "containing not more than 10% artificial wood". What *is* artificial wood?' he demanded of the packed house. Ah, Oxford. But then Mr M. is the only Cavalier Roundhead in the world.

Another time, I was made a life member of a college society which at its annual dinners among other things pronounces a solemn exorcism on the witch Semolina. I shall not reveal the name of this society, but if they read this I would remind them that I haven't had an invitation for some years now; do they think I'm dead? Ah, Oxford, I dare say they do.

So this last time I went as a tourist, as you will, dear readers. Off the A40, down Headington Hill, hooray, managed to park car in that little one on the right. Graffiti on wall just before entering city:

THIS IS THE CRISIS TIME OF THE KALI YOGA
NOW IS THE TIME, YOU ARE THE ROBOT

On foot now, thank God. Little traffic island where roads to Henley, London, etc., diverge, young men must choose where to go when degrees finally earned, alas. (Oxford is probably too beautiful, a lot of them never grow out of it, or grow into very much the same life in the Inns of Court, *q.v.*). Bridge over Cherwell which is eastern boundary of collegiate life, all Oxford that matters is between it and Isis–Thames just south of the city. Magdalen Bridge, weeping willows, private lawns, a *wood*, right in the city. Lush, greenhoused Botanical Gardens behind. Oxford, the supreme architectural example of sudden academic quiets in still pretty noisy city.

Go along High Street, full of buses (no wonder famous old Oxford poem, *Domine defende nos, contra hos motores bos** etc.); it says on them FOR A GOOD LIFE IN OXFORD, THE SCOTTISH AMICABLE. Pass Queen's College on right, look through grand-pedimented arch to shaven lawn, flowers etc., but notice says QUEEN'S COLLEGE CLOSED TO VISITORS. Go into porch though, look at notice board over parked bicycles. *Rugby game against Hertford cancelled by them training* says one in rather immature writing. Go into St Mary's, University Church and Brass Rubbing Centre, lot of builders and scaffolding but can still see lovely exotic south porch and Perp. interior. In north aisle a notice-board says 'If you have a prayer that you would like other people to share, please write it out and put it here'. Pencil and paper provided.

> Dear God, I pray that my family at home are alright and keep my pets safe and they none get hurt. Amen. Sharon.
> Please let me see my father and mother. Erika.
> Dear God, we thank thee for all that I have got.
> Dear God, help my Daddy to get better and be able to work again. Amanda W.
> Help us to forgive the killers of Lord Mountbatten.

Pass Brasenose and Lincoln (actually, at this end, its entrance being in Turl Street, Lincoln College *Library*, formerly All Saints' Church, evidently redundant, now very well converted), then the covered market which forms the corner at Carfax, the nodal centre of Oxford. This street goes on westwards to become Queen Street, best shopping area, northward goes Cornmarket, southward St Aldate's. Carfax derived from *quatre vois*, four ways; if you stood here in medieval times you could see four main gates of old walled town. Covered market has lot of island sites under wooden skylights, rugs, Sex Pistol discs, posters for Haydn *Creation*: clothes, books, china, meat, fruit. Bananas Class I and Class II. What is the difference? I ask stallholder. Well, one is better than the other, he says. Ask a silly question . . .

Go down to Tourist Information Centre in St Aldate's and pay 50p for

*Even non-Latinists can guess 'Lord, defend us against these motor-buses.'

ticket for guided tour to start at 3 p.m. Go back to Turf Tavern off Catte Street, nice, cheap, good pub lunch and beer at table in sunny courtyard. Tour (about 20 people, includes Australians, Germans) led by very erect elderly lady with *very good shoes*. First stop Lincoln, we go in chapel, all fat, rich, dark carved oak. Sir William Davenant and John Wesley were here. Next, Exeter, having passed entrance to Jesus on left, two jolly cherubs on pediment of entrance, lady points out long Welsh connections with this college. Exeter has immense, lofty 19th-cent. chapel by Gilbert Scott, said to be based on La Sainte Chapelle in Paris. Original idea was to have it on northern boundary of college where it would have matched great neighbours, Bodleian Library and Radcliffe Camera. But typical Oxford in-fighting, in the end it is inside quad, like liner stranded in canal.

Sheldonian Theatre, famous round building (by, who would have thought it, Sir C. Wren) where they give honorary degrees etc. Divinity Schools, vaulted roof with hanging central bosses, 'the most beautiful room in Europe', exhibition of wonderful books of hours curiously juxtaposed with memorabilia and letters of Dorothy L. Sayers, the detective story writer. Next door, the famous Bodleian Library, full of priceless manuscripts as well as over 2 million books. If you go in, which you can do at certain times, all you can hope is that there was some truth in the remark made by J. L. Garvin, famous editor of the *Observer* in the good old days, to whom the late Douglas Woodruff—now *there* was an Oxford man—once commented on the huge number of books in his study, and, greatly daring, asked if he had read them. 'No, dear boy. But they're radio-active, radio-active.'

Pausing to note old legends over doors of Schools, *Scola Musicae, Scola Metaphysicae*, go under bridge popularly called Bridge of Sighs, but it's not over river as at Cambridge, merely over New College Lane; it connects two parts of Hertford College. Snug houses, including one where Halley lived, predictor of that Comet. New College has air of Georgian richness, though splendid chapel is noble Gothic, as well it might be, since this college was founded by William of Wykeham (see Winchester). Best thing in it is his pastoral staff, delicious enamelled scenes in curved part, of angels playing triangle etc. Second best is huge painting-on-glass of allegorical ladies, the Cardinal Virtues, in various shades of brown, by Reynolds. Third, or maybe 17th, is Epstein's *Lazarus*. Lady tells us she heard an unqualified guide, stuck for something to tell his party about this, who finally said, 'this is very unusual. There's a lot of work in it.'

In splendid New College Hall with its linenfold panelling, lady disconcerts me because I thought I was the only one who knew the following Spooner story (having once reviewed book about him) which she relates in front of his portrait (he was Warden here). Never mind about merely transposing consonants, he transposed the act of putting salt on accidentally spilt wine on tablecloth—he spilt some salt and was observed solemnly pouring wine over it.

Queen's College (we got in after all), splendid brass eagle, great silver candlesticks; recovered, said the lady, in Cairo when they were stolen. Two other Queen Anne candlesticks from another college were recovered by Interpol in Hamburg.

So we should be grateful, really, that so much of this old-stone, old-lawn quiet should be accessible to the public (and so, even more, should its occupants for their fortunate and sheltered lot). Lady now shows us remains of old city wall in New College garden; it has to be inspected by Mayor every three years. Walls never completely surrounded city, swamps made southern entry difficult.

All colleges so far visited have been between High Street and, running parallel to north, 'The Broad', continuing into Holywell Street, where Holywell Music Room, in which once sang in madrigal concert with Oriana Madrigal Society, is reminder, as oldest concert room in Europe and therefore the world, of what the art was like before today's giant orchestras and halls. Now we cross High Street to see Merton, oldest academic building in *world*, says lady, certainly a magnificent library (1371) also earliest of its type. *Very* radio-active. Chapel with amazingly lofty lateral bit at west end has school-of-Tintoretto Crucifixion with one man painted into it twice. Max Beerbohm and T. S. Eliot were here, fortunately not at the same time; can't see *them* getting on.

So, casting brief longing looks at Merton Fields, Meadows, melting bosky flowered great-soul-haunted approaches to river, to Christ Church, biggest, grandest college, *its* chapel isn't mere chapel, it is Oxford Cathedral, England's smallest cathedral; but some chapel! Lot of Norman, elegant Tudor lierne vault choir, intimate feeling, nice smell of stone. Entrance fee to cloisters, 25p. Picture gallery, probably more rewarding to time-pressed visitor than the Ashmolean, Oxford's somewhat austere answer to Cambridge's Fitzwilliam. Hall perfectly wonderful with great hammer-beam roof. But its best-known feature is the three quadrangles: the enormous Great Quadrangle, 'Tom Quad' with Wren's famous Tom Tower over the gate into St Aldate's; the Peckwater Quadrangle, with the deeply satisfying façade (due to mysterious harmonies of proportion and scale, it's like looking at a Mozart symphony, one has to tear oneself away) of the 18th-century New Library on its south side; and the quad facing Blue Boar Building, opened 1968. They must have felt 'follow that!' even while they were doing it.

Well, a good two hours' worth for 50p (the lady had left us at Merton, I did Christ Church on my own. But the tour was quite enough to give Oxford's special flavour of quiet treasures *hidden*, perhaps all the more moving because of being right there in the uncaring, roaring life of the city. Obviously a lot left out, notably the three great colleges on the north side of The Broad—Balliol, Trinity and St John's with their exquisite gardens. Then there's Worcester College, *very* 18th century, with a lake in its gardens. It is at the end of a cul-de-sac reached when you go on westwards past the Ashmolean.

I once went there to do a piece called 'A Day in the Life of a Don'. Sat in on tutorials etc. Sherry before lunch in Senior Common Room, then as we went upstairs for excellent lunch I found myself in discussion with philosophy don. 'If a train leaves Edinburgh at 10 a.m., what is it doing *exactly* at 10? Is it moving, or not moving?' 'Ah,' I said, feeling smug to know this, 'Zeno's Paradox. Does a point of time have any existence?' A great smile came over his face (after all, the other dons don't have to be philosophy dons). 'Yes, yes, yes! Or, where exactly *is* the edge of this newspaper I'm holding?' Then it got out of my league, with someone called Gottlob Frege.

Of course there is also an area to the north-east absolutely stuffed with laboratories and schools ranging from geology to astrophysics. But I like to end this attempt to present Instant Oxford (so obviously doomed to failure, Oxford is the most un-instant place in the world) with another story from that book about Spooner. In the good old Latin-and-Greek-dominated days, the wife of a previous Warden of New College said scornfully, 'of course the Warden could get up Science in a fortnight if he wanted to'.

Perhaps the only thing to follow Oxford with (although you can't follow Oxford really) is **Blenheim Palace**, at Woodstock a few miles north. But it is a wonderful contrast; everything in Oxford so hidden, everything here so open and flamboyant. This last and greatest private palace, an immense symmetrical Italianate glory of pale yellow stone, Queen Anne's and the nation's gift to the Duke of Marlborough for his history-changing victories over Louis XIV, is the last and greatest piece of triumphalist architecture. Everybody knows the epigrammatical epitaph on its architect Vanbrugh, whose *chef d'oeuvre* it was:

> Lie heavy on him, Earth! for he
> Laid many heavy loads on thee!

—although not so many know who wrote it, indeed I didn't myself till I looked it up. It was Abel Evans, 1679–1737.

Painted ceiling showing Marlborough, dressed as a Roman general (as he also is on the column three-quarters of a mile away in the 2,700 acre park, with its splendid bridge and Capability Brown lake made years after the 1st Duke's death), or on triumphal chariot in clouds; towers showing fleur-de-lys upside down, just in case anyone forgets whom it was that Marlborough beat; marble, splendour, pictures of later generations, notably a Gainsborough of the 4th Duke and family . . . they planned a similar house for the Duke of Wellington when history repeated itself over a century later, but it came to nothing, just a very splendid private house, Stratfield Saye, in Hampshire. (And what was the name of the house where Montgomery wrote his memoirs, again?)

There are, in fact, marvellous views, and a delicious water garden, as well as a restaurant and cafeteria, gift centre (in the old Palace Dairy), garden centre (with 'wide selection of plants, shrubs, bushes, garden supplies and houseplants to suit the requirements of the discerning gardener'), and a miniature steam railway with an engine called *Sir Winston Churchill*.

There is also, of course, the little bedroom where Churchill was born; and, a mile away, the unremarkable church of Bladon on its hill, with the tombstone. It just says WINSTON LEONARD SPENCER CHURCHILL 1874–1965. *Leonard*. Leonard Churchill. That doesn't sound the same at all, does it? Still, it does come from Germanic roots, 'lion hardy'.

Blenheim Palace.

The Midlands

You don't see it at all nowadays as you whizz along the motorway between Coventry and Birmingham. But the old A45 went through Meriden; and on its pleasant village green there was, and of course still is, a cross said to mark the exact centre of England, as the name itself seems to imply. (There are several other claims to this. There used to be a man in Leamington Spa who had a pillar in his drawing-room and he said *that* was the centre.)

Coventry

Clearly, under modern conditions, with Coventry about an hour and a half up the M1, it is perfectly logical for it to be considered here under London as its nodal point; and it would probably surprise most of the inhabitants, even now, to discover that for centuries it very much came under the nodal point of Chester (to which, as a matter of fact, it is slightly nearer).

Everybody knows the story of Lady Godiva—even if they don't also know that she and her husband Leofric, before the Conquest, built a house for an abbot and 24 Benedictine monks, which grew into a house as great as Edward the Confessor's Westminster, later still into a huge cathedral which simply disappeared after the Reformation. (St Michael's Church, which only became 'Coventry Cathedral' in 1918, was the one destroyed in the German air raid on 14 November 1940.) After the Conquest the already famous city was divided into the two halves: the northern, Prior's half, belonging to the monastery, and the southern, Earl's-half, eventually belonging to Ranulf, Earl of Chester.

A lot of fine old rows about markets and other rights there were later, too involved to go into here. But you can see that this apparently humming, roaring, concretised, ring-road-crossed, soulless modern industrial city is also a very ancient, mysterious place, whence came that most tender and heart-piercing of all Christmas music, the Coventry Carol; and the miracle plays of the famous Coventry Pageants. Chester, Coventry and York, those were the places that produced the *first* English drama, the seed-bed for Shakespeare. When Hamlet gives the First Player his advice, true then as now, that there is nothing worse than ham-acting, seeing 'a robustious periwig-pated fellow tear a passion to tatters', he goes on that it 'out-Herods Herod'. In the Coventry plays Herod brandished his 'bright brond' or sword and spoke great rolling lines:

> For I am evyn he thatt made bothe hevin and hell,
> And of my myghte power holdith up this world rownd.
> Magog and Madroke, bothe them did I confounde.

As Mary Dormer Harris remarks, in my well-thumbed copy of *The Story of Coventry* (it is my home town), 'What megalomania! "Magog and Madroke" are undeniably fearsome names and suit well with Herod's vizor, his falchion and towering crests'.

Administrators and speculators between them have been responsible in this century for far more destruction of the medieval past than can be attributed to the Luftwaffe. I myself remember a perfectly wonderful complex including Butcher Row and Ironmonger Row being demolished in the Thirties to make way for a dismal non-road called Trinity Street (ha!), and there was another one called Corporation Street (ha!) where for years there was nothing but new gas showrooms and a cinema called the Rex. Nor can post-war Coventry be said to have been wholly on fire with enthusiasm for the idea of the new Cathedral. There was a lot of mumbling about money being wasted that should have been spent on Houses for the People etc., regardless of the fact that a lot of money and gifts specifically for the Cathedral poured in from abroad. One of the most moving things about it, in fact, is to see these gifts, from the Chinese Kweilin Marble to the Windows of the Chapel of Unity, given by German Evangelical Churches. (After the première of Britten's *War Requiem* in Coventry I was in the shuffling-out crowd, overwhelmed by the experience, and I happened to be right behind the Bishop of Coventry, who was with his sister and some friends. When we got to this beautiful circular chapel, with its marble mosaic floor, a gift from the people of Sweden, the Bishop said to a rather cross-looking man who was standing on the other side of the crimson rope barrier, 'may we come in?' 'No, I'm sorry, it's closed', said the man).

Well, people will argue for ever whether the cathedral is a total 'success', since its brilliant architect, the late Sir Basil Spence, did in a sense stake everything on the enormous, inescapable visual focus the moment one enters, the vast Graham Sutherland tapestry (biggest in the world, etc.) of Christ in Majesty hanging behind the altar. Well, this is a cathedral, not an art gallery; and it's a cathedral of the religion which says that one particular Man, born as a human baby, was also the Second Person of the Divine Trinity, so although this is an age either bored by, or frightened of, or incapable of representational art (maybe all three), it is not an abstract philosophical religion, so it's no good running away into abstract art. And even as one says this one thinks that the greatest single *artistic* impression that is immediately made on almost every visitor is the breathtaking sunburst glory of the Baptistry Window (designed by John Piper, executed by Patrick Reyntiens), its vertical lines falling to the majestically simple centrepiece, the Bethlehem Font, just a huge lump of Palestine rock standing on the polished marble floor (it arrived on Christmas Eve 1960).

But it's no good fussing, with one part of your mind, that the representation of *knees* in such a dominating figure is a problem that even Graham Sutherland couldn't solve, while another part of it admires his 'brilliant' treatment of the four Gospel symbols (St Mark's lion, St John's angel, St Luke's bull, St Matthew's eagle). There are plenty of individual splendours in this cathedral which so boldly eschews the dim religious light and shows you everything; what matters is not only its overall presence but its deeply moving, permanent dialogue with the burnt-out shell of the old St Michael's, to which it is set at right angles, the huge 'west' (actually south) wall of clear glass etched with angels facing the cobbled churchyard through which people not visiting the cathedral at all go about their daily business.

It would be a hard man or woman who (possibly after climbing the noble spire, still standing, one of the finest in England, and looking down at the green grass where once there were pillars and pews, and the apse slightly at an angle to the nave, often said to represent the head of the dead Christ hanging to one side), could stand unmoved in front of the famous Charred Cross, made simply out of two blackened beams, backed by the words FATHER FORGIVE. Dresden and Hiroshima as well.

There are plenty of other things to see in Coventry, apart from two other fine churches. There is the splendid St Mary's Guildhall, in the even-now quiet little Bayley Lane nearby, and Bond's Hospital in Hill Street (just above St John's church) where you step through an archway in a very ordinary street into a beautiful little Tudor almshouse group.

You have only to compare the dismal industrial Foleshill Road leading northwards out of Coventry, or the one going north-west to Birmingham, with the tree-lined Kenilworth Road's almost instant suggestion of the melting south, 'Shakespeare country', the Cotswolds, the far-off hint of south-western seas, to realise that Coventry seems to have within itself the starting-points of both the north and the south of England.

It seems rather tough on **Kenilworth Castle**, unless you have plenty of time to spare and can go through and see this nobly melancholy ruin on your way to **Warwick**, undoubtedly *the* castle in these parts, to say that the best way to Warwick is the back way which I am now about to recommend to you. I knew I would come to this problem sooner or later, the problem facing all topographical writers. If you know a secret magic place, why tell the secret to your 3 million readers; suppose they all go there on the same day?

All I can say is that if, turning off the little road that goes from Coventry via Stoneleigh to **Leamington** (a jolly little sub-Bath, with Pump Room and splendid Jephson Gardens, contiguous with Warwick; Leamington, who would have thought that Borg-Warner clutches and such things would be made there now? Not so when I was a lad) you do manage to find **Ashow**, go along the little path round the little church with its fine roof, and if you see a lot of people in the meadow clutching copies of this book, wait till they come out again (which they will have to do to get to their cars, this being a cul-de-sac village), or come on another day. You cross the infant Avon by a footbridge, and if you are lucky and are there on your own (for you are not likely to be a 14-year-old Coventry Grammar School boy making a long detour home with a couple of contemporaries, as I was), you watch the long green weeds swaying in the clear current, you hear larks and cows and rustling trees, you see dragonflies and, my God, a *kingfisher*; and you think, this is England. Ashow. Sounds like a sneeze. But it is a magic place.

Well, Warwick Castle has pretty well everything (since, unlike Kenilworth, it is not one of the ruins that Cromwell knocked about a bit). Avon frontage, peacocks, Capability Brown gardens, classical examples of medieval defence ideas, two enormous towers (Guy's and Caesar's), hideous sadistic torture displays including oubliette, magnificent State Apartments; State Dining Room with, surprise surprise. Van Dyck of Charles I, Great Hall much admired by Sir W. Scott, as well it might be, Red Drawing Room, Cedar Drawing Room with wonderful Adam fireplace, Blue Boudoir (well, whoever heard of a Red Boudoir, the word *means* 'sulking-place') . . .

Splendid St Mary's church in Warwick too, lovely subaqueous green light on noble tombs etc. But now it is time to go to a place which not all the commercialism in the world can spoil, the town where the world's greatest, most human and universal poet-playwright was a grammar-school boy—

Stratford-on-Avon

(I've never actually heard anyone say out loud 'Stratford-*upon*-Avon' which is the way maps and books and everything insist on printing it.) Actually the commercialism sneer is a bit overdone. After all, a lot of people come here, and they have to eat and drink, nobody is compelling them to buy plaster Bards. I always wanted to get a complete set, buying one more each time, of those tiny little Nelson editions of the plays, about the size of matchboxes but perfectly readable, but I still have only *Henry IV, Parts I and II*.

Here again, it is much better to go the back way (which we always did anyway on our bicycles, since you keep to the Avon level instead of climbing that long hill, from which admittedly you get far views of the Cotswolds. Through snug Georgian Barford, then turn off to Charlecote, where scholars now say Shakespeare *didn't* poach because Sir Thomas Lucy didn't have a deer park then, although there are plenty in the fat, green, lush park now. To Hampton Lucy, where a huge church stands up from the meadows, as though built for some medieval Brasilia, and turns out to have been built between 1822 and 1826.

Getting warm now. The Women's Institute scrapbook for Charlecote says:

'. . . mechanical cutters used on the grass verges have decimated the numbers and varieties of the wild flowers. *Kex* and *paigles*, beloved of Shakespeare, have suffered so much that it is almost impossible to make many cowslip balls or to implement the wild bouquet with the cow parsley, so resembling Gypsophila. However, any country child can still gather Wild Yellow Toadflax, nicknamed Eggs-and-bacon . . .

Actually, when I was there last, in spring 1980, there seemed to be a lot of cow-parsley; perhaps it is coming back, like many wild flowers now that people are fractionally more careful about spraying and mechanical cutting. There is something about this area that makes you know what Shakespeare meant by 'spongy meads'. Here, in these meadows, grew that lofty imagination which could encompass not only the whole range of human character, but fairies, echoing human quarrels,

> And never, since the middle summer's spring
> Met we on hill, in dale, forest or mead,
> By paved fountain, or by rushy brook,
> Or in the beached margent of the sea,
> To dance our ringlets to the whistling wind

and, after the blood of *Macbeth* and the wild storm of Lear's madness and the fury of wars,

> Every fairy take his gait,
> And each several chamber bless,
> Through this palace, with sweet peace;
> Ever shall in safety rest
> And the owner of it blest.

Ah, those simple, terrible, heartbreaking, heartmending rhymes, after the blood and thunder, the heroic lines. The scrapbook goes on: 'When Shakespeare wrote "I know a bank whereon the wild thyme grows" it is said he referred to a bank at Hatton Rock . . .'

There is nothing new to be said about Stratford. There is the theatre with its sweeping river view, there is the birthplace, there is Trinity Church, the tomb, there is New Place, the home he later bought.

I myself have always had amazing luck in getting in to the theatre on the off-chance when I have been anywhere near. Of course, there are huge tourist block bookings, but do not let this discourage you from trying. Stratford (0789) 292271.

If you are even luckier and have the tickets in the morning and a nice afternoon to fill, the whole area between Stratford and Banbury is worth exploring. You are often aware of the blue ridge of Edge Hill to the east, of the great oak trees standing in the hedges, of hidden wonderful houses—some famous like **Compton Wynyates**, only just *in* Warwickshire, perfect house in perfect valley setting; some not so well known, like the beautiful 17th century **Honington Hall** with the Roman busts so surprisingly let into its comfortable brick façade (it is just above Shipston-on-Stour), or **Compton Verney**, splendid classical mansion with all the great names—Vanbrugh, Adam, Brown. The point is that to get from one to the other you would be going along the **Fosse Way**, the great Roman road that goes from Lincoln to Exeter, no less. For part of it you would be on a narrow, hardly used country road all the more striking in its Roman straightness through these quiet fields and over these gentle rises, and partly on the A429, the main road to the Cotswolds. But they come, however arbitrarily, under our next great nodal point. And besides, you can't go on to the Cotswolds now; you've got to get back to Stratford for the play.

Bath and Bristol

Bath

Like Rome, Bath is built on seven hills; and its fantastic 18th-century splendour, the noble golden-brown terraces overlooking the city below with its rich 15th-century Abbey and the great squares and streets laid out by John Wood, the whole concept of this elegant pleasure-city from which green hills are always visible, overlies something very much older. In this soft west-country air, over this rock from which spring waters heated by fire somewhere down there, is the perfect marriage of art with nature; earth, air, water, fire—and Beau Nash, Sheridan, Jane Austen, Dr Johnson, classical civilisation.

There are hundreds of books about this unique city, so simultaneously invigorating and restful. In one of them, called simply *Bath*, R. A. L. Smith (who wrote it in 1943, a year before his death at the age of 28, in another of those periods when people have other things to think of than wit under the chandeliers) says, of the Roman baths, 'when the eyes first become accustomed to the gloom of the dungeon-like apartment that serves as a sub-vault to the Pump Room, it is only to make the horrifying discovery that such priceless archaeological treasures as the famous Bath Gorgon are dumped here, ill-guarded and ill-preserved'.

Not so now. There is a well-organised museum down there, beneath the big Georgian room where you can still have coffee to the sound of Palm Court type music, and where you can look at the oblong of dark green, steaming water, surrounded by Georgian colonnades and with a kind of plaque that modern historians with their fiddling obsession with verification wouldn't pass. It says:

> BLADUD, SON OF LUDHUDIBRAS, 8TH KING OF THE BRITTANS WHOM BRUTE, A GREAT PHILOSOPHER AND MATHEMATICIAN BRED AT ATHENS AND RECORDED THE FIRST DISCOVERY OF THESE BATHS EIGHT HUNDRED AND SIXTY THREE YEARS BEFORE CHRIST THAT IS TWO THOUSAND FIVE HUNDRED AND SIXTY TWO YEARS TO THE PRESENT YEAR 1699.

Now you can see the archaeologists actually at work as they uncover mosaics and hypocaust fragments and generally rediscover the enormous complex that was here in the time of Agricola, when the Sixth Legion was at York and the Twentieth was at Chester. For this was the temple of Sul-Minerva, a fusion of the Roman goddess of healing (there's a marvellous straight-nosed gilded bronze bust of Minerva in the museum) with the Celtic goddess Sul. Indeed, the place was called Aquae Sulis. And although it is on the Fosse Way it was not one of the great garrison centres; almost it seems to have been for the Romans what it was for 18th-century England: a health resort.

They have blow-ups and translations of some of the tablets found there.

Julius Vitalis, armourer of the 20th Legion Valeria Victrix of 9 years' service, aged 29, a Belgic tribesman with funeral at the cost of the guild of armourers lies here.

Romulus and Victoria Sabina set this up to their dearest daughter . . .

And they report the dialogue, '*Barbarian*: "Why do you bathe once a day?" *Roman*: "Because I can't bathe twice a day." '

They have a blown-up version of an Anglo-Saxon poem, with all those consonantal rhymes, all too conscious of the decay into which this splendour had fallen:

Tumbled, crumbled in gravel's hard grip
Till hundred generations of men pass away
War-clang frequent, mead-halls many, merriment frequenting
Till all's overwhelmed by fate unrelenting
While erewhile many a baron joyous and jewelled with elaborate splendour
Haughty and hot with wine, shone in his harness . . .

There were splendours in Bath between this medieval decay and the Georgian flowering, of course. There was a Norman cathedral on the site of the present Abbey which was started in 1499 and is therefore unusual among English cathedrals in being entirely of one style—in this case Perpendicular at its finest, a real 'box of light' with its high, narrow transepts and its supremely beautiful fan vaulting. Not surprisingly, lots of florid monuments, including one to a Sir Richard Hussey which comes more of an essay than an epitaph, it must have taken months to carve; how awful if the mason, having started *Few men have descended to the tomb* . . . and gone on for about 500 words till right at the end . . . *every duty was more uniformly and correctly fulfilled . . . noble and honourable feelings*, had spelt *feelings* wrong and had had to start the whole thing all over again. Quite near this is the Birde Chantry, like a kind of doll's church, with the same kind of roof as the Abbey itself; and a very chic portable font, an elegant wooden affair with lead basin, still used.

Well, of course, there were these four men who *made* the Bath we all know and love: Ralph Allen, whose quarries supplied the luminous Bath Stone; John Wood the Elder, architect of York Street, Duke Street, all the 'new Bath' near the Pump Room, Queen Square, the Circus, 318 feet across, in three sections, each of eleven houses in Tuscan, Ionic and Corinthian tiers (and you realise that the neat classic Palladian Georgians could have their Gothic fantasies too; I saw in fanlights over successive doors knights' helmets, crossed spade and rake, flowers, birch, music, clock with wreath, water wheel, oysters, keys, armorial shields, sheaves of wheat, palette . . .); his son J. W. the Younger, who did Brock Street and, many other things (and there were many other architects, but it was mainly the Woods), his supreme achievement being the noble, deeply satisfying Royal Crescent; and of course Richard, Beau Nash.

He was made official Master of Ceremonies by the Corporation. He took it seriously (for pleasure and gaiety to succeed they need to be taken as seriously as, if not more seriously than, the more solemn things of this world. You watch the faces of a good orchestra playing the fizzing last movement of, say, a Mozart symphony).

A gentleman must consort himself with dignity and elegance no less in the manner of his dress than that of his behaviour. Riding boots are not to be worn at fashionable gatherings. Swords are not to be seen in public places . . . order and decency should be the aim . . . begging and vagrancy should be eradicated, thus enabling the gentleman and the gentlewoman to move without molestation . . . bathing should begin at 6 and finish at 9 a.m., and this should be followed by general assembly in the Pump Room for intelligent discussion and for drinking three glasses of Bath Spring water. After a public breakfast the residents should hire sedan chairs . . . a late luncheon is to be followed by a walk in the gardens. Twice-weekly costume balls . . .

Nash was a kind man, for all that. No. 10 of his famous 11 Rules was 'That all whisperers of lies and scandal be taken for their authors'. Crowds came to his funeral; there are a statue and portrait of him in the Pump Room. After his death his mistress Julia Papjoy (there is now a restaurant named after her in the Sawclose) refused to live in a house any more, and for years lived in a hollow tree in the village where she had been born, until she died.

When you have explored the Pump Room, the Museum, Baths, and Abbey, you can turn in any direction and see some of the most graceful urban architecture in the world, a marvellous combination of classical purity with human life, which can be enjoyed pulsing warmly through the streets all the more now that so many intimate smaller alleys and squares are for pedestrians only, like the charming little Northumberland Place, lamp standards bursting with geranium and trailing lobelia (there are flowers at every level in Bath) and the arcades and colonnades. You will obviously want to see the great things, yet one of the nearest things when you come out of the Pump Room is the Burrows Toy Museum in York Street; just one lovely little tinplate bus turns out to be worth over £300 (and up by the Assembly Rooms is, as a matter of fact, the best toyshop I have ever been in, called Tridias).

You could go east through the Parade Grounds (surprisingly for England, not free; adults 13p) facing on to the river pouring calmly over the weir under the famous Pulteney Bridge, which has shops on it like the Ponte Vecchio in Florence (Bath Stamp Shop, Tina and Peter, the Venice Coffee Shop, Duck Son and Pinker Ltd, Organs Pianos and T.V., est. 1848 . . .) with slightly further on a very grand-looking ironmonger's with the admirable name of Rich and Cooling. Nor are you likely to find a more elegant covered market than the one opposite this bridge, with its central dodecagon lanterns pouring down a glassy light on to a central array of fruit and vegetables so colourfully arranged it almost seems a pity to buy anything for fear of disturbing it. And there is a little sit-down snack bar, not one of your hurry-along-please cafeterias. This isn't any old market. *W. Bennett & Son*, it says, *licensed to sell game, pheasants, partridges, woodcock, snipe, venison and hares.*

The splendid Bridge Bookshop across the road in Bridge Street has, like most of the shops here, elegant old fascia and exterior; in this case Corinthian pillars and a polished sloping brass window sill on which it says *Dispensing Chemists*. And a very intelligent selection of books inside.

Or you could go north from the Pump Room, up pedestrianised Stall Street which becomes Union Street and eventually brings you to Milsom Street, where Anne Elliot, in *Persuasion*, came across that splendid old Admiral Croft looking at a marine picture in a print-shop. 'Did you ever see the like? What queer fellows your fine painters must be, to think that any body would venture their lives in such a shapeless old cockleshell as that?'

It still has elegant shops, as well as a Pizza Parlour and something called Sweeney Todd, and in the elegant George Street which crosses it at the top there are not only posh-looking wine merchants but Charlie Brown's Club and Nero's Disco and a sauna. But these are only extremer examples of the obvious fact that Bath is a thriving, busy, lived-in city, not just a museum. It was heavily bombed during the war (when the Admiralty was evacuated here

Bath.

from London). The most disastrous casualty was the Assembly Rooms, but they were faithfully rebuilt, and you can still walk round them, looking at the portraits and the brilliant original chandeliers (which fortunately had been stored elsewhere) and trying not to look at the dismal modern chairs.

Like any beautiful city, Bath is best explored on foot. If you go to the Tourist Information Centre in the Abbey churchyard you can join a party taken round by one of the extremely well-informed Mayor's Guides (and it is free, so they are entitled to charge 13p for the Parade Garden!). Of course you could spend a week cheerfully looking at Bath, although it is amazing what you can take in in one day. Be a pity to come away for instance, without also seeing, just across the road from the Assembly Rooms, the unequalled Carriage Museum, with hansom cabs (little knee-shaped doors), marvellously shiny-maroon, red and black mail coach, curricle (gentleman's chariot with very high wheels, lot about them in *Northanger Abbey*), sociable, police van, demi-phaeton and a horse hearse I wouldn't mind having for my funeral, with its kneeling black angels (the whole thing is black), vaguely sub-Egyptian-looking corner pillars and floriated top. Can just see it being pulled by black horses with nodding plumes, weeping mourners.

You still can go for calm rides in wagonette, holding 15 adults, clop clop clop through those elegant streets. They hire coaches out for weddings too, with attendants in the proper livery, of course. 'With two horses it costs about the same as a Rolls-Royce, with one horse it's about like hiring a limousine.'

A last tip. If you are driving about Bath there only seems to be one car park if you make the usual motorist's mistake of wanting to start too near the centre, and if you haven't come in from the north and forked left down the one-way Walcot Street, heaven help you; where Bath isn't pedestrianised it's one-way. But there are plenty of other parks down by the river (find Green Park Road). You won't have to walk much farther (although you'll want your car to get up to the higher delights of Camden Crescent and Lansdown Crescent, in which case make sure your handbrake is in good order). This city was built for and lived in by pedestrians—like Burke, Goldsmith, the Earl of Chesterfield, Nelson, Sheridan, Fanny Burney, Horace Walpole, William Pitt, Josiah Wedgwood, Sir Isaac Pitman, Clive of India, William Herschel (who discovered Uranus), Edward Gibbon, Beckford the eccentric of Fonthill Abbey fame, who somehow got the altar rails of the Abbey for his railings in Lansdown Crescent (they are back in the Abbey now), and of course built a great mad tower up there. And, ah yes, Beau Nash. And now you.

Bristol

It is not surprising that Sir John Summerson, that great authority on English architecture, once wrote: 'If I had to show a foreigner one English city and one only, I should take him not to Oxford or Cambridge, which have developed in one special direction, nor to cathedral cities where nothing very much has happened since Henry VIII quarrelled with the Pope, but to Bristol, which has developed in all directions, and where everything has happened.'

One reason why the motorist merely passing through from north to south (on the old through road, the A38, never mind the M5, from which of course he wouldn't see it at all) could miss this eye-delighting, history-layered, surprise-round-every-corner, oddly up-and-down city is the 'City Centre' itself. Where, within living memory, destroyers used to sail right into the city and office workers could hear bosun's whistles, there are now some nondescript municipal lawns, a big new office block on your right as you come in from the north, a vague sense of mainly Victorian building on your left and of honey-coloured Georgian slopes on your right, and you would be out, over a bridge (fleeting glimpse behind you on your right of Brunel's famous suspension bridge as the huge bluff on which Clifton is built slid past, and on the A38 to Taunton, none the wiser.

But when you stand in that City Centre facing south, the old city, with its tumultuous past of glory, drama (and shame, with the infamous slave trade), its memories of the Merchant Venturers, of sieges by the Royalists under Prince Rupert *and* the Roundheads under Fairfax (both successful, both costly to the merchant ratepayers who just wanted the war to go away) is already behind you to the left.

Slightly *ahead* of you on your left, did you but know it, is elegant Queen Square, quietly lawyer-fringed now, but in October 1831 a key scene of the wild Reform Bill riots when the people burnt the Mansion House and the Custom House and anything else that would burn, opened the jail, looted cellars, got communally drunk and were eventually charged by Dragoons, hundreds being killed or wounded. One man, later dug out of the vaults alive but with an arm burnt off above the elbow, is said to have walked away. It was always a tough place.

A lot of the elegance came late, though not all of it, when you think of a splendour like St Mary Redcliffe, that airy marvel of Early Perp., 'the fairest goodliest and most famous parish church in the Kingdom', said Elizabeth I.

The key word for Bristol is *hidden*. All sight or smell of the sea, in this town which gave us the phrase 'all ship-shape and Bristol fashion', is hidden from you as you stand at the southern end of this same Centre, cars swirling round you. It is in fact eight miles of narrow water, soon to turn westward between the beetling cliffs of the Avon Gorge, away from you.

By a statue of Neptune you face a quite small stretch; you are standing over the built-over river Frome, which a few yards down joins the two-mile-long 'Floating Habour', the lock-regulated, dock-and-warehouse-lined section of the Avon built early in the 19th century with the help of French prisoner-of-war labour. This, alongside the new by-pass channel for the river, the New Cut, makes a large artificial island between the two parallel strips of water.

It all has to do with a late-starting, and eventually losing battle with Liverpool to capture the Atlantic trade (or, from Bristol's point of view, to keep it). That many-sided genius Brunel not only designed the magically graceful bridge over the gorge (not to mention a fair section of the entire Great Western Railway, including the still-used bridge over the Tamar, just outside Plymouth, which divides Devon from Cornwall) but was deeply involved in the shipbuilding side of this battle. But the very size of his revolutionary vessels meant that deep-water, Severnside Avonmouth and Portishead and Portbury, opened in 1977 by Queen Elizabeth II, were inevitable.

The 1,370-ton *Great Western* (1837) soon started to use Liverpool, and only six years later came the magnificent *Great Britain*, 3,270 tons. But only eight years after *that*, in 1851, the stranding of the 3,000-ton *Demerara* right across the Avon (she was only pulled off with a mighty effort of ox-teams and men on an exceptionally high tide) was the writing on the wall for inner Bristol as a modern big-ship port.

All the better for tourist pleasure! After an epic tow from the Falkland Islands the *Great Britain* is now the centrepiece, on that same man-made island, of an imaginative scheme to re-plan all this as a leisure centre with marinas, walkways, floating restaurants and all sorts of goodies for a city which has moved on to other things. (Just up the road for instance, they built the Concorde.)

A splendid lofty Victorian warehouse, the Granary, has for some time been the Jazz Club, where Mr Acker Bilk and others rose to prominence. Another has become the Arnolfini Gallery; there is to be a Technology Museum, and among the cobbles and preserved steam cranes and gulls, a floating pub.

It is pretty dramatic to walk over the enormous shell of the *Great Britain*, like an upside-down cathedral, with its great iron ribs and hand-forged plates, some think from that start-of-the-whole-thing Ironbridge, just up the Severn. There is a sense of great things having begun here. You get the same feeling by that Neptune statue, on that municipal-looking pavement; for there is nearby a bronze plate saying:

FROM THIS PORT JOHN CABOT AND HIS SON SEBASTIAN (WHO WAS BORN IN BRIS-
TOL) SAILED IN THE SHIP MATTHEW A.D. 1497 AND DISCOVERED THE CONTINENT OF
AMERICA.

Well, Newfoundland, anyway.

It is one of those numinous spots where a great turning-point of history is, so to say, physically located. From here, from *here*, began that huge expansion, that impact of the dynamic west on the then passive east, with all its consequences for good and evil. Oh, I know you can also feel like this by the statue of Henry the Navigator by the Tagus at Lisbon. But it's a strong feeling, in Bristol, all the same.

Bristol was founded by two legendary giants, Brennus and Belinus (and there were two other giants, engagingly named Vincent and Goram, who made the Avon Gorge—not to mention a real historical giant called O'Brian, 8 ft 4 in., who lit his pipe at street lamps and died in 1806).

Bombs destroyed a lot. But they left dignified Corn Street, now also pedestrians-only, with its four brass tables, known as 'nails', outside the Exchange—hence the expression 'paying on the nail'. There are wonderful mad buildings, like the Art-Nouveau, faintly ecclesiastical printing house of Edward Everard, ceramic-fronted with the Spirit of Literature and William Morris and his Golden Alphabet and some dotty pepper-pots (its architect W. J. Neatby also designed Harrods' Food Hall); Christmas Steps, with the curlicued, turreted, scrolled Foster Almshouses at the top, like the setting for some Weber opera; the historic Theatre Royal, associated with the University in drama training; many glorious and comfortable old inns.

There is the unbuttoned atmospheric charm of the market, with strange boiled sweets, magnetic pencils, yards of cake, velour, old prints, hideous anodised-metal Gifts, jeans, browse-all-morning bookstalls, under cast-iron pillars and high glass lights in All Saints Lane.

As for churches, you have everything from the noble cathedral, G. E. Street's 19th-century nave repeating the high-transomed 14th-century choir aisles of this unique 'hall-church', through the elegant white-and-gold Renaissance St Stephen's, and Christ Church with one of those clocks where people stop to watch the little figures, Quarter Jacks, striking with their hammers, to the absolutely fascinating new Catholic Cathedral, set above the huge-towered university and Clifton's gorgeous Georgian terraces. It is one of those funnelled cake-tins from outside, but inside, with everything, from candle-holders to chairs, based on the same basic 18-inch module, the natural light pouring down on to the altar, and perhaps above all the Stations of the Cross, apparently simply done while the concrete of the wall was setting so that they are simply *part* of it. Lovely blaze of abstract glass where you come in; always a mysterious wind thrumming high above, as though it were a permanent Whit Sunday; a numinous, living building—in a city where they have always known how to build.

The West Country

This book began with London as its nodal point. With the exception of the Isle of Wight, all the places so far mentioned have been ones that you *could* manage in a day from London, although this is not recommended if they are more than fifty miles away, if that. It is as a tribute and compliment, not a slight, to their deep independent non-London richness and character that the remaining places—including the entire countries of Scotland and Wales—receive a length of treatment which is almost in inverse proportion to their attractiveness to the visitor, who can safely be assured that at any office bearing the *i* sign there is a wealth of regional information beyond the scope of this or any other book.

As Belloc remarked, let us not 'be too hard upon the just but anxious fellow that sat down dutifully to paint the soul of Switzerland upon a fan'. As a matter of fact that would be easier. When you've seen one Alp you've seen the lot, but when you've seen Somerset you haven't seen Cornwall.

Somerset, Devon and Cornwall

Even though there are sodium street lights, and traffic jams on narrow roads through grey stone hilly towns, and about ten million caravans and chalets, and an increasing number of pylons, dish aerials and assorted masts, this is still, in the European mind, let alone the British, the land of *romance*, before that word was devalued. Of Atlantis, of Lyonesse (the Scilly Isles, say some), of King Mark's court with Tristan and Isolde endlessly approaching on a magic, doomed sea, of King Arthur in Tintagel Castle on that magnificent north coast (rubbish, says a D. of E. booklet, it was built by Reginald, a Norman).

The west country has a marvellously diverse geography. There is actually some footling new bureaucrats'-convenience county called 'Avon', said to include Bath and Bristol and the northern parts of the old Somerset, but let us ignore this and be grateful that at least the southern boundaries of Somerset take in a nice western bulge, to include the essential mass of the great, free, airy heights of **Exmoor** before its eastward bulge to the boundaries of Dorset.

Lynton and **Lynmouth**, in their sea-cleft, are joined by a lift with a water-tank counterweight (George Stephenson used a similar idea on his Inclined Plane on the Yorkshire Moors railway when it got too steep for those early locomotives) and just in Devon, but it's all *Lorna Doone* country; **Oare**, where R. D. Blackmore's father was rector, has a church where they solemnly point out the window through which she was shot at the altar.

The lovely maid, fair Lorna Doone
She lived on a heath as bare as the moon

And she dreamed of a lover, the bold Jan Ridd
Who'd seek her out where she lay hid
  Oh over Exmoor the wind blows free
  And none can find where that love might be
  The rocks hang over the waterfall
  But lovely Lorna's not there at all.
O she was lovely, and she was fair,
The brightest jewel in that robbers' lair
And he was a wrestler, a king of men
With muscles of iron, and the strength of ten
  Oh over Exmoor, etc.
They vanished away, that robber band,
They found a valley in another land
And Lorna, the lady of all men prized,
Was a voice on the wind, or a bird disguised.
  Oh over Exmoor etc.
O Jan may seek her, and Jan may search
Where the coaches park by Oare village church
Or by Badgery Water that flows by the trees
To the place that sells all those cream teas.
  Oh over Exmoor, etc.

Music on request.

The only way to know about Exmoor, that ex-Royal Forest and moorland with its unique breed of stocky pony, its marvellous atmospheric
names—Dunkery Beacon (highest point, wonderful views over to Wales),
Larkbarrow, Buckethole, Little Black Hill, Great Black Hill, Wallover
Down, Ricksby Ball, Desolate, Hangley Cleave—is to go boldly up one of the
little roads marked in yellow on the Ordnance Survey map as far as you can
and walk. It's all beautiful.

Devon is the first county to have a north and a south coast, and it of course
has the even greater and wilder and grander massif of **Dartmoor**, that
overlooks naval Plymouth to its west and ultra-civilian, palm-treed, sea-
view-hotelled Torquay to its east. Here, more than ever, you *must* turn down
the inviting road. One of the most exhilarating rides I had in my life, on a
perfect summer day, in an open car, was from the edge of Exmoor to
Torrington, utterly unvisited, unbuttoned farmers' town (no, they *were*
visitors eating in that lovely hotel, the Plough) to Okehampton. One high
horizon left for another; at points on the road I could see both.

But before we leave Somerset (which nobody must without seeing **Wells
Cathedral**, with its unique egg-timer chancel arch which seems to make the
purist angry but which I adore, and its famous swans that ring a bell for their
dinner) let us not forget that as well as heights it has depths, underground
marvels like **Cheddar** or **Wookey Hole**. The former tends to frighten the
more aesthetically-minded away from seeing its stalactite marvels by giving
them such names as The Fonts, Ring of Bells, Swiss Village, Pixie Forest,
Fairy Grotto, Bunch of Carrots, Ladye (!) Chapel. Pity, because both the
caves and the gorge itself have something much more *wild* about them than
any photograph could convey. Something very mysterious here, as though it
were nature's subconscious. Wookey Hole down the road, although it is now
owned by Madame Tussaud's and also offers a fairground exhibition with
galloping horses and one of those lovely rococo organs and a paper mill
where you can still see that curious moment when suddenly it's not liquid
scum at the top, it's paper, is more restrained in its guide, merely referring to
1st Chamber, 2nd Chamber . . . 25th Chamber. From this complex, whence

Wells Cathedral.

the river Axe emerges from underground, Coleridge probably got *his* mysterious subconscious inspiration for *Kubla Khan* . . .

> Where Alph, the sacred river, ran
> Through caverns measureless to man

—an inspiration broken, it will be remembered by the intrusion of the Person from Porlock. You've got the prosaic too, in Somerset as elsewhere. But you've also got the mystical, all that is summed up in the word **Glastonbury**, with its legend that Joseph of Arimathaea planted a graft from the Crown of Thorns here. This is also Avalon, the old Celtic paradise where no one grew old, and the blossom and apples are on the tree simultaneously—in fact the word simply means Island of Apples.

The cider apple is called the Kingston Black. But oh, the poetry of the names of its companions, long may they survive the dismal EEC standardisation rules! Foxwhelp, Ashton Brown Jersey, Chisel Jersey, Hangydown, Porter's Perfection, Loyal Drain, Slack-ma-Girdle, Cheatboy, Bloody Butcher . . . it's quite easy to go round a cider works, but it's easier still, asking around in the pub (where you should remember that

> Cider on beer makes you feel queer
> Beer on cider makes a good rider

and that a *Commando* is bitter with cider, a VC is *Vimto* with cider, a *Snakebite* is ginger cordial with cider), anywhere in the Vale of Taunton, and someone will put you on to a marvellous red-faced old boy like the one I met in his ramshackle shed, with his own press in which he squashes the apples, separating the layers of solid remainder known as *pomace*, fermenting, racking, storing 30 or 40 hogsheads of very dry cider indeed, selling it to anyone that comes round.

Giving a lot away too. 'The rat-catcher's always here, I give him a pint before he starts and maybe a pint after. There wasn't any rats before he came, I tell him he must 'a brought them with him. Ah, a dozen pints of this an' the policeman'll never catch me on my bike.'

Curiously, Devon is less mysterious than either Somerset or Cornwall. Historical, heraldic, atmospheric, beautiful, yes. The rich county town of **Exeter**, once a curse-name to holiday motorists on what was laughingly called its by-pass, is now fortunate in being even more by-passed by the M5, so you can enjoy its cathedral, one of those which is miraculously bigger inside than it is outside; this is because of its glorious roof, the rich Purbeck marble nave pillars, the general perfection of its Decorated (late 13th and first half of 14th centuries). It is also the only cathedral which instead of having a central tower at the crossing has two, one over each transept; a beautiful arrangement anyway, but the more so because these are *Norman*, with white-capped turrets at the corners which instantly remind you of the White Tower in London. But you will find that rich turreted towers are a noticeable feature, the first thing you see in fact, in many west country churches of later periods.

I may just have been lucky, but I've always found it easier getting into and parking in the centre of Exeter than driving round it. My wife and I stayed once at the Royal Clarence Hotel, when the Clarence Room, with a painted ceiling, was the dining room (now, more's the pity, it is what they call a Function Room; nor is there any more a brown door on which it actually says *Barristers' Mess*, although barristers do still eat there during the Assizes). We asked the chambermaid to keep an eye on our 18-month-old in her cot while we went to breakfast in this deeply satisfying room, in which every meal was a Function. When we came back it was like Act I in *Die Fledermaus*; there were a maid with a duster, the chambermaid, a man in a green baize apron, a lady in a white overall and a young waiter all clustered round the cot talking to its occupant graciously smiling at all this homage. We went to the window and there saw a splendid civic procession with the judges in their red gowns just entering the cathedral.

Even if you are in the train to Cornwall you can see it crowning the hill, before you see the widening estuary of the Exe on your left, then the sea, right next to the line, which around Dawlish plunges through overlapping rocks in one of the most dramatic railway scenes in Britain. Pity to have missed **Sidmouth**, up the coast on the east side of the Exe, and in fact only still just *in* Devon; set in a bowl of red Devon hills and cliffs, on the way to nowhere but itself, a terminus, all blue and white and pink Regency and 19th-century buildings with a lot of white woodwork; yet a sense that people live here all the time. I was there on a sparkling February morning, people were walking up and down the long paved seaside walk with dogs, raising their hats, smiling, as if they all knew each other. A week there would be very peaceful indeed.

Well, of course, every place on the coast here is a Resort. Some more hidden than others, naturally. Here's a nice map-readers-only road, you might think, congratulating yourself on getting in at the Tower Inn in **Slapton**, village of free-standing white cottages, flowers, narrow road, overlooking Sands of same name. In many-cornered, wood-smokey bar, Dish of Day written on blackboard, lot of family parties containing young men, athletic-looking, no long hair, unobtrusively well-dressed, knowledge-able about the wide varieties of Real Beer stocked here. They are cadets from Royal Naval College at **Dartmouth**, long Edwardian-Queen-Anne-style stone ship on green hillside above boat-rocking town. If you are lucky enough to be there for big ceremonial, band of Royal Marines, long waiting at attention, inspection, precision marching, wild cheer from inside and tension broken when last file goes through great front door and it is slammed shut, you see one thing they've all learned; how to pass out without passing out.

This whole promontory well worth exploring, to Start Point, Prawle Point, superb views, creeks of Kingsbridge estuary; but Cornwall beckons.

From here obviously you do approach via Plymouth, in which case do not fail to turn right moments after you have crossed the Tamar to see **Cotehele**, solid grey-granite house as old as, say, Compton Wynyates, but already having tough sea-look about it, style best described as Cornobethan; full of tapestries, four-posters (I still have six of their postcards of a tapestry detail, fat jolly cherubs with cymbals and pipes accompanying Bacchus), the most unclocklike clock you ever saw since it was made around 1480 before clocks had dials, let alone pendulums. Also marvellous water-garden in hidden bird-loud combe, with medieval dovecote. Peace. Also very good cream teas. And if you happen to be there on the right day, Mozart or something in acoustically perfect converted barn.

However, I was a midlander before I was a southerner, and for me Corn-wall is to be entered from the north. This always used to mean the A39 from Barnstaple. And here again, although you can, long before you get to Pen-zance (in this extremely hypothetical journey), become increasingly aware of sea light coming from your left as well as your right as England narrows down to a point, there is always, until you are actually at Land's End, that marvellous sense of more intricate space, of something else round the corner, down that turning.

I hesitate about what to say of the first of these turnings off the road from Barnstaple, while you are still in Devon, before the coast takes its decisive right-angle turn due south at Hartland Point, and from hereabouts you have Cornwall's rugged, rocky, gale-facing, Atlantic north coast, so different from the snug palmy creeks and inlets of its southern one (when I arrived in Falmouth in 1978 I saw something I've always had an ambition to see—snow-covered palm trees. The snow had melted by the time I was parking in the town, then there was a tremendous clap of thunder and all the electricity in the town went off for two hours. Thus was my arrival to give a music talk heralded).

This turning is to the well-known **Clovelly**, the famous cobble-stepped, one-street, carless 'fishing' village. Well, it *is* beautiful, although the people living in those fresh-painted houses and shops with their little patios and pots of flowers looked more like souvenir-sellers and retired insurance managers than fishermen to me. It is a *locus classicus* of the tourist problem, and has been for years. My aunt's house was named after it before 1900, and so were thousands of others.

So try and see it at dawn, or in the off-peak season. But as the A39 doesn't actually touch the sea all the way down to Truro, there are any number of other possible turns-off. It was only last year that I left it to go to **Bude**, for instance. Admittedly it was only April, but I was totally unprepared for the colossal, airy blue vista of its enormous, sandy, rock-edged bay, which looked as if it could contain the entire human race, never mind the few figures seen against the westering light, against the majestic Atlantic breakers. 'Oh, but you should see it when all the surfers are here', said a resident, rather gloomily I thought. I should quite *like* to see it. I got the feeling that enough people by-pass Bude for it to be fairly unspoilable.

Well, everybody knows that Cornwall had a lot of saints, many of whom came over from Ireland, often on a millstone, and they lived in beehive cells and were hermits. You could spend a lot of time in Cornwall finding out about its saints. Who was St Issey? St Tudy? St Teath? St Keverne? Well St Keverne, who gave his name to a delightful village below Helston,

> came from Ireland or Wales in the period between 500 and 800 A.D., though there are no written records. There are two stories about him. One is that, disrespect having been shown to him by local inhabitants, he caused the mineral lodes to become barren. Hence the saying 'no metal will run within the sound of St Keverne's bell'. The other is that his friend, St Just, coveted his chalice. After a visit St Just took it away with him. On discovery of the theft St Keverne set off in pursuit, picking up three stones on the way. He overtook his ungrateful friend and threw the stones, whereupon St Just dropped the chalice and fled.

I find this very encouraging. If you can throw stones after people who pinch your chalice and still be a saint there's hope for us all.

Well, of course, that brings us to mining, in which the Cornish people are pioneers, in the literal sense of that word. The bare uplands of Bodmin Moor, where the rare trees all bend the same way—no need to ask where the prevailing wind comes from—are dotted with old workings and buildings and beam engines and other fascinating bits of industrial archaeology. Around St Austell it's not archaeology at all; the great white moon-mountains of the china clay industry workings are a reminder that Cornwall continues an industrial tradition it had when Lancashire was simply a place where they made cheese; and let us not forget that Richard Trevithick, who in 1801 made the first steam carriage that ever carried people, a good time before Stephenson, was born near Camborne (there is a splendid working beam engine at East Pool nearby).

Miners know all about the earth. Earthy and mystical are not opposed terms in this context, they are the same. The ancient Chinese, it is said, used to put a human embryo into a new furnace, believing that metal was a concentration of the earth's living power. Nothing like that in Cornwall. But if you turn off the A39 (to get back to *that* again) to **Padstow**, it probably won't be May Day, when they have a great drum-thumping dance, the Horse (a man inside a curious frame) and the dancers (the Pairs and the Teaser) taking you to an unknown antiquity; and what about this for a lyric:

Oh where is Saint George, oh where is he oh?
He's out in his long boat all on the salt sea oh.
Up flies the kite
Down falls the lark
Oh, Aunt Ursula Birdood she had an old yow
And she died in her own park oh.

Helston's dance, better known, is inevitably more self-conscious, just as **Helston** itself, a rich-looking town with fine Georgian houses and a lovely high street from which you see green hills, as you should from all proper high streets, and deep open gutters which have ruined the back axle of more than one 300-mile-tired motorist incautiously backing in to park, is smoother than grey, gull-haunted, real fishing town Padstow.

So to the southern coast, with the aforesaid snug creeks, none more worth exploring than that of **St Just-in-Roseland**, in Falmouth Bay, where you will find a waterside church set among specimens of the African strawberry tree, the Chilean myrtle, the palm and six different varieties of bamboo. It is one locale of the persistent Cornish legend that Joseph of Arimathaea visited England with Christ as a child. An old lady told a previous rector, 'Jesus passed by here, and blessed these parts. I think it is because it is the end of the world' (meaning Land's End).

Well, you can't be this far without *going* to **Land's End**, though not before seeing **St Michael's Mount**, on its tide-covered spit off (evocative Cornish name!) Marazion, England's answer to France's Mont Saint Michel, not to mention the Sacra San Michele near Turin (St Michael liked high places). And not, if you have the chance of hearing some such play as (except that there *is* no such play as; but you guessed!) *A Midsummer Night's Dream*, without visiting the delightful cliff-edge open-air theatre of Minack, near Porthcurno.

But if you go straight from Penzance, you go through a village called Drift. A lot of lacy Edwardian woodwork. A fascia says GROCER, BUTCHER, THE LAST SHOP IN ENGLAND. *The Last Inn*, 100 yards. Sea light, distant buildings profiled on open landscape. *Sea View, Vacancies. Caravans to Let*. A lot of aerials. Turf, wind, gulls. Breakers far below. A barn-like cafeteria. A car park facing America.

Of course, the moment you turn round it is Land's Beginning. By this time they won't have let you forget about Cornish Cream (clotted, like Devonshire, only more so), Despatched To Any Part Of The World. But let me recommend something those fishermen know about, especially when the wind is blowing: rum and shrub, the latter being a cockle-of-the-heart-warming cordial, much appreciated by the old tin miners. Ah, goes well with a pasty (pronounced *parsty*). I got rather a taste for mead in Cornwall too. As well as a taste for Cornwall.

Meanwhile, north of Bath–Bristol . . .

. . . you could have a nice exploring cross-country run to **Fairford**. This is within reach of an area already considered. Indeed, when I was there I was collecting material for a book about four disused railway lines, one of which went from Oxford to Fairford, where it stopped, apparently in the middle of a field (and always had, being part of one of several failed attempts to beat the Great Western Railway to Wales in the 19th century).

In Fairford you would of course see the justly famous windows of Fairford Church: a homogeneous picture of the complete Christian faith, and by no means a placid and undisturbing one. There are a delicious cool green Garden of Eden, an Annunciation, a Flight into Egypt, little receding flowery land-scapes, horizons, palaces, houses, and what is said to be the first windmill represented in stained glass; but there are also the Passion, and the extra-ordinary turbulent crimson-centred Last Judgment (the entire great west window) with, as well as angels, some terribly realistic tortures of the damned being impaled and put through mills and roasted in crucibles.

And Concorde's test flights were made from Fairford. Well, that's England.

If you really did come from Bath your route would have been via Malmes-bury, and after this dreamlike stone town you would turn perhaps with some relief off the inexplicably lorry-infested road to Cirencester to go along the pleasant B4040 to Cricklade where you can see the source of the **Thames**; then you would want a nice detailed map to get across to Lechlade, preferably via Down Ampney, after which one of Vaughan Williams's noblest hymn tunes is named, and you can see why, apart from the fact that he was born here.

You are thus reminded that the Thames is a Cotswold river. In fact, stone for the dome of St Paul's was put on barges at Lechlade. The **Cotswolds** means Gloucestershire; not only a special county, but the one where you meet the first lusty hello-me-hearty true west-country types. I used to think Laurie Lee was making it all up—no, no, making *some* of it up Laurie!—in *Cider With Rosie* until I went into a pub in Lechlade and the moment I told the man next to me at the bar that I was doing this railway book he launched into truly amazing stories of the alleged love-life of the guards on that long-defunct line. Talk about a girl in every station . . .

If you drew a line from Stratford-on-Avon to Bristol a lot of it would pass along the steep western Cotswold escarpment. In fact it seems all wrong to be approaching them from the south. For me the Cotswolds mean Stratford, the first climb at Mickleton (for ever remembered as a climb if you have done it on a bicycle!) and first sight of the golden-brown stone (and the proper Cotswold houses have stone-tile roofs also, none of your slate), of the amazing frequency of hollyhocks against old walls. Then Fish Hill, **Broadway**. A snug, rich, lowland village, unavoidably a bit touristy but still beautiful, and a characteristic example of the ancestral instinct for building in conformity with the landscape; for when you climb out of it up Fish Hill, perhaps stopping at the tower with its huge prospects into blue Wales, you are on instant windswept upland, where the rolling fields are divided by stone walls and towns like the descriptively-named Stow-on-the-Wold seem much more compact, as if standing together against the wind.

Then you could go down again to see this verified at Bourton-on-the-Water, where there is grass beside the main street with little low stone

Bourton-on-the-Water.

footbridges across the water. Most of the snug lowland ones, in fact, and some of the steepest low-gear climbs, are to be found in the many combes and sudden valleys with which the eastern sides of the Cotswolds are indented, giving rise to rivers with magic names—Windrush, Evenlode, Leach—and of course Thames (Cirencester, the 'Capital of the Cotswolds', already thinking of Bath and the smooth south, is *very* snug and elegant). But to continue along that western edge, from another evocatively named height, Cleeve Cloud, at 1,083 feet actually the highest in the Cotswolds, you plunge down to Cheltenham, now a curious mix of Regency gentry and aerodynamics and other boffins; then up again to Birdlip (tremendous hill), along airy uplands to Painswick, Stroud. And all the time a growing sense of blue opening distance, of the huge opening out into the Severn valley, to the sea.

But of course we were coming northwards, from Bristol. There is actually a lot of Cotswold almost as soon as you leave. There is always a place to see for the first time; last year for me, in this southern block, it was Wotton-under-Edge, yet another decent, untarted, sloping main street, good bookshop, good ironmonger, good toyshop. Good atmosphere. Good views. Good.

Absolutely no one could write down a best-of-Cotswolds tour. The only way to absorb their unique atmosphere is to get a large-scale map and wander about in them. If you have half a chance, on foot. I noticed in that Tourist Information office at Oxford a pamphlet giving details of Cotswold Walks. There are pamphlets about *everything*.

Yet another view north from Bristol–Bath is to the inverted triangle, with Gloucester at the bottom, formed by the three cathedral towns which have given their name to the oldest music festival in England, the Three Choirs, which dates from 1724. **Gloucester** a wonderful mixture, where the choir and transepts pioneered Perpendicular style (and for me memorable not only for its cloisters, including the brilliant medieval tiny-leaded glass above the stone trough where the monks washed in the cloisters, but for the reply given by a surpliced choirboy in an excellent TV programme about the cathedral, to the question 'whom do you sing for?' 'Well,' said the child, with a toothy smile, 'during the service, I suppose Jesus. But during rehearsals it's for Mr Richards.'). **Worcester**, with its west front facing, over grass, the still inland Severn, the cricket ground, and the blue bulk of the Malvern Hills, from which William Langland saw the fair field full of folk and wrote the first recognisable great English poem, *Piers Plowman*. **Hereford**, solid, already suggesting the red earth from which it springs; Norman nave, and the best chance you are ever likely to have of seeing a medieval library with nearly 1,500 chained books, and the famous *Mappa Mundi*, map of the world with Jerusalem in the middle—this was 1305, remember—Asia at the top, Europe and Africa below, with England and Wales bottom left, and covered with charming drawings—Celtic-looking Ark, the Pyramids, known as 'barns of St Joseph' drawn as medieval barns.

Hereford is a frontier town; you're on the edge of Wales here, in the romantic air. Hardly a dud village or town, but if you *have* to choose don't miss either **Weobley**, the full splendour of black-beam-and-white-plaster vernacular architecture, or **Ledbury**. Like Worcester (where he grew up) Hereford is redolent of the music of the arch-Romantic Elgar, who was discovered as a boy by his mother writing down 'what the wind was saying to the reeds', and who in adult life said 'the air is full of music. I just take as much of it as I want.' There is a marvellous account in the little book by his daughter of an evening and long night when he was living at Plas Gwyn in Herefordshire when they took food to his study door and were warned by a growling voice not to come near. The women sat, silent in the lamplight in that silent turn-of-the-century, pre-mechanised deep country. The clock ticked. Finally the door creaked open, and out he came, pale and strained. 'Come and hear this.' And they were the first to hear the noblest music in that noble work, *The Dream of Gerontius* . . .

And still we have not finished our northern scan from Bristol–Bath. For the westernmost sector of it, the other side of the Severn, takes in, first, some of the most romantic scenery in Britain, the **Wye Valley**, where this fast-flowing river flows past the famous high wooded-cliff viewpoint of Symond's Yat and **Tintern Abbey**—not only Visited, but very properly Re-visited by Wordsworth. To put the cart before the horse in terms of his poem, he was not the only one who, having heard 'the still sad music of humanity', could say

> how oft
> In darkness and amid the many shapes
> Of joyless daylight; when the fretful stir
> Unprofitable, and the fever of the world,
> Have hung upon the beatings of my heart—
> How oft, in spirit, have I turned to thee,
> O sylvan Wye! thou wanderer through the woods,
> How often has my spirit turned to thee!

And beyond that is the **Forest of Dean**, *its* wooded hills dotted with mysterious one-man coal mines, run by mysterious Free Miners with rights and institutions going back for centuries. To be a Free Miner you must have been born there and worked in a mine for a year and a day. They rarely, if ever, go below 200 feet. Still . . .

One of the many remarkable things here, and somehow characteristic of the area, is **Clearwell Castle**, a stately home bought, when he heard it was falling into unoccupied ruin, by a man whose father had been under-gardener there in the old days. Mr Frank Yeates sold the bakery business he had built up in Blackpool, bought the castle as a semi-retirement venture, and by sheer hard labour restored it, copying elegant plaster cornices, reflooring, refurnishing, seeing about grants, until there was another great house saved; a work carried on now by his family.

Come to think of it, Hereford would make a good nodal point too.

The North-East

Lincoln

Back to the A1, the Great North Road. Of course, to get to Lincoln you don't
have to have come up the A1, in fact you might have been taking a leisurely
trip up through Suffolk and Norfolk and/or the Fens (much more interesting,
although that would mean missing Burghley House, see p. 118. Decisions,
decisions, decisions), and via Boston and Woodhall Spa; suddenly the road
climbs a little from the fenland (though not to breezy Wolds height, they're
still to your north) into woodland, and there is this bosky little Poor Man's
Baden-Baden. Then you would get the full glory of Lincoln Cathedral
crowning the ridge, visible for miles, drawing the surrounding landscape to a
point as Chartres does. This glorious—

—there must be those among you, dear readers, who are saying, and who
shall blame you, 'not another cathedral! What about the **fishing**, for God's
sake, when are we going to get on to the *fishing*?' All right then, the Teifi is
one of the best salmon and trout rivers in Wales. Mr Duncan Fitzwilliams,
who used to be a coracle (Ancient Briton's leather boat still used on rivers
from Wye westwards) champion, has opened at Cenarth, Dyfed, the country's biggest fishing museum, containing poachers' gear, a salmon 25 inches
long and 15 inches round etc. The address of the School of Casting, Salmon
and Trout Fly Fishing is PO Box 10, Inverness. That's one of about a
thousand useful addresses in *Scotland for Fishing*, of all good tourist offices.
There are pamphlets about everything—

—this glorious building, not only the crown and flower of England's
second largest county but a major glory of the country as a whole, is no doubt
the reason why, when the *Sunday Times* brought out England's first colour
supplement, to the intense rage of every other paper which then had to do
likewise, it was all about Lincoln.

There is doubtless some engineering and light industry scattered around,
but the predominant impression you have from the city is of large-
windowed, high, 19th-century wholesale corn merchants' houses of brick, of
capacious old shops perhaps not so prosperous as they were. But you never
forget for a moment the calm majesty awaiting you at the top. Through the
Exchequergate (only survivor of several when the precincts were walled
from the city) and there is this huge, many-niched west front with its two
towers, and if you stand far enough back you can see, looming vaster above
them in the airy distance, the great central tower over the crossing with the
Great Transept. Inside, you walk holding your breath through this cool
underwater graceful stone forest, pausing to look through the marvellous
circular window, the Dean's Eye, so formal and geometrical yet so wild, like
Euclid in Technicolor, then past St Hugh's choir, then past the east transept;
these things can be studied at leisure, when you have seen, while you are still

fresh, what you have come to see, what all the world comes to see, the famous Angel Choir.

It isn't the angels themselves, that divine stone orchestra tootling and clashing and singing away for ever between those tribune (triforium, or gallery) arches high up there, it isn't the arches themselves with their polished marble shafts interwoven with stone ones, it isn't their relationship with the clerestory windows above *them*, and the roof vaults, or with the graceful Early English aisle arches to the ground beneath. It isn't any one element, it's the whole thing. The Angel Choir at Lincoln (1256–1280) is one of the great things in this world. That men should have been able to do this, with stone. I say it again, and to hell with Pseuds Corner: it reduced me to tears.

And then there is the chapter house, another, like Salisbury's, with one stone pillar at the circle's centre spreading out into graceful vaults. There are the Cloisters, of which one side is not Gothic at all, but an elegant Renaissance arcade over which is (here he is again!) a library by Wren. There is—

—but I hope I have already persuaded you not to go into Yorkshire, as Jane Austen would have put it, without seeing Lincoln first, by whatever route. I also hope that Lincoln will not be insulted at finding itself, in this book, coming under York as its nodal point. There was a Celtic city here (*lin*, pool; *dun*, hill fort) before the Romans (Ninth Legion) got here and made a Roman city, with baths and colonnades; it became a behind-the-lines settlement or *colonia* (Lindocolina in a 4th-century document) *after* they had pushed on to their obvious strategic north-guarding citadel of—

York (Eboracum)

This county town of the largest and most varied county in England, containing some of its most beautiful scenery—wild moors, sweeping dales, no, can't have a small d, sweeping Dales, seascapes with a coast on whose rugged cliffs beats a real sea, summer-blue or winter-black, not the mud-brown, pale blue shallow waters off East Anglia—and some of its grimiest and most unprepossessing industry.

The first thing that strikes you as you enter is the realisation that this is a walled city. In fact, with Chester, it is the *only* city which you can walk right round (or almost) on the walls. Naturally your eye is continuously drawn to the great towered white bulk of the Minster riding over it all like a ship (and that's what *nave* means, I am the 3,422nd writer to point out, just in this century). The last time but one I was there the whole vast interior was one nest of steel scaffolding, alive with men in protective clothing and sounding more or less the same as any factory on a busy day. They were in the middle of the £2 million operation (for which more than half the money was raised in Yorkshire) of saving it. Divers went down into the water surrounding some of the great piers which were perilously resting on not very much, and there was an amazing operation of putting girders through them, anchoring in concrete and I know not what; and very moving it was to see twentieth-century skills brought in to save this marvellous product of those of the 13th, 14th and 15th centuries.

So this time I thought I would approach it on foot from the outer gate, as a pilgrim should. In this case, Walmgate. Lot of shops selling tiles, baths, elements for electric kettles, brass and anodised stuff. Slightly run-down air. Echoes of past, shop selling saddle soap, curry combs, has sign saying *Cover Makers* and effigy of horse outside. Street becomes Fossgate. Notice in pub window says VIOLENCE: THIS HOUSE OPERATES AN EARLY WARNING SYS-

TEM WITH THE POLICE. Cross small river, the Foss. One shop with large circular alcove bears legend ELECTRIC CINEMA, go in, manager points to upper floor, that used to be balcony, he came there as boy on Saturday mornings when they had those children's serials.

After Whip-ma-Whop-ma Gate it gets smarter, better kept, wonderful medieval-cum-Georgian roofline. Nice Anglo-Saxon way of describing pedestrianisation, signs point to (e.g.) Stonegate *Footstreet*. Best-known medieval street, The Shambles, v. picturesque. Nice little vulgar market behind rather posh shops, Arts and Crafts, Ristorante Bari, Natural Jute, and, I swear, Fudge Now For Winter. Actually heard man say 'not £2, not £1, not 80p, 70p, to the lady over there'. Trinket stall with mugs saying *See all, hear all, say nowt,* and *A Yorkshireman's Advice to his son: Eat all, drink all, pay nowt, and if iver tha does owt for nowt allus do it for thissen.*

All right, splendours coming later. But if you walk about York like this you realise that this city, second in England in old days, producer of famous Miracle Plays (performed still, triennially) still has warm medieval sense of community. St Sampson's Church (who he?) damaged by cannonball 1644, now centre for old people, gassing merrily over coffee. Church of Gilds (which did Miracle Plays), Pavement, with its wonderful lantern, just across wide, flowers-down-centre Parliament Street, has chained book on stand open at contents page: *The Pope with his Cardinals as negligent as the People. The Pope Fifty Times greater than the Emperor . . .*

Stonegate, perfectly magnificent. It was Via Praetoria, part of square grid plan, leading straight to Principia, military HQ, where Minster now is. Something to delight the eye wherever you look: figureheads, carved gables, arches, roofs of all shapes, marvellous shops e.g. selling 'Ripe Mangoes Ecstatically Sumptuous Direct From Israel', 'Fresh Asparagus By Air From The Cape', 'Large Seedless Grapes From Limassol, Cyprus', etc, but (sorry to go on about this) still friendly. In smart coffee shop (I was tempted in by delicious aroma) waitress said 'I'll bring you some more milk, it's curdling, luv'.

Very well then, here we are, outside one of the greatest churches in Christendom. Across road from it, Roman column with bull. Notice says it 'once stood within the great hall of the HQ of the VI Legion, whose emblem was a bull, 4th century A.D. It was found in 1969 during excavations of the South Transept, lying where it had collapsed. It was given by the Dean and Chapter to York Civic Trust who in 1971 erected it on this site to mark the 1900th anniversary of the founding of the city by the Romans in 71.'

There are times when I wish I lived in York.

I shall not attempt to describe the Minster. Everybody has heard about its wonderful windows; the Five Sisters, and the largest east window in the world (made of Coventry glass, hooray), its chap—no, *got* to leave space for Durham. I merely say that the world should be grateful to the people responsible for making this miracle safe for later generations.

There are plenty of other things to see. Far too many for one day, what with the Castle Museum, that pioneer reconstruction of period streets with every detail correct so that you really can walk about in another century; the numerous Georgian splendours, notably the Assembly Rooms; the National Railway Museum, removed from London after a frightful north–south tug-of-war; a Guildhall rebuilt after wartime bombing with cheering evidence that we can still make jolly, grotesque, painted wooden figures; the Viking Excavation in Coppergate; the Roman Bath Inn . . . clearly to get the best out

Colterdale, Yorkshire.

of this deeply rewarding and pleasant city you need to stay for a day or two. And if you are able to do that, it's a good idea to spend the first three-quarters of an hour at the Heritage Centre, Castlegate, where you get a very good 25p's worth of film and other information.

Moors and Dales

When you do tear yourself away a fearful decision awaits you. Should you head through the fat, comfortable Vale of York north-west to the Moors or north-east to the Dales (the industrial area now being comfortably south-west, behind you)? Both areas are National Parks. The **Moors** and **Cleveland Hills** offer huge heathery landscapes, the lonely cries of birds and sheep the only sound, reaching all the way to the coast, with places on it ranging from up-and-down, many-gardened, unexpected, splendid Scarborough, past Robin Hood's Bay, just a lot of fishermen's and/or smugglers' cottages improbably crammed into a rocky cleft, to Whitby with its great Abbey ruins on the high cliff, and Staithes—another Robin Hood's Bay. After that you find iron and steel works.

The aristocracy of this area are undoubtedly a group of lunatics called the Lyke Wake Club. To qualify for membership you must have walked the forty miles, ascending and of course descending about thirty thousand feet on the way, from Osmotherley on the western edge to Ravenscar on the high coast cliff, where the bar of the Raven Hall hotel is the official finishing point, *within twenty-four hours.*

They take their title from the famous, haunting old dialect poem (memorably set to music by Benjamin Britten), the Cleveland Lyke Wake Dirge:

This yah neet, this yah neet
Ivvery neet an' all,
Fire an' fleet an' cannle leet,
An' Christ tak' up thy saul.
When thoo frae hence away art passed
Ivvery neet an' all
Ti Whinny Moor thoo coms at last
An' Christ tak up thy saul . . .

Fleet was probably a dialect word for embers, kept burning, as was a candle, while the corpse (*lyke*) remained in the house. The extraordinary local and physical imagery for the passing of a soul must have grown naturally, out of the earth. Anyone who has done the walk must obviously have felt it seriously from the moors in all their moods. Since Bill Cowley (from whose *Dalesman* paperback these facts are quoted) founded the Club, records have been shattered in a way that makes the Olympics look prosaic. One participant couldn't get out of his bath afterwards without assistance and was off work for seven weeks. It has been done by a clergyman on his 81st birthday, by a man in a dinner jacket and top hat with an umbrella and briefcase, by Durham policewomen and by three artificial inseminators from the Cattle Breeding Centre at York. An incredible man called Arthur Puckrin did it once across in 6½ hours, twice in 16 hours 17 minutes, and *three* times (that is 120 miles) in 32 hours 15 minutes. The Club have cheerfully lugubrious-sounding annual dinners with officials such as the Cheerless Chaplain, the Melancholy Mace-Bearer and the Horrible Horn-Blower.

Still, you don't have to be as athletic as that to enjoy these exhilarating uplands (and their valleys, in one of which you will find the lovely ruins, living up to the calm and melodious promise in their very name, of the great Cistercian Abbey of Rievaulx). You drive in and out of forests, cross cattle-bangs, ascend ridges with great, broad, soul-expanding views, and everywhere there seem to be little paths almost compelling you to get out of that car and be as athletic as you can yourself. And don't forget the steam train from Pickering to Grosmont (about an hour). Towards the end of it you are in an area where every rise seems to bring you within sight of the Fylingdales Early Warning Radar System, weird looming things like giant golf balls, strange pearly colour; a reminder that you can't escape this century for long, even in these solitudes. At one end of the Park, Fylingdales. At the other, Rievaulx. *And Christ receive thy saul . . .*

As for the **Dales**—well, here is another area where many people come year after year to spend their entire holiday. If you are energetic enough you can follow the course of one of those east-flowing rivers from a brown peaty trickle in high fells, through an ever-widening gully till it flows chattering over stones beside the road of a broad but still high valley, past the broader valley with more and more farms, till it flows under stone bridges in less romantic towns, generally to join the Ouse (York's river) and thus eventually the Humber and the sea.

And they are all marvellously different. You see a blue line on your left as you speed up the A1 but you wouldn't believe what there is up there unless you tried it. The road signs were already saying THE NORTH & SCOTCH CORNER when I turned off and made the gentle climb to **Richmond**. This comfortable town may stand as a type to be found all over what used to be known as the Ridings (especially East R. and North R.) before that fool re-naming came in. Solid, wind-proof stone Georgian houses, tree-dotted enriched, if the place is the size of Richmond, by some such building as its castle, with its keep visible from the big, sloping, cobbled market-place, or the pretty little Georgian Theatre below.

Richmond, where the Sweet Lass lived (she was called Frances l'Anson) gave its name not only to over 50 towns throughout the world but (long before the last re-naming) to Richmondshire, and stands at the head of Swaledale, most northerly of the ones in the Dales National Park (not that there aren't plenty more north of that, right up to Teesdale and Weardale, and, after Hadrian's Wall, flowing from the border Cheviots).

Passing in and out of woods—at this stage deciduous trees often reached half-way up the other side of the valley—above them I could see what looked like very small farms indeed, up to the moor skylines. I climbed a stone wall, in the middle of this celestial nowhere, to read a very municipal-looking notice which turned out to forbid me to do all sorts of things, such as

> 4. loiter or commit any nuisance or behave in any indecent or unseemly manner or engage in prostitution . . .
> 5. assemble, attempt to assemble or cause to assemble or bring upon the military lands any number of persons for the purpose of a private or public meeting . . .
> 6. canvas by word of mouth . . . play or take part in organised games . . . camp whether in tents, caravans or other wise, bivouac or sleep out . . .

And if I did I could be 'taken into custody without Warrant and brought before a court of summary jurisdiction to be dealt with according to law'.

Military lands, eh? Well, devil a soldier did I see, only birds and clouds and green fields turning to grey-brown moor, till I came to the enchanted village of Reeth, sitting comfortably facing its huge green in a huger bowl of hills in the high, zesty moorland air. Then on to Muker (nearly all moor now) where I turned left to climb (splendid name!) Buttertubs Pass (not before noticing a signpost to Crackpot). This leads over into the next joy, the broader, richer Wensleydale.

I turned right (i.e. west) before going down the valley a bit to Askrigg to have a look at **Hardraw Force**, 'the highest single-drop waterfall in the country'. Well, it does resound nicely, falling into a hidden rock cleft, but it's no Niagara, it looked about fifty feet to me; some French tourists in bright anoraks were cooking on sophisticated little stoves and standing on rocks. You have to go through a pub called the Green Dragon, which charges you 20p, if I remember rightly. Nice pub, and lavatories say bluntly MEN and WOMEN, no rot about Ladies and Gentlemen. But I have seen more impressive waterfalls; bit of an anti-climax after the stupendous views of Peak heights from top of Buttertubs (would that great flat-topped one be Ingleborough?).

Then down road to Askrigg, perfect moorland market town, has been since Domesday. Their (1965) scrapbook gave a tremendous list of everyone's nickname; they all obviously know each other and make their own life up here:

Mrs M. Weatherhead	Mary Michael
Mr H. Kirkbride	Lile Harry
Mr John Percival	Bogey
Mr J. Fawcett	Fawcey Fowce
Mr W. Metcalfe	Flute
Mr Carl Metcalfe	Splash

and so on, for pages. Part of the attraction of the Dales is the thought of the tough but somehow simultaneously cosy human life that went on for so

many centuries in these wild hills long before tourists had heard of them. At
the pub where I stayed the bar was the old kitchen, great fireplace, old
wooden chairs, mysterious hooks, so full of local laughter that we visitors felt
we would have been intruding (not that they were anything but kind to us). It
had a visitor's poem written above the bar, in part:

> Level with the singing lark
> Hear the far-off farm dogs bark
> Squat grey roofs and ribboned Ure
> Patchwork fields below the moor
> Short to look and long remember
> August dale in town December . . .

Up the road, at **Hawes**, in the old station (oh, to have heard steam whistles
blown through the windy night up *here*!), there is the Upper Dales Folk
Museum, yet another reminder how idiotic it is ever to be put off by that now
often corrupted word 'folk'. Full of lovely stuff about Wensleydale cheese
(invented by Cistercians, particular character comes from herby limestone
pastures; two kinds, crumbly white new, and blue, probably originally from
mould cells in cheese room where they kept it till Christmas); and about
knitting. 'Men, women and children all knitted and were so skilful that they
could do it as they tended their sheep or walked to market.' Funeral cake
markers, knitting sticks . . .

I should have liked to take the road from Hawes to **Dent**, between the great
hills of Great Knoutberry and Whernside (at, 2,414 feet one of the highest in
the Pennines), and thus approach that idyllic cobbled stone village from the
east, and not from the Lake District west as I have always done previously
(another knitters' place; Southey heard of the Terrible Knitters of Dent and
wrote about them). But my intention was to have another, reminding look at
the spacious urban splendours of **Harrogate**, that fine Victorian spa with
Pump Room and elegant gardens and the rest of it. So up I went over Dodd
Fell, then down to adjoining ever broader, greener, cultivated Wharfedale. At
first, no one but the odd hiker, a family car on the grass between the road and
the purling infant river, or a flock of sheep. Then the dale became more
park-like and occupied.

Finally, Skipton. I had forgotten what an awful road, for all its beauty, the
A59 is. Not a straight 50 yards all the way up to Blubberhouses Moor, let
alone to Harrogate. Never out of bottom gear for three-quarters of an hour
while hundreds of us ground along led by a lorry carrying what appeared to
be a piece of the Forth Bridge. I swore a mighty oath (well, several mighty
oaths actually). Never again would I go on the A59.

Well, you don't have to go to Harrogate, at least not on a Saturday
morning. But there's the charm of Yorkshire, why should I not see **Fountains Abbey** instead? So I cut off north across country from that damned
A59, found an excellent pub lunch at Summerbridge, paused before dropping
from the last high ridge on the road to Ripon to enjoy the vast blue views
eastward over the Vale of York to the moors, and found this absolute miracle
of peace. Who would have thought there could be something more moving
even than Rievaulx? I don't think I have received anywhere such an impression of lofty calm as in those colossally tall yet graceful arches of the Chapel of
the Nine Altars, of the general impression of shafts of sunlight falling on to
quiet grass of the nave, of the cloister, refectory etc. of what is said to be the
finest monastic ruin in Europe. Decline and fall. Thirteen Benedictine monks
from York came here in 1132, to Skelldale, 'thick set with thorns, fit rather to
be the lair of wild beasts than the home of human beings'. Dissatisfied with

the laxity at York, they joined the strict Cistercian Order. Their first winter was spent sheltering under an elm. Subsequently Fountains became the wealthiest Cistercian house in Britain. Now . . .

Now, it is surely a medicine to the soul of anyone who goes there, both then and whenever he conjures up the memory of it.

I went on to **Ripon**. (There was said to be a fine exhibition of Jacobean furniture in Fountains Hall, but it is better to see such things, splendid though they no doubt are, before the Abbey. After it you don't want to see anything for a bit.)

Of this pleasant town I will say nothing, or nearly nothing. There is no space for the Ripon Spa Hotel, the Victorian portico of its swimming baths, its solid austere Early English cathedral with astonishing bronze pulpit on marble pillars which turns out to be a great compliment to the year 1910, of the famous misericord carvings—Samson grinning to himself as he carries off the gates of Gaza, dragons, foxes, two pigs dancing to bagpipes played by a third (maybe they *were* all frightened of Hell, but they sure seem to have enjoyed being alive in those days)—of the facing Old Deanery Restaurant, (Swiss Touring Club, Fodor Guide of America) . . .

. . . because here we are, believe it or not, at the Last Cathedral. For years, ever since seeing this majestic holy fortress tantalisingly from train windows, which one can do for quite a time as the line curves obligingly round, I have been resolving to go and see it, and at last writing this book gave me the excuse to make a special trip.

Durham

I have to report that *Durham* is simply overwhelming. People are absolutely right when they go on about it like, say, Alec Clifton-Taylor: 'The noblest example in England of Norman cathedral-building, and indeed the finest Romanesque church in Europe.' You would have to go to the Parthenon to find such a resonant correspondence between the siting of the building and its nature. It may have begun as a Benedictine monastery and shrine of the two great saints of the north, Cuthbert and Bede. But it developed, if only because of that height-in-bend-of-river defensive position of so many ancient cities, into something expressed in the lines of Walter Scott; 'Grey Towers of Durham, Yet well I loved thy mixed and massive piles, Half church of God, half castle 'gainst the Scot'.

Durham was the only English cathedral to have 'Prince-Bishops' on the Continental model, ruling over a County Palatine with many royal privileges, and with their own army which they often led in person. In fact the southerner is always faintly surprised to be reminded that it's a long way to Scotland yet. Newcastle may be only ten miles north, and Hadrian's Wall (still walkable through mile upon mile of sweepingly beautiful country) may run more or less due west to Carlisle from just above Newcastle; but above Newcastle there are forty miles of good rolling Northumberland before you get to Berwick-on-Tweed at the eastern end of that sloping border. All the same, it *is* a fortress; the only one never taken by the Scots during those turbulent centuries, till 1640; and ten years after that 3,000 Scottish prisoners of Cromwell at the Battle of Dunbar were kept, characteristically, in the Cathedral.

They destroyed everything made of wood in it, except the fantastic Prior Castell's Clock in the south transept (perhaps because of the Scots thistle at the top). You wouldn't notice unless you had been told; the dark oak choir stalls look old enough, though they are merely 17th-century. The beauty of Durham is that whether you first see it end on from across the river, with its twin west towers apparently rising straight out of the steep wooded bank, or approach it broadside, as you have to to get in and see its enormous, breath-taking bulk, at once airy and solemn, across stone pavement and lawn, you have an overpowering impression of unified Norman strength. The thing to remember is that the basic structure—nave, transepts and choir—was all built between 1093 and 1133 (the great central tower was rebuilt in 1470).

Delicate (though Norman!) Galilee Chapel, with simple marble slab mark-ing Bede's tomb, nave with those famous incised pillars cut in spiral or zig-zag grooves, first triumphant solution of stone vaulting problems on this scale, crossing, choir, St Cuthbert's tomb, end-on easternmost Chapel of Nine Altars (sounds familiar?) achieving exactly the same effect as at Foun-tains of aspiring height, perhaps even more so here since we're into the Decorated (post-1250) period—and they got even more height by the simple expedient of lowering the floor.

When you come out, dazed by this magnificence, you will find there is a snug up-and-down Georgian intimate townscape round you down to the river, you hear people tootling flutes and playing pianos, half the buildings seem to be part of the Durham University, which has a strong music tradition. So they should. If architecture is frozen music, they've got the Beethoven of cathedrals here.

Wales and the Welsh Border

There is an overwhelming case for approaching the majestically romantic loneliness of Wales gradually, from the first far-off rolling fieldscape viewed from some dismal industrial plain, then the first mound, then the line of blue hills, then the great mountains (and everywhere the wide-vowelled sounds of that Other Language).

So what are we doing starting with a bang in **Chester**, which is still in England, though only just? Because geography and history combine to force us to regard this fascinating city as a classic nodal point. At the Battle of Chester, in 607 (said the first account I read, closely followed by another which said 'about 614'), one King Ethelfrith destroyed it and killed about 2,000 Celtic monks who were praying he would lose the battle. If he had, Wales might have included the Lake District (where there are still plenty of Welsh-sounding place-names, like Glaramara and Helvellyn).

For the Romans it was the top left-hand corner of the box, the other three corners being York, London and Caerleon, which was the framework of their command structure. It was Agricola's winter quarters, it was the HQ of the 20th Legion. In those days the town was washed by a curve of the river Dee, and the street called Watergate led down to the Roman harbour, where now is the flat area called the Roodee, where they have the oldest race meeting in Britain, though not old for Chester, merely 1540 (long after their famous Miracle Plays were established, for instance).

Once you have been to Chester the centre of any other city seems to be rather boringly on one plane. The unique Rows turn the whole place into a kind of fantastic climbing frame for adults. You can walk along the pavement, sheltered by an arcade of pillars, looking at the street life and the marvellous doorways and frontages or at the shops, then you can pop up the next flight of steps and be as it were on the city's mezzanine floor, and do exactly the same, for there are more shops up there.

There's an amazingly harmonious jumble of styles, the black-and-white timbered style characteristic of Cheshire predominating, of course, but mixing in nicely with 18th-century Classical and with Gothic; and quite a lot of the black-and-white turns out to have been done (and very well, too) by two Victorian architects called J. Douglas and T. M. Lockwood.

It's the only city in Britain which you can walk right round on its walls, from which you can get a splendid view of the Welsh hills if the weather is right. I met a man who remembered agonising decisions, when he was a child, about whether there would be a family picnic excursion, depending on the look of the clouds round Moel Fammau (1,852 feet) from some city vantage-point.

It is not surprising that in the converted church of St Michael's they should have Britain's first Heritage Centre, very well equipped to help you understand this many-layered city. In fact they are very well organised for tourism altogether. There is a free guide service, and any foreign visitor who phones Chester 43128 or 62338 can visit 'an English home' between 8 and 10.30 p.m.

As a matter of fact, even if you do start your visit to Wales via Chester—say, turning off the M6 at Exit 15 and going through Whitchurch—you begin to pass signposts with strange names like Wem, Prees, Bruera; there is already an unmistakable feeling that you are in frontier country.

It is a feeling I have always had when taking my usual route into North Wales along the classic route, Telford's road from Holyhead to London, the A5, which passes a few miles east of my native Coventry. This last time, however, I followed a route which not only goes gradually from plain to mountain but also offers a dramatic transition from industrial to pastoral; what you might call the two polarities of modern life, and *experienced* as such perhaps more in Britain than in any other country in the world. We invented the whole thing, it was we who had the Industrial Revolution that changed the world for ever. But we also had the first Luddites, the first doubts about it, and, even in these post-war days of tower blocks, we have far more gardens per capita than any other country: and Wales, with its totally industrialised southern valleys, its lonely sheep-covered central uplands and its classic northern mountains—quite apart from its separate nationhood and culture; how far is this a *pastoral* ideal, a reaction from the soulless internationalism of industry?—offers a clear, quasi-textbook example of these contrasts.

The A5 skirts the northern edges of Wolverhampton and passes through the Black Country, indeed I have often thought that in the pre-industrial days when these ridges of wasteland and low brick houses and old factories were covered with trees there must have been a hint of Wales even here (and can there be something of Welsh accentuation already in that sing-song speech of Birmingham? 'Whur are yo goin' then?'). So, this time I left the A5 where an amazing confusion of huge, raw, new traffic islands announces the short bit of nowhere-leading motorway M54 and the New Town of 'TELFORD, BIRTHPLACE OF INDUSTRY'. You don't actually see any industry from the roads, just a lot of close-packed, treeless, machine-made workers' houses, like Haverhill in Suffolk (no, not as bad as *that*), the slums of 2000 (the only pleasant New Town *I* have ever seen is Cumbernauld, east of Glasgow); and I picked my way a few miles south to **Ironbridge**.

Here, in a still-beautiful wooded gorge of the Severn, you may see the first iron bridge in the world (1778). The whole valley is full of unequalled industrial archaeology and very well presented as such. Just down the road is the Coalport China Works museum; just up the road is the famous Coalbrookdale; and since the great founding families of Darby and Reynolds were Quakers, there are fine ironmasters' and workmen's houses (some with cast-iron chimney-pots) and (now being converted into a youth hostel) the Coalbrookdale Literary and Scientific Institute, 'erected in 1859, where the traditionally high educational standards of the Coalbrookdale workmen were maintained through evening classes'. I bet people aren't going to be as fascinated by the New Town of Telford when *it* is 200 years old.

A mile up the Severn valley there is a most tremendous modern power station with four huge cooling towers, still against the backdrop of the wooded hill. Another mile or so—and I was on a long, gentle climb through the trees into a totally different world. I was on **Wenlock Edge**, the country of the poet Housman, with occasional tremendous views to the north over the rolling border county of Shropshire, and so to **Church Stretton** and the **Long Mynd**.

Ironbridge.

Although still in England, this is clearly the last outpost of the great rolling hills of Radnorshire and central Wales. With a summit of 1,606 feet there are obviously marvellous views to be had in every direction; but I had another experience, for misty fine-rain clouds had now descended (old joke: how can you tell when it's summer in Wales? Well, in summer the rain is warmer). I drove through the inland-resort, walking-tour centre, many-tea-roomed Church Stretton and, Engaging Low Gear Now, went up the narrow Burway that leads to the top. Almost immediately I was looking down over very steep drops indeed on to little houses hundreds of feet below. Soon there were no houses; just extraordinary swooping clefts, and great bare summits appearing and reappearing through the drifting curtains of rain. I got out, and there was absolutely no sound but the cry of birds and the baa-ing of sheep on the bright green, very short, springy turf almost compelling one to walk even in this weather. As for what it must be like on a good day with sunshine and a Spring wind . . . God knows why Housman was so *melancholy* about Shropshire. All that book-larnin', I dare say.

Then I went down the dreadfully lorry-infested A49, which only goes from Shrewsbury to Hereford, for heaven's sake, though that afternoon it might have been from Essen to Dortmund, or Pittsburgh to Cleveland, only not so wide. But this was the last evidence of industry I was to see, for I turned off to see the perfect town of **Ludlow**. Even there the hill which leads to its crown is rather trafficky (and they don't seem to have pedestrian crossings, you just have to take your life in your hands as in Bath). But oh, what a marvellous harmony of wooden-framed Tudor and Jacobean, on the grand scale, with classical Georgian! Very living and lived-in, even if the Feathers Hotel does have a board outside in wonderfully phony Olde Englysshe. *Dinner at noone, supper at five, served by comelye and complyante wenches. Succulente hares guaranteyed not to cause the Shropshire melancholye and the subsequent throat-slittynge. Home-brewed Ayles, Meade.*

St Lawrence's church; the classic mini-cathedral focus of a rich agricultural town, Broad Street, every façade down the hill delighting the eye, arcades over pavement, elegant bay windows of all shapes, a tea room with the perfect name De Grey's, women with umbrellas greeting each other outside it. Castle; view of nothing but hills from churchyard (and what delicious misericords and magnificent east window in there!), King Street splits into Bull Ring leaving two island blocks of those fairy-tale black-and-white buildings, almost like the set for an English *Hansel and Gretel*, or perhaps a pantomime principal boy could come out slapping thigh, *Hell-OH, girls and boys* . . .

What a delightful town, what could *they* ever be melancholy about?

North Wales

On to **Knighton**, miniature version of the same thing, do not on any account by-pass it, it has hilly little streets, views of forested slopes all round. Butcher's shop A. L. Marriott has long, thin, mural painted over nameboard, showing hunting scene with king rather like Henry VIII, nobles on horseback, river, sea, meadow with sheep, forest, peacock, wild boar. By local painter Tony Weston. Further up hill, past antique shop containing e.g. brass pony and trap, £27, tiny square with more house-wall paintings, this time of sun with face, Polish eagle, and *trompe-l'oeil* quoin stones. Inhabited by Polish cobbler, but paintings done by previous occupant.

Intonations heard in street now sound very Welsh. Not surprising, because now I *was* in Wales. In this part, more than any other, the best rewards are almost always to be found by taking the thinnest-looking road you can find on your map and exploring. Accordingly, after passing over the sheep-covered, hill-surrounded high common before Pen-y-bont I drove to Cross Gates and then turned north a little up the A438 (which cuts right down through the centre of Wales from Chester to Brecon, after which there are only the wild Brecon Beacons before the industrial valleys) before finding the thin road, in this case leading to **Abbey Cwmhir**. *Cwmhir* means a long narrow valley. The Abbey is a ruined Cistercian one, proving yet again that those monks knew better than anyone else, and *before* anyone else come to that, how to pick what is now known as a beauty spot. It's a pleasant little village, with a pleasant pub (with accommodation) called The Happy Union; but it's what comes after it, on the road to Rhayader, that makes it so rewarding. Up on to very high land, through lonely, sighing pine forests, huge bare hill opposite you, no sound but (when I was there) larks, cuckoos and sheep.

Perhaps it's different in high summer and at week-ends. All I can say is that I had this magic landscape entirely to myself. Like any travel writer with a vestige of conscience, I had some twinges before writing about this, and only did so in the end because there are so many more, which I haven't tried but which look just as tempting on the map. Do not go up there. Say to yourself, 'Everybody who reads this book will be up there, I'll find another one on my own'. Explore the thin roads on the map.

I don't in the least mind writing about **Rhayader** (where, when I arrived, there was a sudden glory of sunshine. I had left the rain behind in England, for a change). It is bang in the middle of Wales, a well-known centre for walking and pony-trekking (surprisingly inexpensive. Trevor's Treks there, for instance, cost £7 if you do one day, £6 per day if you do 5 days or more. This is not including accommodation, but that's not very expensive in these parts, as you will later see). Hire of essential hard hat, 20p per day. You can hardly call that money-grubbing.

Then north-westwards along the A44, which goes to the great Plynlimmon range and the central seaside resort of Aberystwyth. Somewhere around here, of course, is the decision-point, if you *have* entered Wales by this unconventional middle route. If you are 'doing' the country for the first time the obvious way is to start with the north and Snowdonia, then come down through as much of the middle as you can, then get across to the bottom left-hand corner of Pembrokeshire (whatever that's called now), drive back eastwards till you come to that industry, then get on to the main road and the motorway back to the Severn as fast as you can. But by this route you have to choose; north or south.

I had never approached Snowdonia from the south before, so my decision on this particular trip was to turn north towards it. The shades of night were drawing on, Llangurig looked like a good place to stop. The mountains that came down steeply to the road just past Rhayader on this beautiful road began to draw out on either side of it as the road climbed—a curious reversal of the usual narrowing as one approaches the head of a pass.

But here, as the valley below the road began to fill out and hold farms and trees beneath the ever-present backdrop of great rounded bare hills, as though a young god had enjoyed himself making gigantic mud-pies, lovingly smoothing them out, I was climbing to what is in fact the highest village in Wales, if you define village as an inhabited place with a church. This was **Llangurig** (*Llan*, originally a piece of land, then a sacred piece of land, usually with a church, and St Curig, a 7th-century saint). There is indeed a good, ancient, solid church, much restored by 'the Chevalier Lloyd Verney' who became a Catholic, picked up and kept this very 19th-century title, but reverted to his original faith and became a church history enthusiast; there's a marble obelisk to him in the village.

I stayed at the excellent Bluebell Inn (v. good, in fact Egon Ronay recommended, dinner with glass of wine, coffee, double-glazed chintzy little bedroom with radio, and of course breakfast: £14.84). It may be a main road, of sorts, that passes through this village; but my chief memory of it is a peaceful post-prandial stroll in a high upland bowl, down to a river (with a hideous concrete bridge over it, that's another thing we don't seem to do as gracefully as the Cistercians did) and from all round—but you guessed—the sound of sheep and (this being early June) lambs. Incidentally, they seem quite *bright* sheep: they seem to know about traffic, and move quietly to the side of the road when a car approaches.

The next day brought an even better justification for taking the thin road—in this case, after Llanidloes, to **Machynlleth** (pronounced, as near as one can spell it, Mach-int-leth; the plain of Cynllaith, nowhere further explained, doubtless he was some hero). Here you go for miles well above the 1,500-foot mark, and I didn't meet anybody at all. I know it's very unpastoral, but there's nothing like a bit of land with no other motors on it at all for giving you the god-like, Toad of Toad Hall feeling that the original motorists must have had. At the absolute summit of this paradise for Sheep And The Single Motorist there was a signpost saying PUBLIC FOOTPATH: GLYNDWR'S WAY, leading over the moors miles and miles to some timeless nowhere, indeed by this time I shouldn't have been surprised to find some great medieval hall where Glyndwr, alias Glendower, and his fellow warriors were quaffing mead from great horns.

As it was, however, I passed through the village of Staylittle and down to Machynlleth, another of those little towns where all kinds of colours adorn the houses—black, white, green, blue; and stone or wood, helm or gable roof, they all fit in to each other in that deeply satisfying organic way of such towns, which have 'just growed' over the centuries. There's also a kind of small Welsh answer to London's Albert Memorial, a charming mad clock tower with angels at each corner playing flute, violin, etc. Turns out to have been Erected by Inhabitants of the Town and District of Machynlleth to Commemorate the Coming of Age of Viscount Castlereagh. Obviously not *the* Castlereagh, since this was 15 July 1878. A man standing underneath it with his dog, watching the world go by, said there had been a movement to pull it down. They'd be fools if they did.

There's a wonderful road from here down the river Dovey to its estuary and Aberdovey (you pass the Outward Bound training school, so you know you are into athletic country now). I was, however, bound for **Dolgellau** (pronounced, in that inscrutable way, Dol-gethly; *dol*, land by a river or meadow, and *gellau*, monks' cells). At one point, climbing up through the woods, I had a view of the long lake of Tal-y-llyn (*Tal*, the end, *y-llyn*, of the lake). I was relieved to see that, as far as was discernible from this distance, there still *was* only the one white hotel at the other end, where my wife and I once had a marvellous summer week exploring this whole area and, of course, sampling the little steam train that trundles down through the woods to the sea (p. 79).

But the road turned right to go up the great gorge which is one side of the noble mountain of Cader Idris. It's the kind of road that often seems to be favoured by advertising agencies to show some new car in lonely country, and indeed there were magnificent screes and fallen boulders on my left as I went up, but it was child's play compared to some passes in Wales. Then left, and through an open wide valley, with the full splendour of Cader Idris still on my left, into Dolgellau.

I once stayed here to cover a National Eisteddfod (more of these uniquely Welsh music tournaments later) and did not have the same experience as Thomas Hughes, who wrote the well-known quatrain:

> If ever you go to Dolgelley,
> Don't stay at the——Hotel;
> There's nothing to put in your belly,
> And no one to answer the bell.

It is, of course, a favoured centre for walking and climbing.

But I was bound for the first of what to me are the three things that must be seen in Wales, no matter how short your visit: **Portmeirion**, Snowdon and Bodnant.

If you can conceive of a holiday village, on a wooded peninsula between two silver estuaries, filled partly with architectural marvels of the past—from colonnades and statues to a carved ceiling or a campanile—bought cheap at auctions to save them, split into numbered pieces, transported and lovingly reassembled at enormous cost, and partly with pink and blue and yellow domes and temples and follies designed by the architect of genius who thought of this whole thing, Sir Clough Williams-Ellis, and by his friends, you will have some idea.

You will have perhaps a better idea when you learn that, in the words of his daughter (who now runs the Portmeirion Pottery of which the ware is sold all over the country), the place was intended from the first as 'an eye-opener to awaken in its visitors the sense of pleasure in Architecture', and that he himself wrote, 'throughout the years of my war service abroad I had to dream of something other than the horror, destruction and savagery—and what *more* different than to build with whatever serenity, kindness and loveliness one could contrive on some beautiful unknown site, yet to be miraculously discovered?'

He spent the years from the end of World War I till his death in 1978 at the age of 95 in the amazing realisation of this fabulous dream. Down in the central hollow, where there are a piazza and a Gothick Pavilion and of course water and fountains and a colonnade dating from 1760 brought from a bomb-damaged house near Bristol, and many other delightful sights, there is a wonderful lion on a pedestal 'presented on his 90th birthday by friends and colleagues, 1973'.

He said himself that he aimed at 'a gay, light-opera sort of approach', and he succeeded perfectly. You park your car in the spacious woods, pass under the arch of the pink-washed Gatehouse built over the road, go by Cliff House with its painted-on windows making a joyful symmetry with the real ones, and you don't know where to look next—up to your right at the Dome—as though Wren had designed the pink decagon with its white pilasters, green-bronze dome topped by lantern, and then seen some Hindu temples and put this marvellous kind of two-storied porch (with the gold eagles at the corners) in front of it—or at the row of white cottages behind it on their ledge, or at the cobbled courtyard, houses and campanile on your left, or at the piazza below. And then there's the hotel, and the Town Hall with its Neptune ceiling, and the old-fashioned petrol pump with a curious mythological

Portmeirion.

helmeted lady splendidly crowning it. It is as though some Disney with a miraculously cultivated 18th-century taste yet completely aware of the modern world had been given *carte-blanche* on this romantic headland (which in fact has twenty miles of paths, leading to anything from the Dogs' Cemetery made by a previous owner to a Camera Obscura).

Day visitors must leave by 5.30 (it costs 90p), but the privacy of holiday residents is cunningly preserved. It has gained increasing fame over the years (as his daughter, again, remarks) 'among the distinguished, the interesting, and the merely rich'. But you can hire a self-contained cottage there from £150 a week + VAT. Do not be alarmed by the address—Portmeirion, Penrhyndeudraeth, Gwynedd. It's pronounced, roughly, Pen-rin-dye-dryeth; *penrhyn*, headland, between *deu*, two, *traeth* beach(es).

Snowdonia was now calling, so with some reluctance I drove past adjoining Porthmadog, gateway to the Lleyn peninsula that sticks out over Cardigan Bay and is alleged to have sunshine when it is raining in Snowdonia. Already you have from here a fine horizon of blue peaks. On the road to Beddgelert, a name well known to all the rock-climbers who come to Snowdon, there was at first a forested hillside on my left, on my right sheep-filled meadows down to an already placid, lowland river bordered by some very exotic-looking yellow flowers among the reeds, the name of which I cannot say escaped me because I hadn't the faintest idea what they were. But if you imagine something like gladioli, with several flowers one above another on a thick stem, only the flowers themselves rather like orchids, that's what they were. Well, you can't know everything. Bound to be pamphlets about them in the many excellent tourist information places.

I did, however, know the name of the amazing purple splendour climbing hundreds of feet up the hills rising steeply behind Beddgelert: rhododendron. To people like me whose idea of a rhododendron is something you see in the better class of garden or at the side of selected roads in beautiful areas like the New Forest, or the road to Orford in Suffolk, the sight of a *mountain* absolutely covered with the stuff, the way Scottish mountains are covered with heather, was a revelation.

Then up the long, gorgeous valley on the Caernarvon road, with a lake on the left and the long mass of Snowdon in all its grandeur towering up on the right. Even from here it looks fairly forbidding, and I can well believe the notice for climbers in the little car park by Lake Cwellyn. 'It is at least 10 degrees F. cooler on the summit than it is here. A breeze here is a strong wind at the top. Erosion is a serious problem in Snowdonia, please keep to path to avoid wearing away vegetation. Do not build cairns or dam streams . . . bring back any litter you see . . .'

Litter! It all looks so wild and lonely, you can't imagine any need for this word, smacking more of a municipal park than the National Park we are now in, and have been in since Machynlleth. It embraces the whole of 'Snowdonia', reaching westwards over to Lake Bala and up the Conwy estuary to Conwy itself, but excluding the historic towns of Caernarvon and Bangor, facing the southern and northern ends of the Menai Straits between Wales and Anglesey; and also excluding the fringe of popular resorts along the top north coast, from Llandudno (quite jolly, with classical Victorian pier 2,000 feet long, cable cars up Great Orme's Head) to Prestatyn, passing Rhyl where you need only go if there is so much rain that you are reduced to despair and feel attracted to their new £4.8 million glass-covered Suncentre with Mediterranean atmosphere, the first indoor surfing pool in Europe, etc., etc.

The great **Caernarvon Castle**, so obviously guarding this strategic sea point, built by Edward I, birthplace of the first Prince of Wales, Edward II, scene of the Investiture of Prince Charles in 1969, combines Norman solidity with a beauty, derived partly from towers let into its great walls which are architectural glories in their own right, particularly the Eagle Tower and Queen's Tower at its western, sea-facing end, and partly from its actual situation. It is the most immediately impressive castle in Britain. It's not surprising that artists such as Peter de Wint, Sandby and Girtin were attracted to it as a subject. Inside it is just grass, stone steps and gulls. It's the outside view that is so impressive.

Just outside the eastern wall, overlooking the car park that goes down to the river's edge with its always interesting array of tough, businesslike fishing boats, there is a statue of the man who had a great deal to do with the revived Investiture procedure for that Prince of Wales who was eventually to become, for a very short time indeed, Edward VIII. This was, of course, Lloyd George, here in bronze frock coat and trousers, right arm raised as he orates, bronze eyeglasses hanging from bronze waistcoat. Two bas-reliefs on plinth show him being brightest boy in class at village school of Llanystumdwy (place, presumably with church, where rivers Dwyfor and Dwyfach meet) and orating at 1919 Peace Conference of Versailles, with Clemenceau looking very bored.

I did not have to debate long whether to go round the long way, when I heard that there was an unmoving traffic block on the beautiful coast road between Bangor and Conwy (as they now spell Conway, it's all different since I was a lad). I turned inland to **Llanberis** (the church, you must realise by now—apparently of Peris, not a Celtic saint but a missionary from Rome). There are five known ways of walking up **Snowdon** (of which I was now approaching the northern side) for ordinary mortal walkers; and at the top of the awesome pass, with the great ridge up there on your right, there is a mountaineers' centre with an Everest Room with the signatures of the team who conquered it to remind you that some of the best rock-climbers in the world train here.

But down at Llanberis there is also the softest option of the lot, for it is the station of the Snowdon Mountain Railway, where steam trains take you up the only rack-and-pinion line in Britain to the licensed bar and gift shop at the top (apart from unparalleled views, of course, if you've chosen the right day) where you may watch the panting figures of those who have come up the hard way with smugness or guilt, according to your temperament. The round trip takes 2½ hours, costs £6.60 for adults, £3.30 for children, and £2 for dogs.

Actually, once you have passed the enormous scars of the defunct slate quarry (good exhibition about this down there) and the very much alive work of huge yellow machines as they construct the Dinorwic hydro-electric scheme, the most extraordinary sight as you really get into the pass is on your left, northern side, where huge boulders that have fallen down the steep slopes of the Glyders lie in profusion.

I turned left along the A4086 to Capel Curig (church of the saint we have already met at Llangurig), along a most beautiful high valley containing a long, shallow lake and no human habitation whatever, and evidently well known to French caravan owners. At Capel Curig there is another famous centre where you can take short or long rock-climbing courses and practise on a dry-ski slope (and incidentally, throughout the National Park there are, in addition to walks you can of course work out for yourself, always remembering your limitations, many guided walks).

Here I was on the A5 again, which goes eastwards from Capel Curig through another magnificent pass, under the great looming height of Tryfan. But I was bound for Bodnant, which meant the lovely ride *down* a short A5 stretch to **Betws-y-Coed** (some argument here about whether it comes from the Old English for *bede house* or the Welsh *bedwas* meaning birch groves, in this case on hilly slope). It's simply no good driving through here, when all you will see is the wooded slopes, beautiful though these are. What you have to see is the Swallow Falls, where the river Llugwy drops into a rocky chasm, and preferably walk down through the woods past the Miners' Bridge, and Ty Hyll, the Ugly House, and the beautiful ancient bridge, and have your chauffeur bring the car down to meet you in the village.

I turned off northwards to go down the road that follows the Conwy valley to the sea, via **Llanrwst** (St Crwst was 7th-century), yet another quiet, stone, riverside market town. Well, in fact I stayed in a pleasant white farmhouse on a hillside a couple of miles outside Llanrwst. We shall hear more about the Bed and Breakfast way of life when we get to Scotland; but let me just say here that it cost £5—and it wasn't just the breakfast. To tell the truth, I had done a bit too much driving and sightseeing and note-taking for one day and had a headache. When I had taken my bag up to the excellent room I just happened to mention it to Mrs Evans, who runs this excellent house, Bryn Rhydd, typical no doubt of several thousand. 'Oh,' she said, 'I'll make you a nice cup of tea.'

It was magic Welsh tea. Ten minutes after I had drunk it and gazed at the quiet sunset hills the headache had gone. There are plenty of good hotels in Wales, but they do tend to have tea-making machines in the bedrooms which couldn't care less if you've got a headache. I drove into Llanrwst and got some first-class fish-and-chips from a Chinese take-away shop and ate them in a lay-by looking at the last shreds of the now glorious sunset and listening to a Mozart piano concerto on the car radio. Tea, dinner, bed and breakfast; the best £6.20's worth I've ever had, really.

Bodnant is an absolute must. It is one of *the* Great Gardens of the West. Difficult to say what is the best time to be there. The magnolias, in which it is famously rich, were finished by the time I was there, but wait till you hear what I did see at the end.

I crossed the lawn in front of the great house, covered with wistaria and pyracantha; facing south, of course, then the glories started with the five terraces at the west end of the house. After the statue of Priapus, god of garden fertility, I stood on the top one, from which there is a view over the other four ever more Elysian terraces, over the river to pastures bounded by mountains called Carnedd Llewelyn, only slightly lower than Snowdon itself, Foel Fras, the Drum, and Tal-y-fan. The next terrace down is the Croquet Terrace; as its name implies, a perfect piece of grass, with a wall on the house side in which there is a fountain surrounded by the kind of shrubs which like this west-facing shelter, particularly some fine magnolias. Next comes the Lily Terrace—another shrub-covered wall on the house side, then this formal water-lily pond, with two noble cedars, a blue and a green, on either side of it, the blue one with its lower branches actually in the water.

You can get down here by paths at the side or via a sloping lawn-and-shrub bit on your right as you come down, called the North Garden. It was rhododendron and azalea time when I was there, so I expected colour, but not the absolutely breathtaking red—the very essence, the Platonic Form of red, of one called *Repens sanguineum*. And the profusion of it all, the exuberance, the overspill, the sheer abundance! The whole thing reminded me of the remark made, in another context, by Harold Ross, founder-editor of the *New Yorker*, to whom, according to Thurber, they practically had to explain the facts of life when his daughter was getting married; including the fact that there are millions of spermatozoa each time but only one is needed to fertilise the ovum. 'Gee,' Ross is alleged to have said, 'ain't nature *prodgidal!*'

Next comes the Pergola and Lower Rose Terrace, all warm herringbone brick paths, roses (on the way down, *Clematis viticella*, not one of your garden clematises but a huge, opulent flower nine inches across) and then a shrub called *Crinodendron hookerianum*, with hanging red flowers often likened to Chinese lanterns; and of course roses roses roses.

Last comes a classic example of what man and nature can do when they really get together; the Canal Terrace. At the southern end you stand in front of the Pin Mill and look along a stone-bordered stretch of water, with water lilies, bordered by perfect grass and herbaceous beds (I don't know how the eleven gardeners there co-ordinate their planting, but on this day everything on the left or western side as I did this was some shade of blue) to a raised natural stage at the other end, in which the wings are perfectly trimmed blocks of yew hedge, with a great classical green wooden seat in the centre, copied from a design by William Kent. Then you can go to that stage and sit on that seat flanked by two little classical garden statues, and look the other way down the 'canal' at the Pin Mill, a delicious little fantasy building, tower flanked by two double-arched wings, mirrored in the water.

At this point you could go home and remember it for the rest of your life, but you haven't seen a quarter of the area yet. There is the Dell, full of rare trees and tinkling water and secret paths (and more rhododendrons, if you are as lucky as I was). There are rock gardens and other lawns, on one of which an

Bodnant.

enormous chestnut tree has two huge branches that come down to the ground and then curve up again (good place to sit on and admire the distant house and wish you were Lord Aberconway, to whom it belongs; well, no, it belongs to the National Trust, but he lives there). Then, on the way out, a real miracle, the Laburnum Arch. This is an avenue about 100 yards long with pleached laburnum trees forming the roof. I got the feeling that even if you walked down it at night it would still blaze with yellow light. Glorious. The bees were going mad, and I'm not surprised. I was quite disappointed to find that *Bod* simply means dwelling place and *nant* means stream. At the very least the name should mean Heavenly Petals to Inspire the Soul.

Back up to the A5 and down to **Llangollen**. Obviously the best time to be here is at the height of summer when they have the International Eisteddfod, when a man in mere slacks and shirt or girl in ordinary dress looks a bit odd, since the place is full of Greek and Balearic folk singers and Zambian drummers and Spanish dancers and Irish dancers and Polish dancers and German dancers and Italian and Dutch and American and English chamber choirs and joy and music. I tell you, it is something to sit in the huge marquee, which holds about 9,000, and marvel at how different the set piece, as it might be by Palestrina, or Monteverdi, or Handel, or Britten, can sound when sung by different choirs—and yet how the same. The more I read about sport bringing the world together the less I believe it when I actually look at, say, international soccer matches; but music and dancing—ah, that's a different matter. And I fancy they get nearer to the heart of the matter in this delightful valley (St Collen was another 7th-century saint who was Abbot of Glastonbury but very sensibly spent his last years here) than in that dismal UNO building in New York.

And the Welsh, who started it, have every reason to be proud of the tradition of musical competition in their own country from which it sprang, and which culminates in the *National* Eisteddfod held each year in a different town, in spite of a lot of rather vague talk about building a permanent centre for it (which I hope they will never do. There's something so festive about that huge marquee, and the tents, and the temporary loudspeakers, and the sense of an *occasion* magically conjured up in quiet fields and hills).

At the one I covered, in Dolgellau, they finished with everybody combining to do Bach's *St John Passion*. In Welsh. From tonic-sol-fa sheets which to an Englishman looked like a mad typist's nightmare. But you should have heard the sound that echoed up to the mountains.

South Wales

A lot of the participants, of course, came from *South* Wales. Well, if I had gone on to Aberystwyth I could have made the other decision to turn south and go to the extreme tip of **Pembrokeshire**, where we once had a holiday in the excellent hotel overlooking Whitesands Bay, wonderfully empty in the morning, filling up during the day with car visitors, but big enough to hold them all without the slightest feeling of crowding. All dunes and grass and wild flowers—and just along the road the magnificent surprise of **St David's Cathedral**, the finest in Wales, with the adjoining Bishop's Palace, with its pink-ochre delicate arcading like something you would expect to see in Provence rather than Wales. And when you read all that about rain, you will be surprised to hear that this is one of the sunniest parts of Britain.

Or I could have gone from Aberystwyth straight down to **Carmarthen**, along the road which seems to run through one long private valley, with still a slightly mountainy, upland air about it, piles of firewood logs outside many houses, such as you see in the Jura or Switzerland. The roughcast or concrete houses with their square stone door frames and lintels have almost a French appearance—and yet there is something of Ireland here too. You get the feeling that they all know each other for miles up and down the road. There are couples strolling about, two or three miles from a village, people sitting on bridge parapets or outside their houses, chatting.

I went down from Carmarthen to a village on an estuary. Colour-washed houses in a soft evening light. I had come to read the village scrapbook as part of the research for my book *The Living Village*. It was in a house down a steep little road where there were houses wherever there was room. No pavements. One might have been on a Greek island:

> The shops of the district are all family concerns, as are the eight public houses. It is said that every other house used to sell beer . . . we have seven grocers' shops, two drapers, two butchers, one post office, one newsagent, one sweetshop and one betting shop . . . we can buy tomatoes at the bakery, fresh lettuce at the chemist, pork chops at the grocer's and bananas at the butchers, and even antiques at the newsagent's . . .
>
> When the recently deceased Mr James J. Roberts was discussing the future renovation he remarked how the piles of old papers in the upper storey would have to be disposed of. They were Bills of Loading and Unloading the boat called *Lively*, captained by his father and grandfather, plying from Bristol . . . the milkman was a student at Aberystwyth University where he secured his Bachelor of Laws degree and was destined for the law . . . Mr R. H. Pearse, more often called 'Dicky', converted a disused carpenter's shop over an old brewery into a modern flat for Mrs Nancy Morris . . . Evans and Edmonds converted the butcher's shop at Abercorran House into a betting shop, run by Mr Howard Lewis . . . the late E. V. Williams, ex-schoolmaster at the Carmarthen Grammar School, and organist and choirmaster at St Martin's, was a figure so loved and respected that when he died in 1964 a gloom settled over the whole town. Mr Bradshaw, the headmaster (of the village school) said how the morning after Mr Williams's death a little boy of seven came into his office and said 'Sir, E. V. is dead. I am very sorry, sir, because I loves him.'

Dicky Pearse, the B. A. Milkman, Up Street and Down Street, E. V. the Beloved Organist, Howard Lewis's Betting Shop, Grandfather the Captain of the *Lively*—such names will have a familiar ring to anyone who has ever read or seen *Under Milk Wood*; for the village was **Laugharne**, Dylan Thomas's not-so-fictional town of Llaregub, that virtuoso evocation of a Welsh community, a murmur of life among the murmur of the sea. You can see the Boat House where he lived, perched over that wide tide-creeping estuary.

There are other glories of nature down here, notably the fine rocky splendours of the **Gower Peninsula** which flowers out westwards so unexpectedly from industrial Swansea, after which you find yourself humming along through huge oil and steel and coal and tinplate and chemical plants (the steel ones facing a very uncertain future). Then you are on the M4, and as good as out of Wales.

Well may we make the distinction between the industrial and the pastoral, the prosaic and the poetic; so it is as well to remember that the greatest poet to come out of Wales in modern times should have come not from somewhere in its idyllic mountains but from Cwmdonkin Avenue, Swansea.

The Lake District

> The vales in north Wales . . . are not formed for the reception of lakes; those of
> Switzerland and Scotland, and this part of the north of England, *are* so formed; but
> in Switzerland and Scotland, the proportion of diffused water is often too great, as
> at the lake of Geneva for instance, and in most of the Scottish lakes. No doubt it
> sounds magnificent and flatters the imagination to hear, at a distance, of expanses
> of water so many leagues in length and miles in width; and such ample room may
> be delightful to the fresh-water sailor, scudding with a lively breeze amid the
> rapidly shifting scenery. But, whoever travelled along the banks of Loch Lomond
> . . . without feeling that a speedier termination of the long vistas of blank water
> would be acceptable . . .

Thus Wordsworth, the topographical writer of all time, whose guide-book prose was the subsoil for towering trees (as well as weeds) of poetry. He put his finger right on it. Even some Scottish lakes, let alone the big Swiss ones, lack the infinite, ever-changing variety of the English ones. I came across that when I was doing the research for a Yorkshire Television film about the Lake District. It was in a lecture by an ecologist, Mr A. G. Lunn, who also pointed out that because of the geology of its glaciated uplands and a combination of other factors, everything is perfectly in scale and the place seems bigger than it is—what he called the 'moon illusion'. The image thrown on the retina by the moon on the horizon, he says (and you could have fooled me) is the same size as that of the moon at its zenith, where it only *looks* smaller because it is perceived through clear emptiness instead of against points of reference such as trees, chimneys, etc. The Lake District looks bigger than it is (mind you, when you see, peering through binoculars at climbers, tiny figures hundreds of feet above you on sheer rock at a place like Dungeon Ghyll, they *are* hundreds of feet above you).

Already, we have come to the two types of aristocrat inLakeland; the Poet and the Climber. The whole area is only about thirty-five miles across in either direction, but it is the classical example in England (and therefore the world) of what I described on the first page of this book as the conquest of inner space. Its intensely concentrated atmospheric beauty of constantly changing cloudlight over wild fell, frowning crag, forest and gentle farm-dotted valley, its woods and villages and pastures, and of course lakes, brought forth the Lake Poets: Wordsworth, Southey, Coleridge, De Quincey. Shelley, Scott, Matthew Arnold, Fitzgerald, Keats, Gray, Tennyson and many others were besotted visitors. In a way the climbers followed them. The first practitioners of this amazing peace-through-conquering-self sport were all professional, educated gentlemen.

Nowadays **rock-climbing** is for all social classes (if there still are such distinctions). Everyone knows that Joe Brown, one of the world's greatest, was a plumber. But take, for instance, the (to a groundling like me) still terrifying-looking Napes Needle, an isolated pillar on Great Gable. It was first climbed, alone, long before there were such things as Mountain Rescue, by Walter Parry Haskett-Smith (absolutely characteristic name) in 1886, when he was a young barrister. 'This tattered Old Etonian,' says Mr A. H. Griffin, to whose delightful book* I am indebted for this information, 'with his ragged moustache and a glint in his eye, who would turn out, on the hottest days, in a long, heavy check tail coat fitted with huge outside pockets', went up again at the age of 74. The top is only a few feet across, remember. He was 'roped between the present Lord Chorley and late Mr G. R. Speaker. Many hundreds of people watched the slow, careful ascent on Easter Sunday, 1936, and when the old man clambered on to the top of the most famous bit of rock in English climbing the crowd below gave him a cheer. Haskett-Smith had a reputation of never being at a loss for words and his gift of repartee did not fail him even on this particularly important occasion. 'Tell us a story,' shouted someone, and the old man seated on the spire a hundred feet above their heads replied, in a flash: 'there is no other story. This is the top storey.'

There are seven or eight other ways up Napes Needle now, and over the years more and more climbs, with their pitches detailed, and graded into official classifications of difficulty, have been discovered by ever more daring, skilful and (they will not mind my saying this) democratic climbers. There are more, and more varied, climbs to the square mile here than anywhere else in the world.

And the people who do them are the aristocrats (for we seem to have run out of poets). There are certain bars where, if you do not go in with those special boots and coils of nylon rope, and your socks over your trousers and preferably, if you are a man, with a beard, and, if you are a woman (it seems to the cowed outsider) wearing glasses for some reason, a sudden silence will fall. The talking, let alone the singing, will be interrupted. Too late, too late, you will try frantically to remember what the hell an *abseil* is. They are the rightful owners of the heights, they and the ravens and the eagles. Between you and them there is no middle way.

Well, come to think of it, as a matter of fact there is. Anybody can do fell walking (and many people, to the rage of the endlessly patient wardens and rescue people, blithely do, in the wrong weather and clothes, and find themselves above the 2,000-foot contour line lost in a sudden menacing, drenching mist). I have been to the Lake District every two years for the past twenty years, and even I have managed each time to get to a glorious ridge, of which I will say no more than that you can see God knows how far over the Irish Sea, as well as enjoying stupendous views both of the adjacent Yorkshire fells and of the Langdale Pikes, from its 1,500 feet.

Of course, that is nothing compared to the aristocrats' view from the top of Scafell, at 3,162 feet the highest (remember La Paz, p. 7!) or even mere 1,970-feet Black Combe, in the bottom left hand corner, on the Cumberland coast, from which you are said to be able to see the hills of Staffordshire, Snowdonia, the Isle of Man, Ireland and Scotland.

People are always going on about the danger to the Lake District now that twenty million people are, because of the M6 motorway, now within a three-hour journey from it. As a visitor myself, although from more than three hours away, I can only say how I marvel not only at the way the most modest enterprise can bring you to a silent forest or a high moor where you are alone with nature, but at the way there always seems to be room even by the most popular lakes. I have always been there with children who count any

Inside the Real Lakeland (Guardian Press, Preston, 1961).

The Lake District, near Keswick.

day irretrievably lost, even if it is pouring with rain (and everyone knows there's plenty of that in the Lake District), on which there has been no swimming. How often, after a wet morning pleasantly spent in the town of Kendal (of which more anon) and a return to base, have I heard the cry 'oh, come on, it's *bound* to clear up', and set off from base to the nearest convenient lake, which for us has been **Coniston**.

But even on cloudless warm days, as we drove along the narrow road along its eastern shore, sometimes with a couple of stone-walled fields between us and the water, sometimes, tree-hung, right on the lake's edge, as we waited in wider bits for oncoming cars or cumbrous coaches to squeeze past, thinking that this time every possible car-park and inlet would be taken, by people with elaborate picnic equipment, rubber boats and canoes ('ah, *there* it is!' shouts someone as we get the first view of the Old Man of Coniston, that instantly recognisable shape mirrored in the water), somehow there always has been a place.

And the people already there have been overwhelmingly family parties like ourselves. Before I started on that Yorkshire TV film I was told sternly, 'we don't want a lot of wind-and-Wordsworth stuff. The average visitor is a chap from Manchester who says to his wife, "it looks like a nice week-end, let's go oop to Lake District", and is bored when he finds there is nothing to *do*.' Not so. Even the people who sit in their cars as near as they can get to Windermere have some kind of ideal about this area, otherwise they would have gone to Blackpool. Inside all of them there is a rock-climber or a botanist or an ornithologist or a poet screaming to get out.

For many people their first view of the whole thing has been on the Instant Lake District trip when you come over the rise by Staveley, half-way from Kendal, and suddenly see the melting panorama of **Windermere**, that long thin lake (like most of them) in its bowl of blue hills. Well, of course there's a long queue for the car ferry if you want to cross the lake westwards at its waist. Of course, you must drive slowly though the town of Windermere, thronged with people of whom an astonishing number are in shorts and carry knapsacks, but who are also members of coach parties eating ice-cream (and why not?).

There is a lot of traffic on the road to Ambleside at the northern head of the lake. If this is your first day here and you really want to find out where the best walks, accommodation, bird-watching hides, poets' houses, or whatever things interest you, are to be found, do stop on the way at Brockhole, the National Park Information Centre, which is not only very helpful, including excellently researched short films and literature, but is also a lakeside beauty spot in its own right with magnificent terraced gardens.

Then, if you have a single poetic nerve in your body, you follow the road north a little past Rydal Water, slightly under a mile long, and the practically adjacent Grasmere, just *over* a mile; and there is **Dove Cottage**. Here Wordsworth lived from 1799 to 1808. You have already passed by Rydal Mount, where he lived the last 37 of his 80 years (he died in 1850). But Dove Cottage was his home when the great mysterious poems, with their profound post-Christian reverence before the marvels of what used to be called Creation and is now called Nature, were composed. Never mind the inevitable crush of tourists—you are a tourist, I am a tourist, everybody is a tourist except in his own town; in these tiny rooms (you notice his hat, a pair of spectacles on a desk), were written, never mind 'I wandered lonely as a cloud' etc., works like *The Prelude* and the *Intimations of Immortality*, that will keep their organ-like resonance as long as the English language is known and loved. Thoughts that do often lie too deep for tears, indeed.

In the same village there is the larger house of Allan Mount, where he lived from 1808 to 1811. And Coleridge moved to Dove Cottage, and when—

—but if this is the Instant Lake District trip it will be time to go back down the main road, get up to the high little lake of **Tarn Hows**—and, I was going to write, on to Hawkshead and Far Sawrey, even if you only stop for a few minutes, where, if you are lucky, you will experience the small miracle, in a car park with one of the best views in England, of simply holding out your hand with a few crumbs in it and *having a chaffinch come and perch on it* and calmly eat them till chased off by other chaffinches clearly anxious to do the same thing. I am not making this up. I have witnesses. I tell you, it made me feel like St Francis.

Let me observe in passing, however, that Tarn Hows is a well-known and popular spot; we have been there on a Bank Holiday Monday when the car parks (the discreet enlargement and tree-screening of which is National Parks policy) were hopelessly jammed, and one had to get anywhere off the road where one could, but when we walked down to the water, alive with kids splashing about in rubber boats and rafts, it was perfectly possible to carry our picnic and bathing stuff down and find a little family nest among the ferns and boulders which was ours for the whole day.

But if you can't do this, well, on to Hawkshead, utterly unspoilt village with characteristic white-painted, black-lintelled Lake District cottages (four of them are National Trust) and on past the charming little Esthwaite Water to **Far Sawrey**, where you will find the residence of the late Mrs William Heelis, a very tough character indeed, wife of an Ambleside lawyer, noted for her knowledge of the finer points of sheep judging, a dumpy, tweed-clad figure happy with locals and often rude to strangers.

Better known as Beatrix Potter.

So universal have her children's books, seemingly of a timeless pre-mechanised age, become that it is something of a shock to realise that she only died in 1943, and from Hill Top Farm, which is now preserved as a museum (surely, you think, that *is* the landing where Samuel Whiskers pushed the rolling-pin in front of him 'with his paws, like a brewer's man trundling a barrel'), she saw the sky reddened by fires in air raids on Lancashire and Cheshire. But so it is. And when you look at the amazing, sharp, delicate colours of her inimitable paintings, many of which are displayed here, they seem a great deal fresher and sharper than they do in the books.

The natural course now would be to go on down the steep hill which brings you to the western side of the Windermere ferry. But you haven't seen Coniston yet, so you probably go back, passing Tarn Hows, to Coniston. Not the town itself (unless you're thinking of hiring a boat), which is on the western side of the top end of the lake. Not only is the town itself not particularly interesting, but the road south from it is just a main road, and often actually out of sight of the lake, unlike the aforementioned eastern road, which has the added advantage that Brantwood, the home of John Ruskin is on it.

Since you will now already, for practical purposes, have embarked on more than can be done in one day (there's no point in rushing in the Lake District. Even if you want to pass a couple of cars in front of you, on most roads you won't be able to for miles), you may as well, when you join the A590, the rather boring main road that forms the southern boundary of the Lake District, take the road at Newby Bridge which leads up to the southern tip of Windermere and turn off it to the right to find Cartmel Fell, where there is a magic little rough-cast church all by itself in a little churchyard full of wild flowers. It has always been utterly silent every time we went there till the last, when we found people from two cars sitting down to a tremendous meal, chairs and tables and radio and everything.

You can't win them all, even in the Lake District. Nevertheless it was really the exception that proves my rule, that even in this most popular and crowded part of the Lake District a very small enterprise will bring you rich rewards of solitude and space and height and beauty. In the **Grizedale Forest**, for instance, on the high land between Windermere and Coniston, there are paradisal walks and trails (and suddenly you come on rustic wooden picnic tables and seats in the quiet woods), of all kinds, with or without guide, of which you can get details at any tourist office or at Brockhole.

This is not to be confused with Grisedale, another excellent area for walking, which debouches into the majestic Ullswater, a dozen miles away north-east over all sorts of complex hills; nor with Grisedale Pike, twenty miles to the north-west, where the Whinlatter Pass, a beautiful roundabout route, over 1,000 feet, from Keswick to lovely remote Crummock Water and Buttermere, goes between it and the grandly-named Lord's Seat. They don't seem to mind repeating names up there. There are two Staveleys quite close to each other, there's another Borrowdale besides the one at the other, non-Keswick end of the divine Derwentwater; it runs down eastwards to the M6, and in fact Langdale Fell, well over twenty miles from the Langdale Pikes, is nearly in *Yorkshire*. They are all Norse place-names. *Thwaite* = clearing, *scar* = rock face, *gill* = torrent or ravine etc.

Obviously you could spend a lifetime getting to know the Lake District, and all I have been able to mention here is a few absolutely classic views. There is one other I simply must mention. If you can resist the temptation, going westwards along that A595, to turn right at Duddon Bridge, go on till you find the turn right to Santon Bridge and then to **Wast Water**. A tough lake (though not so cold to swim in as it looks) with those wicked Screes just across from it. As E. M. Forster wrote, 'dimpling Windermere can never gloom like Wastwater, awesome even in sunlight'. Even so, as you go along its western shore you come to one of *the* views, Great Gable framed between two other hills. In fact, it is the view which you see stylised as the National Park emblem.

I said 'resist the temptation' because in going to Wast Water you will have passed, at Duddon Bridge, the point where you turn right for the Duddon Valley. If you did choose this magnificent journey you would come to the world's most beautiful T-junction, where you would then have to decide whether to turn west, go over Hard Knott Pass into the widening beauties of Eskdale (till you come to the head of the famous small-gauge railway which takes people in its little open cars down to the sea at Ravenglass, trundling through fields of that tall and varied grass that only railways seem to know about)—or east and over Wrynose Pass and round the Old Man Of Coniston and down to a superb view of the lake (and in either case you had just better be sure there's nothing wrong with your brakes and clutch).

Wast Water would have been a journey where you would have to come back the same way; the other two would be round trips. If you're in a car, that is. To the walker there are of course an infinite range of larger possibilities, and you will be surprised to find what famous names are within range of the ordinary visitor. Skiddaw, for instance, the grand northern monarch, is climbable by people with no other equipment than good legs, good nerves and common sense (if in doubt about weather, ring Windermere 5151). If you are not feeling *that* ambitious, Lough Rigg (right in Wordsworth country at Grasmere), or Claife Heights above Windermere, or the previously mentioned Grizedale Forest, and several thousand others, are warmly recommended.

Infinite geography, infinite choice. But of course you can't live with geography all the time, there have to be pubs (and I don't know how they've got round that law, so irritating to the family tourist in Britain, of not being able to take children into pubs, as though they were still full of Hogarthian drunks and prostitutes; I can think of several with people sitting happily with their pints and kids all over the place). There have to be towns; and here I must admit to a soft spot for **Kendal**.

I know it's the county town of Westmorland (and if that's another county They have written out of history, too bad; it will always be Westmorland to me). It is true that, even now they have built the M6, its hilly main street is still loud with traffic. People going to the Lake District will have got off the M6 by now, anyway. But whereas Windermere and Ambleside and even the curiously Victorian Keswick give you a blurred impression of many of the kind of shop that spills out on to the pavement with racks of postcards, straw hats, rubber boats, walking sticks, ice-cream, etc., Kendal is full of a kind of decent jollity which is a reassuring reminder of the solid, farm-based life that goes on here when the tourists have all departed. You can get a hint of it at any sheep-dog trials, or at the famous Grasmere Games (Thursday nearest to 20 August; as everyone knows, they *run* up fells, and there is Westmorland wrestling—not so many have heard of a type known as 'Hype, Hank and Buttock'). But Kendal is the place to remind you that the whole thing isn't just a holiday dream, People live here. Of course there are shops called Glad Rags or The Pantry, just like anywhere else. But there is also an elegant old-fashioned chemist's shop front with a beautifully painted notice saying *No Dogs. Please use hook provided*, and there is the hook on the doorstep. There is L'Ile Shop, a *very* small tobacconist's. Outside the Highgate Hotel one sign says 'Edinburgh *155 miles*, and *on* the hotel are the words *To dwellers in this place God grante peace*.

It is one of those towns where you look through archways and see gardens and secret life, right behind the main street. I heard one woman say to another, 'a bit like Truro, isn't it?' It's not in the least like Truro. It is Kendal. It gave its name to something I should not have thought possible: for Kendal Mint Cake is a confectioner's oxymoron, a kind of Roundhead fudge. (What a marvellous language English is; fancy giving such a blunt name to such a cloying, sweet, basically Cavalier confection! Fudge. *Fudge*). Kendal Mint Cake is the only sweet that can be eaten entirely without guilt, indeed with a distinctly worthy and moral feeling. It *must* be good for you. For it was included in the rations which Edmund Hillary took on the conquest of Everest.

It wasn't the only link, of course. Many Alpinists and Himalayan climbers have learnt their rock-climbing in the Lake District. And countless more have discovered that

> . . . there's not a man
> That lives who hath not known his god-like hours,
> And feels not what an empire we inherit
> As natural beings in the strength of Nature.

Scotland

I suppose there must be plenty of Englishmen who have been to Majorca and have never been to Scotland. More fool them, with one of the most beautiful, romantic and varied countries in the world on their doorstep. Yet if you asked me what was the first thing that the word 'Scotland' suggested to me it wouldn't be the scenery, the cities, the people. It would be the *air*.

And it's when you do a tour of Scotland that you really notice the air. One glance at the map will show you that it's not a country you go through, it's one you go round; and there is something about the south-west-to-north-east orientation that predisposes you to do it clockwise. Apart from anything else, if you did it the other way Edinburgh would come at the beginning instead of as the glorious finale, as it should.

Of course this must be qualified by the admission that geography gives a heavy bias of interest to the fantastically convoluted west coast with its myriad inlets and islands and magical views of water and hills seen against Atlantic light, and the great eastern end of the Highlands below Inverness. But on this tour I noticed the air everywhere, even in what are laughingly called the Lowlands—say around Hawick and Teviotdale.

I have lived in Edinburgh. I have had a family holiday on the island of Jura (boat journey from Gourock, blue water, dreamlike summer day, up Kyles of Bute, stopping at landing-stages of snug retirement bungalow-and-palm-fringed resortlets—Colintraive, Tighnabruaich. At Tarbert, five-minute bus journey across narrow neck of one of those multitudinous south-west-pointing isthmuses, second boat to Jura, where seals on rocks). I have been to the island of Eigg, to do a story about the enterprising Yorkshireman, ex-Olympic bobsleigh team and mad motor racer, Keith Schellenberg, who has bought it and seems to be succeeding in the mighty task of making it economically viable, halting depopulation etc. without tarting it up, even though tourist accommodation is modestly increased. I have been to Glasgow and many other places in Scotland on various journalistic assignments. I cherish memories of a wartime glimpse of St Andrew's, that grey sea town on the east coast with the students in their proud scarlet gowns . . .

But it wasn't till I came to write this book and made this tour that I had this continuous, slightly intoxicating permanent awareness of that *air*. It is a mixture of heather and peat and general boskiness and sea and seaweed and sand and grass and bracken and pine and something which one must simply call Ingredient X. I've been to other countries, notably Norway perhaps, where you might expect the same thing. But no. It's surprising, science being what it is, that no one has yet discovered a way of getting it into Aerosol sprays. It would sell as well as Scotch whisky, which in some effects it resembles. No wonder they have at long last recognised the effect of it on their respiratory and vocal system, and have suddenly started producing world-class singers from the blossoming Scottish Opera, and in the Edinburgh Festival Chorus have one of the most exhilarating-sounding choirs in the world. Get the vowels right, you see.

The other thing we discovered, in a big way, was the bed-and-breakfast way of life, as you shall see. We've always had children and tents or convenient friends on other occasions, otherwise we should have discovered it before. I mean, jolly good luck to hotels, at £30 a night or whatever; obviously somebody has to cater for expense-account business men and the richer type of tourist and civil servants with those index-linked pensions, and those laggers getting £300 a week, to quote the strike at the time of writing; but wait till you hear about (for instance) Mrs McLellan at Pitlochry.

Galloway

This time we got in to Scotland gradually, passing through the delightful, still utterly unspoiled bottom left-hand corner of Galloway. On many previous visits I have *woken* to find myself in Scotland, having gone by rail. And there is a certain magic about getting into your sleeper at Euston, dozing through the journey so admirably evoked by poets like T. S. Eliot (with *Skimbleshanks, the Railway Cat*: 'there's a funny little basin/You're supposed to wash your face in') or W. H. Auden (in *The Night Mail*: 'In the farm she passes nobody wakes/But a jug in the wash-stand gently shakes'), and opening your window, to let the London air out and that Air in, to a fantastic opal dawnscape over the greens and browns of Rannoch Moor. And if you are doing a tour and do want to start straight in you can always Motorail your car to Stirling or Inverness (fares depend on the season, but for the average car with two people the return fare from London, with sleeper, is around £100).

This time, however, we simply went on from the Lake District and turned left for **Dumfries**. A fine town with the kind of public building (the Town House with its off-centre Mid Steeple) which instantly reminds you with its distinctive style that you're not in England any more (not quite sure *where* you are with that very Assyrian-looking St Michael with his spade beard). Certainly not, for in the churchyard is the tomb of Robert Burns.

The town slopes down towards a pleasantly wide riverside area where all the forthcoming-event posters seem to be (who would have expected to find the Drystone Walling Association announcing an 'Impressionistic, Informal, Illustrative Talk on Dry-stone Dyking in Scotland by Dr Anne-Berit Bouch-Grevink of *Oslo* University'?). But our main reason for coming off the main road (which goes ultimately to Stranraer and the boats for Northern Ireland) was the white tower visible on the facing hill of the town, like a lighthouse. This is the Camera Obscura—one of three in Scotland, the others being at Edinburgh and Kirriemuir.

Well, it must have seemed quite something in 1836, when they put it up 'installed on the wet afternoon of the 28th of July by Morton of Kilmarnock, instrument maker to Sir John Ross, the explorer, who had recommended him', says the memorial plate in charmingly unmemorial-type language). It seems quite something *now*. About a dozen visitors crowd round the flat table under the domed roof while the girl manipulates and focuses to any desired part of the town. You see a couple of women's expressions as they talk to each other, sublimely unconscious that we can see them from hundreds of yards away. You see distant traffic, birds flying, smoke blowing across the town or—'let's come in a wee bit closer,' said the girl; 'Och, he's at it again!' This was a man whom we actually saw look round cautiously before throwing dead flowers and other garden debris over the next-door fence one street away from where we were. And all, of course, in the most beautiful natural colour. I can't think why they don't have one on the top of every police station.

I'd been wanting to see a camera obscura for years. There is one on Clifton Down just above the Suspension Bridge at Bristol which must be something to see; it's just that so far I've never found it open.

Another long-nursed ambition has been to see one of the great gardens on this side of Scotland, with its Gulf Stream mild climate. The one we did see, **Threave**, just outside the comfortable little town of Castle Douglas ('caravan in comfort by our loch' says a hospitable civic notice) is only a quarter of the way to what is clearly the greatest, the Logan Botanical Gardens, on the extreme tip of Galloway, twenty miles south even of Stranraer, and laid out by the McDouall family with the specific intention of encouraging warm and temperate climate plants and trees. I have heard rapturous accounts from friends who have been there, and the more I look at photographs of its amazing avenues of palms, Africa in the Atlantic but with all our deciduous splendour as well, the more I long to see it; but you really would have to be staying in the area to do so, and we were on this tour.

Which is not to depreciate Threave, on the way to which is a signpost to the left which I shall always remember, since it looks like an attempt to spell the sound of a man clearing his throat. Haugh of Urr, it says. Well, you try it. *Haugh* means 'piece of flat alluvial land by the side of a river', but even so . . .

It's amazing how there's always a first time for everything. I must have seen a weeping ash before (bound to be one at Stourhead!) but that was the first splendid thing we noticed on the lawn at Threave. Above the lawn there's a marvellous woodland walk and arboretum. There is a peat garden which is a revelation of what you can do facing north, a bog garden, a winter border, a woodland garden (foxgloves and rhododendron in May and June, lilies and gorgeous feathery multi-coloured estilbes when we were there. There are also particularly rich greenhouses since there is now a Gardening School, with a two-year course, run by the National Trust for Scotland who are continuing the expressed desire of the last owner, Major A. L. Gordon, to run it as 'a typical small estate of a type once common in Scotland but now on the decline'.

Lucky old lairds, if *this* was ever common. It may have been a lucky month (*August?*), but I'm reminded of the late Ruth Draper's sketch of the lady showing off her garden. 'You should have seen it last week, it was a blaze of colour!' I'd never heard of *Cynoglossum firmament* before. Like many of the things you see in these marvellous gardens, it's not the kind of thing they ever seem to have at your friendly local nursery; but I still cherish the memory of that fantastic blue mass, and indeed of all the gorgeous herbaceous beds. None of that smart high-class garden rot here about flowers being faintly vulgar, what you should have is grass, shrubs and trees. A memorable visit.

We went on to cross the first of our many peninsulas, the trees in the sea-haunted meadows all leaning the same way as a reminder that this windless summer calm was not permanent, to **Kirkcudbright** (pronounced Kir*koo*bry, it simply means 'church of St Cuthbert'). It is Scotland's answer to St Ives, having for years had a colony of artists, originally of the Glasgow School (and one of its attractions is a fortnight's Summer Painting School for which the tuition fee is a mere £24).

We saw a house simply in the middle of fields which bore the surprising sign *Jeweller. No VAT*. And this seems to be the place to observe that Scotland seems somehow to have lifted the word 'crafts' from the folky, jokey curse that somehow hangs over it. Even though the sharpening of a national 'folk' consciousness has obviously played some part in it, in the admirable booklet *See Scotland at Work* you will find the addresses not only of kilt-makers, curling-stone polishers (for that quintessentially Scottish game, like bowls on ice) and of course weavers and potters and woodcarvers, but also shipyards and cosmetic manufacture and indeed nuclear power (though for that you'd have to go as near to the North Pole as you can get in these islands—Thurso in Caithness). And of course if you were mean enough, in the Highlands you could go round one distillery after another and enjoy the sample of their product which they give you at the end. And I have rarely seen such a collection of desirable objects as in the Highlands and Islands Development Board's display centre in Inverness.

Kirkcudbright seemed little changed from my memories of a wartime leave there (the aunt whose house was called 'Clovelly' in Coventry moved there after it was bombed). Those houses not of stone are painted in pleasant seaside colours. The Tolbooth (Scots for town hall) is now a memorial to John Paul Jones (1747–1792), a slave trader and privateer, later founder of the American Navy. In 1778 he actually attacked the British revenue cutter *Hussar* off the Isle of Man, and a few days later raided St Mary's Isle, the Kirkcudbright peninsula tip, hoping to capture the Earl of Selkirk as a hostage (does all this sound familiar?) to exchange for American prisoners of war, but the Earl was not at home, so they just took the silver—which Jones himself later returned to the Earl.

It was in the Selkirk Arms here that Burns wrote the famous grace:

Some hae meat and canna eat
And some wad eat that want it
But we hae meat and we can eat
Sae let the Lord be thankit.

Pleasant waterside streets, quite large Teesport tanker moored. Steam Packet Inn. The Paul Jones Bakery. Drinking fountain with verse I suspect *not* by Burns

This fount not riches—Life supplies
Art gives what Nature here denies
Posterity must surely bliss
St Cuthbert's sons who purchased this.

I should have liked to try the long-remembered warm sea bathing at our favourite Carrick shore, indeed to stay a week and explore the trails in the 240-square-mile Galloway Forest Park. But the tour beckoned, and we went via the pretty little town Gatehouse of Fleet back on to the main Stranraer road, now with huge sea vistas of Wigtown Bay on our left. Just when it got most beautiful there was a large caravan camp, shrieking with the glossy colours that caravans seem to find indispensable. It must have been visible from miles out at sea. Again, this may have been luck, but it was the only example that we came across. When we later got to Loch Lomond we were to wonder where all the caravans were, until we noticed the signs at every lay-by forbidding overnight camping, and the many pleasant, usually tree-screened sites. I know there's more *room* in Scotland, but it did seem very unspoilt indeed after some parts of the Lake District.

At Newton Stewart we turned back for an absolutely unforgettable journey, with many lovely straight bits as well as climbing zig-zags, through the southern part of the Forest Park, in and out of trees, past heathery hillsides, past the south side of the wonderfully-named Clatteringshaws Loch, through the delightful Moniaive (roses everywhere, over little low white houses), a half-mile detour after Kirkland for a quick look at **Maxwelton House**, where Annie Laurie (1682–1761) lived. She never actually married the man who wrote the song, William Douglas.

But Maxwelton Braes certainly *are* bonny, and so is the sober, tall, white moated house; although it has won awards for the loving reconstruction of period life in its interior, we only had this quick look because we intended to join the A76, at Thornhill, and get across to the next main road to Glasgow, the A78. Not that the A76 is exactly an ugly road, leading as it does up to the head of **Nithsdale**, full of castles and abbeys and a Henry Moore group and I know not what marvels (including, on the next pass north of the one we took, Wanlockhead, at 1,380 feet the highest village in Scotland, beating the best the Highlands has to offer, Tomintoul, by 220 feet). We had heard that the Dalveen Pass, through the Lowther Hills, was the finest road in the Lowlands. Well, of course, I haven't seen them all, but I can report that the climb to 1,100 feet between those rolling, rounded, splendid hills was wonderful. I can remember that Air now. Lowlands indeed!

We did not go to **Glasgow**. Well, of *course*, it has that marvellous Opera and the best art gallery outside London and the Art School for ever associated with the name of Charles Rennie Mackintosh and the Transport Museum (which includes huge ship models) and lots of High Victorian architecture and the Cathedral and the University and a carpet factory built as the Doge's palace and Sauchiehall Street and of course Glaswegians . . . but Glasgow is a tour in itself.

Skirting the southern and south-western conurbations with their tower blocks standing up against the great sunset building up from those western seas, we found the M8 motorway, crossed the new Erskine Bridge, the latest and most westerly across the Clyde, and, it seemed in a few minutes, were driving up the west side of—

Loch Lomond

I've never arrived there in the morning, so of course I can't say with complete certainty—but I simply cannot imagine a better time than the evening to get your first view of it. I've always been fascinated by the relationship, if any, between the fame and reputation of something and your actual feelings when you yourself see it—in art as well as nature, Sometimes there is a let-down. They always go on about *The Night Watch* at the Rijksmuseum in Amsterdam, and I found myself thinking heretically 'is that all?' and moving on to be put into a trance in front of the picture by Nicholas Maes of the old woman, cottage loaf on table, cat clawing at cloth, saying grace before eating. Similarly at the Prado, Exhibit A is the Velasquez *Las Meninas*, all that brilliance with mirror-images and dwarfs, well yes, marvellous, but in the next room there is this luminous, numinous *Los Borachos*, 'the tipplers', brown, earthy clothed drinking peasants kneeling before calmly ecstatic divine naked Bacchic gods—

—well, everything you have heard about Loch Lomond is true, only more so. No song, no legend could prepare you for the sight. You have already caught sight of the mountains from high ground south of the river, of course; and you have only to look at a relief map to see that the massif of which Ben Lomond is the highest point is the climactic, magnificent statement of the Highlands to the Lowlands. But to see across the calm water, the islands, the sloping shore fields and the miles of golden aqueous air between you and the great darkening shapes must be a revelation.

We had not booked in anywhere, and we did not discover till next day, in a little tourist information caravan further up the loch, the admirable 'book-a-bed-ahead' scheme they have; you tell them roughly where you think you are going to be by the end of the day, pay them a £1 fee, and they fix you up there and then. (They have it in Wales, too.) So we turned down the first drive to the right saying Bed and Breakfast. It was a farm. A man was talking to the owner in the doorway, and as I got out he came back to his car. 'Sorry,' he said, 'We've just got the last one. When the man saw you getting out of your car he hadn't seen my wife and he said "it's no two *men*, is it?" ' Quite right too.

So we went on to the next one, over a private concrete track through fields in the middle of which, framed against this celestial view (it seemed ridiculous, surrealist, that Glasgow should be less than half an hour away) was another farm. And yes, they could let us have a room. Would we like to see it first, said this admirable Mrs Keith, of Midross Farm, Arden, Loch Lomond; as if we would have turned *anything* down after such a long and eventful day. It was a big, high old room, with wash-basin. We took our stuff up and changed. She gave us the key (they *always* give you the key, I suppose they can tell if you're a criminal, but it's very trusting of them these days) and we went back down the road for an enormous, winey and reasonably priced meal.

At the time of writing this (June 1980) I had mislaid my note of the place where we had this meal, so I rang up Mrs Keith to ask her. 'It's the Duck Bay Marina', she said. (Of course. All those boats bobbing cheerfully outside the huge window-wall, the lone water-skier using the last minutes of the long northern twilight) . . . 'Can I really believe my note here, that your bill for the two of us was £9' I asked.

'Weel,' said the voice on the telephone. 'I'm afraid we've had to put the charge up this year. It's £5 each now. Yes, Duck Bay Marina. We've just had some Americans—no, they were Canadians—yesterday and they went to it and they said it was the best meal they'd had since they came here.'

The next day, after an immense bacon-and-egg breakfast (proper pink, crisp, back rashers, not that greasy stuff) we went on up the loch side, wishing we could explore its many islands (some of them nature reserves, some with abandoned 18th-century *clachans* or hamlets; and one has a *very* ancient causeway just below the surface leading to it). It was a grey day, but that gave the endlessly differing views, as new mountain shapes appeared, a calm, opalescent charm. I imagine the only time when Loch Lomond doesn't look beautiful is when there is fog and you can't see it at all.

We turned westward at Tarbet, before the end of Lomond (which is 21 miles long, every mile convincing me that Wordsworth (see p. 177) was wrong on this point at least, and a couple of miles brought us to another block.

Look at a road map and you will see what I mean by this term. All roads in this region go round a huge block of wild mountain country, across which you will rarely see the most minor, light-vehicles-only (preferably with four-wheel drive) connecting road. This isn't the Yorkshire moors. For instance, the block to the east contains the famous Loch Katrine and the Trossachs, a perhaps inevitably more touristy area since a motorway aims at its heart from Edinburgh and Stirling. In our case we came to Arrochar, at the head of the aptly-named sea inlet of Loch Long, then through a quite wild and

stony valley (Glen Croe—and the r is not a mistake, as you will see) which led
to my favourite place-name in the whole world; *Rest and Be Thankful*. Lower
down we did, it now being opening time, although it seemed early to me.

Inveraray

Our intention was to push on to Inveraray; but it's no good having too rigid
notions of where you're going on a tour, and the moment we saw the signs
telling us that it contained the tallest tree in Britain we went to the splendid
forest garden, dropping down to the eastern shore of the end of Loch Fyne, at
Strone. There was one of those we-trust-you machines in the car park but
absolutely nobody about and no one to take money as we wandered under
these solemn, beautiful, tremendous trees. It's a very sloping garden, so you
can get almost to look down on the top of the Tallest Tree in Britain; *Abies
grandis*, a notice says it was measured in 1969 and 175 feet, and by 1976 it was
188 feet. Well, thank you, whoever manages all that.

Inveraray is, dare I say it (for it is meant as a compliment), one of those
places where to come on something like its castle, seat of the Dukes of Argyll
(the Campbells), surprises you with one of those final articulations of gracious living; glorious tapestry drawing room with Adam ceiling, elegant and
exotic china (e.g. Meissen, a Chelsea asparagus dish actually made to look like
a piece of asparagus, all displayed in the China Turret—so *that's* what they
have in those round bits at the corners with the fairy-tale conical roofs) in this
building in what can best be described as Scottish Palladian Gothick; dining
room with charming mad filigree silver-gilt boats on wheels, called nefs,
surely not just for pepper and salt; splendid pictures, Opie, Gainsborough,
Raeburn, etc. And nothing behind but wild mountains and the little grey,
calm, loch-side town. How did they *get* it all here, to make this dream-capsule
of great art against a background of great nature?

Well, of course, you don't survive as a top family, least of all in Scotland,
without a fair amount of blood and turmoil and side-changing on the way.
Before things settled down and the 9th Duke of Argyll married a daughter of
Queen Victoria and became Governor-General of Canada, the 2nd Earl was
killed at Flodden, the 4th was one of the first Scottish lords to turn Protestant,
the 5th supported Queen Mary. The 8th opposed Charles I, the 9th fought on
the Royalist side at Dunbar (and both were executed when their sides lost).
The 10th Earl (who was the *First* Duke, a reward for inviting William of
Orange to be King of Scotland too) organised the Massacre of Glencoe.

The head of the family is automatically the head of the Clan Campbell,
about which there is some surprising information in the Castle. The septs
(divisions) of the clan include such names as Arthur, Burns, Conachy,
Denoon, Kissock and Isaacs.

Nice little airy town by the water, full of wool shops; and very well done
restoration of tall whitewashed houses in vernacular style, Relief Land.

Islands

Even if you keep looking at the map, in this part of the world you never know
whether a long arm of blue or against-the-light silver-grey water, with hills
on the far side of it, is going to appear in front of you, or on the left, or on the
right. We went on up through the gently open Glen Aroy, saw the head
waters of Loch Awe ahead, and then on the left as we rounded it and went
through the Pass of Brander (not memorable, as passes go; just a road

Inveraray.

between rocks. Your standards of what constitutes a memorable pass tend to rise as you move about Scotland). And so to the T-junction with the road that goes five miles down to Oban, or for 110 miles up north-east along the great divide of the Highlands, following Loch Linnhe, Loch Lochy, Loch Oich and Loch Ness, with the interconnecting bits of the Caledonian Canal, to Inverness.

T-junctions are symbolic of decisions—in this case of a basic decision you have to make in Scotland; are you going to an island or not? Perhaps it is not quite so difficult to decide, now that (for instance) you can fly from Glasgow to Skye in an hour; though when I go (not on this tour, and in any case, what's the point of trying to follow Johnson and Boswell?) it will be by the cheaper method of going up to the Kyle of Lochalsh, where the mainland practically touches it and the ferry takes five minutes. *Then* I shall make that famous trip down to Elgol, where Bonny Prince Charlie embarked, make the boat trip over the sea loch of Scavaig, and walk up the little stream to Loch Coruisk and stare up at the great blue-black Cuillins in what everybody says is the best view in Scotland (if it's not raining, for which the best bets are May and June) . . .

Oban is a nodal point for island journeys, whether somewhat less romantically in the high-speed passenger-only catamaran to Tobermory on the island of Mull or (another future hope) what I can't help thinking of as the Mendelssohn Trip round the south of Mull to Staffa and Fingal's Cave and (of course, it's the St Columba trip really) Iona, on some perfect blue day.

This cannot, however, be relied on. There is that splendid story about the Catholic Bishop of Argyll and the Isles visiting one of the Catholic islands (for there are some that the Reformation never reached) where there was no priest, and asking an old man why he had not been to confession on the mainland for seven years. 'Well, my lord, ye ken these are vairy difficult waters,' was the reply in that soft Highland voice, 'and I've aye thought if it was a venial sin it didna matter, and if it was a mortal sin it's too bloody dangerous.'

In any case you can't stay on Staffa. An island really has to be stayed on, not visited. It's then you get the true sea peace stealing into your soul, where you are alone on enormous seaweedy beaches watching some dreamlike panorama of water and other distant blue hills. It's then you see what inspired the author of the Canadian Boat Song of which (perhaps) you may not recognise the chorus:

> Fair these broad meads—these hoary woods are grand;
> But we are exiles from our fathers' land

—but you may well recognise the second verse, which I am not the only one to think has four of the most mysteriously moving lines in the language:

> From the lone sheiling of the misty island
> Mountains divide us, and the waste of seas—
> Yet still the blood is strong, the heart is Highland,
> And we in dreams behold the Hebrides.

And we in dreams behold the Hebrides. *And we in dreams behold the Hebrides.* It appeared in *Blackwood's Magazine* in 1829. No one knows who wrote it.

With so many islands it is no problem to find somewhere to stay where you can realise the dream. It is only one example from hundreds; but on **Eigg**, for instance, you can stay in a converted shepherd's bothy or little stone house, with a shower and cooker etc., hire a bicycle and go and get your own food at the kind of shop where a half-hour conversation is nothing uncommon, climb the great Sgurr (it's the same word as *scar*) which gives it the outline of some huge aircraft carrier from the mainland thirteen miles away, visit the *singing sands* of its western shore (they *do*, in certain wind conditions), talk to crofters or be utterly alone, as you wish. And the little boat, often piloted by Keith Schellenberg himself, a very unusual laird indeed, will take you from Glen Uig, past the hills of Ardnamurchan, the most westerly part of the mainland of Britain, when it's 'too bloody dangerous' for the big official boat from Mallaig . . .

Glencoe

But our tour meant that we must turn right at that T-junction. Along constantly-changing sea-loch views to Ballachulish, where the literally *awful*, or rather *aweful*, Glencoe is a few miles up to the right. Scottish history, to the outsider, seems as convoluted as its geography. Bruce established its independence more or less completely by his victory over the English at Bannockburn in 1314, Edward II not proving such a tough egg as Edward I. But oh, what interminable trouble those early Scottish Stuarts, one James after another (their James VI became England's James I in 1603) had with those terrible nobles, first the Black Douglases and then the Red Douglases. They killed James III at Sauchieburn in 1488. And the Scottish disaster of Flodden, where James IV was killed, was after all not due to the English invading Scotland but to James invading England. And the terrible religious ambivalence! The outsider tends, again, to equate Jacobitism and support for the Stuarts with Catholicism, in a general sort of way. And with bishops and spiritual authoritarianism. Yet Culloden (which we are coming to in a couple of pages), the terrible death-blow to the Jacobite cause in 1746, the last battle on British soil, is somehow in the lore as a victory *for* authoritarianism. But of course this was *English* authoritarianism . . .

To get back to Glencoe, the Chief of the Sept of Macdonald of Glencoe had fought with Claverhouse at Killiecrankie, the last Jacobite victory (in 1689, against William of Orange's forces). This was the man who had directed the cruel operations against the Covenanters, spiritually democratic, fiercely anti-bishop, let alone anti-Pope. (By cruel I mean things like tying women to stakes on the beach and letting the tide drown them, as you may see from memorials in Wigtown Bay.) After Killiecrankie there was an order from William (than whom there couldn't have been a more anti-Pope king: you see what I mean about religious ambivalence) that everyone must take an oath of allegiance to him, or else. Macdonald, after some difficulty finding a magistrate to administer the oath, did take it, though five days late; upon which Government soldiers, led by a Campbell, who had been billeted on, and hospitably received by, the Macdonalds, massacred them, starting with the chief in his bed. Thirty-eight were killed, many more fled and perished in a snowstorm.

Well, that was the bad side, and so was what was laughingly called the Pacification of the Highlands by the Duke of Cumberland. The good side is that every valley has a long, twisted saga behind it, sometimes bloody and sometimes beautiful. It may be wild, but it's not the wildness of an empty continent. History is in that Air as well.

The Great Glen

Every name has resonance—including, clearly, **Fort William**, at the head of

Loch Linnhe, now a railhead town completely dominated by the huge plant of British Aluminium. The first thing you see from the train window is some enormous tubular steel thingummies coming straight down a mountainside. However, it is very easy to turn to more natural and grand sights, since it is also in the shadow of **Ben Nevis**, the highest mountain in Britain (4,406 feet, take *that*, La Paz!); and the surprising thing about it is that you can walk to the top. Takes a little more than two hours, I am told (haven't done it myself, but I will one day). From the top you can see Ireland and Inverness, on the other side of Scotland.

This was where we were aiming, stopping for a moment at **Fort Augustus** (that was the Duke of Cumberland's first name) which is now a Benedictine monastery. We got there just in time for Vespers, where we heard something I thought had vanished from the face of the earth: Gregorian chant. Rather listless, British-sounding, but indubitably Gregorian chant (though the psalms were in English).

The other Fort is twelve miles east of Inverness itself, **Fort George**, built by the Adam brothers and embodying the latest defence ideas of pre-shrapnel Italian military engineers of the day (1773). It is now a museum and tourist attraction.

On the way to Inverness you can choose either side of **Loch Ness**. We chose the northern side, and like everybody else had a good look through binoculars but noticed nothing. What we did notice was the continuing unspoilt nature of the whole area. Notices said *Look for Nessie but don't be messy*.

Inverness

We stayed with a friend who lives just north of Inverness, where she enjoys ravishing views of Beauly Firth, into the south bank of which the river Ness flows through the city. She regaled us with tantalising stories of the trips to be made north and west—particularly, she said, back across the country to Kyle of Lochalsh, turning off the road by which we had come before Fort Augustus, to go through Glen Moriston and along General Wade's Military Road, the famous Road to the Isles, followed by Dr Johnson and Boswell in 1773, past the Five Sisters of Kintail above Loch Duich—

—but not on this tour. The next day we went to Inverness. This spacious, wide-river-divided, gull-screaming city, much less than two hours by air from London (and, as we have seen, motorail terminal), would obviously be an ideal nodal point from which to fan out all over the Highlands if you were really 'doing' Scotland. The extremes of Wester Ross, and the classic Cairngorm and Grampian scenery of the widest area of the country that comes south of Inverness, bulging out eastwards in the same way as East Anglia bulges out in the same relative part of England, are all within a day's car range.

This is the city to which people from as far afield (and asea, if there was such a word) as the Orkneys have for centuries looked as their metropolis. Since we had already seen (at Spean Bridge, on the road up from Fort William) tartan cloth being hand-woven, we thought it a good idea to visit a place which can claim to supply any tartan with a day or two's notice, besides fulfilling a lot of what are now bureaucratically called Ministry of Defence contracts—i.e. kilts for soldiers. There's a workroom above the shop of Hector Russell where you can see them at it—not unaided by modern sewing machines, it is true, but making you realise why it needs so much cloth to get

Loch Ness.

those wonderful, swinging, copious pleats.

As usual in such places we spent far more time than we intended, learning which flowers made the natural dyes (elderberry for blue, St John's Wort for yellow . . .) and discovering a charming bit in the official proclamation of 1792, revoking the post-Culloden ban on the wearing of the kilt:

> This is bringing before all sons of the Gael that the King and Parliament of Britain have forever abolished the Act against Highland Dress that came down to the Clans from the beginning of the world to the year 1746. This must bring joy to every Highland heart. You are no longer bound down to the unmanly dress of the Lowlander.

I hope this is true. I should like to think that any Proclamation said anything as jolly as that.

There was no doubt whatever about the jollity of the most recent addition to Inverness's claim to offer something *metropolitan*, something to accord with a tradition going back, as its guide book says, long before the days when the railway brought the Station Hotel 'patronised by the Royal Family and by most of the Nobility of Europe. Pianos were at the free disposal of the occupants in every sitting room, but a cold bath cost a shilling'; back to the days when Highland chiefs came to buy 'their claret and books, their broadsword steel, Spanish silver, velvet, silks and spices'. This addition is the Eden Court Theatre.

Of the new theatres that I have seen it seems to me to be the only big modern one that combines—well, *modernity* with a kind of human welcoming and comfort. The new Mercury Theatre at Colchester, for instance, is welcoming and modern, the kind of theatre where you could go to their excellent little restaurant and have a pleasant evening if (as was our experience once) you are coming back from a long journey, feel like a pleasant evening out, and are actually too late for the play itself. The National Theatre is big and modern and welcoming but in a rather impersonal, slightly overpowering, London way. Stratford is, well, *sui generis*, it is Stratford. But the Eden Court, which incorporates the old Bishop's Palace of the adjoining Episcopalian cathedral as a minor part of its wonderful design of interlocking hexagons, has one of the best auditoria (well it *is* a Latin word) in Britain and a marvellous come-on-in atmosphere. We never got to see a show there (they do everything—plays, visiting opera, ballet, folk shows, films), as it was morning when we were shown round. A tremendous humming wind made a kind of Aeolian noise through the cantilevered outside structure, giving a curious northern sense of snugness once one was inside (where of course all was carpeted silence). My idea of a perfect evening would be to see something like *The Seagull*, in the depths of winter, with a snowstorm outside, to be fortified with malt whisky in the splendid bar, and then to make the short walk to some welcoming hotel.

I can't think why we haven't seen more in the press about this beautiful theatre. Apparently *The Sunday Times* did say 'the inside is spellbinding', but this must have been on one of the Sundays when the printers, or the journalists, or the electricians, or the other printers' union, or the railways, or the Post Office, or whoever whose turn it was, were on strike and we didn't get our copy.

Then we turned south. Almost every glance at the map here calls up memories of *Macbeth*. Nairn and Forres, says a signpost inviting you to go east along the south coast of Moray Firth, stopping first at the wide-beached, open resort of Nairn and then to the place where in Act I, Scene II, Duncan meets the Bloody Sergeant. You will have passed, before Nairn, a little road southwards to Cawdor, of which, you remember, Macbeth becomes Thane very early on, and where in the castle ('four nature trails, colourful gardens, pitch and putt course, picnic area, snack bar, licensed restaurant and gift shop') its leaflet says firmly, 'King Duncan was foully murdered by the infamous Macbeth'. In my copy the murder, Act II, Scene III, takes place in the castle at Inverness. Ah, well.

We did not go that far along the road to the east, because we stopped, as anyone must, at the site of **Culloden**, the last battle fought on British soil. On that terrible day, 16 April 1746, Prince Charlie's Highlanders, ill-equipped and hungry after long marching, 'facing easterly gales of rain and sleet, lost men in the preliminary exchange of artillery fire. When the charge started, Clan Chattan, raked by heavy fire from Price's Regiment, swerved to the right, compressing the right wing against a stone dyke. This wing although sorely pressed broke through Barrel's and Munro's Regiments but were thrown back by the combined efforts of the second line and Onslow's Regiment on their right. Within one hour this ill-advised battle ended and with it the Stuart cause, and a period of martial law began in the Highlands which was to end the clan system as it then existed.'

So says the memorial. There were 5,000 Highlanders against the Duke of Cumberland's 9,000. The whole place seems about the size of a rugby field, except that you couldn't have artillery fire now, since they seem to have let fire trees grow up all round. The cairns standing where the clans formed their line, marked Glengarry, Keppoch, Clan Ranald, Chisholm, Macleod and Farquharson, Clan Chattan, Fraser, Stewart of Appin, Atholl Men . . . are a few yards apart from each other. We ate our sandwiches at one of the picnic tables under the sighing fir trees, and drove back on to the main road south, past the shop of Culloden Crafts.

Next stop **Aviemore**. This is the most popular and organised sports centre in Scotland, a centre for climbing, pony trekking, fishing, exploring the Spey Valley, Scotland's only major steam railway (see p. 79); and, in winter, it is the nearest thing Britain has to St Moritz.

There is a large complex with everything from dry ski slope and Britain's Second Largest Rink and billiards to 'Santa Claus Land, where his Toy Factory is always preparing for next Christmas', not to mention a Clan Tartan Centre where you 'can trace your clan connections on a computer'. Yes, yes, but some holidaymakers do have children who would enjoy the Santa Claus thing, and people called, say, Isaacs (see p. 190) might well want to use that computer. It *is* a bit touristy-looking, but not more than it has to be.

There is a vast amount of wild and utterly unspoiled Cairngorm grandeur all round it, even if all you have time for on a tour is a trip on the chairlift which takes you in two stages to within 400 feet of a 4,000-foot summit. A curiously restful experience; there's a slight rumbling noise as you pass each tower, then you are alone on your slightly swaying chair, ten or fifty feet above rocks and little tinkling burns on the silent mountain side, vaster and vaster prospects opening out below you. And that was only the lower section, which rises a mere 368 feet (you are quite high up at the starting point). The second section, which disappears over a ridge to rise another 1,425 feet, must be quite something, but it was closed because of wind conditions the day I was there.

Down the road, at **Kingussie** (how pleasant the small Scottish town is, with its wide main street, its stone houses, and always some interesting landscape glimpsed round every corner!), we spent a very rewarding hour in the Highland Folk Museum. Lots of interesting stuff in the pleasant white gabled house, like an illicit whisky still and the moustache cup belonging to Mr Macaskill, the Strathdearn Bard, and the manuscript of the song 'Come over the stream, Charlie' and various exotic musical do-it-yourself instruments; but the highlight is undoubtedly the Black House, an extremely atmospheric and authentic reconstruction of a drystone, thatch-roofed farm dwelling from the Isle of Lewis, with no chimney (peat soot later used as fertiliser on potato crop), box beds separating byre from kitchen, since animals shared the warmth during the long dark winter. Yet a lot of tiny chairs, in this poor dark interior; subsistence farmers may have been poor but they made special furniture for children. A bit humbling, really. What a combination of physical fitness and inner strength those people must have had.

After Kingussie, leaving the Spey valley, the road went through a pleasant open vale, then it was bare heathery uplands again as we passed Drumochter summit and went through Glengarry and the Forest of Atholl, regretfully passing the obviously gorgeous **Blair Castle** (Jacobite history; when it was occupied by a Hanoverian garrison Lord George Murray laid siege to his own home, but now it has elegant Adam dining room, pictures, etc.), not to mention a hotel with a sign saying MALT WHISKY BOUTIQUE; and so to—

Pitlochry

Not, of course, without having stopped just outside to see the Soldier's Leap in the Pass of Killiecrankie (see p. 193).

We found we were just in time to go to the famous Festival Theatre. This began in a marquee in 1951 and blossomed out into a temporary theatre (you can still see great canvas swags in the little restaurant) with a season from May to October, in this delightful town set by the river Tummel between two pine-clad ridges. We walked about a hundred yards from it and at the second attempt booked ourselves for B & B in the pin-bright, luxurious bungalow of Mrs McLellan. Back to the theatre, and an excellent, moderately-priced dinner before the play, a new one about Lizzie Borden (the one who gave her mother forty whacks, etc.); well-made, episodic, gently suggesting that it was Lizzie's Irish maid who dunnit. Not likely to make the West End, perhaps, but interesting (and after all they had just done *Private Lives* and *Arms and the Man*). A perfect end to a day spend bowling through all that marvellous scenery.

Well, not quite the end. Technically B & B means just that, Bed and Breakfast, although you often see a board saying *Evening Meal Provided*, and you have no right to expect one if you don't. But Mr and Mrs McLellan invited us into their living room for tea and a vast array of those Scottish variations on the theme of cake, cookie and shortbread. The other guests were an incredible Australian couple who seemed to have been doing Europe for months. It seemed to include America for them. When they were somewhere in Bedfordshire 'we found we had a week spare. Well, my wife has always wanted to see Disneyland—'

'So have you', said his wife.

'Course I have. Well, we got on a plane and went there. Saw the Grand Canyon as well. Fantastic! Went on one of those Greyhound buses.'

They were doing Britain by coach; not a round trip, they just booked from one place to another. They had enough travellers' tales to sustain a lecture tour. 'Took an open-end trip to John o' Groats, then when we'd got the ticket we found we couldn't get back for a week, so we took it back, we did a week's touring from Inverness instead.'

They did hire a car to do the Continent. 'Yeh, in Vienna, we were trying to park down by the Rhine—'

'That was the Danube.'

'Yeh,' (huge wink) 'the Danube, I kept putting money in this machine and nothing seemed to happen and then a child told us it was for chewing gum.' In another city, in Germany, they were walking and couldn't remember what street their hotel was in. Somebody gave them precise directions, at least they *sounded* precise; but an hour later, as they were still trying, the instruction-giver passed them in his white Mercedes. He invited them in and drove them not to the hotel, but 'into some kind of private basement that seemed to be under a bank. It *was* a bank. He was the manager or something, he had a lot of keys and took us inside because he had to put some papers in the safe. Then he locked it all up and took us to a party he was invited to, and we had a great time, and *then* he drove us to the hotel.'

That's what I mean about B and B. You don't seem to meet people like that in hotels. In fact you don't seem to meet *anybody*, at least in the bigger ones.

The next morning was misty—or, to use the beautifully expressive Norse word the Scots have for it, there was a *haar*. And as we sat eating our bacon-and-egg breakfast, looking out over the town, the opposite pine ridge began to materialise magically out of the empty sky. By the time we had finished and paid our bill (£12 altogether), the whole place was bathed in that clear upland sunlight. And that Air!

We went down to the river, across a charming little pedestrians-only toy suspension bridge, having walked past what must surely be one of the most beautifully situated municipal recreation grounds in the world. On notice PATH TO DAM someone has written with Aerosol spray *naughty word*. On the way to the dam great activity in beautiful wooded slope on our left as we walk upstream. They are building the new theatre on its riverside site. It will seat 540, just the right size, is due to open in 1981, and as far as I am concerned needs no more recommendation beyond the fact that it is by Law and Dunbar-Nasmith, the architects who designed the Eden Court in Inverness.

The dam is visited by everyone who goes to Pitlochry not because they want to see a parcel of turbines in the hydro-electric installation, but because there is a special staircase of 32 pools at the side of the river for the salmon, who each year make that extraordinary journey, perhaps through thousands of miles of sea, to lay their eggs in the upper reaches of the river where they were born. One of the pools has a glass side and is illuminated, and there is usually a little crowd round it. Suddenly someone cries 'here it is! Look!', and there is this great handsome fish. It is curiously moving. The day we were there, after the salmon moved through the meter moved up to 6,993, the total so far that year.

On to Dunkeld, not perhaps such a famous name to the tourist, pleasant though it is, as the little resort across the river (now we are on the Tay), reached by a bridge designed by another of those men whose name crops up all over the place, Telford (see p. 164); for this is Birnam. Its wood had quite a way to go to Dunsinane, which is twelve miles away to the south-east, and still has the remains of Macbeth's castle.

And so to **Perth**, that famous city strategically placed on the Tay before it widens into its Firth, which then narrows again at **Dundee** just sufficiently for it to be bridged, a circumstance which led to the composition of the most famous bad poem in the English language, lamenting the loss of a train, not to mention half the bridge, when it was one year old in 1879. I shall not quote that effort of the noted bard William McGonagall, however. Apart from the fact that it's the one everybody else quotes, there are some lines of his which seem more relevant to our tour:

> Beautiful and ancient city of Perth
> One of the grandest upon the earth,
> With your stately mansions and streets so clean
> And situated betwixt two Inches green
> Which are most magnificent to be seen . . .
>
> The surrounding woodland scenery is very grand,
> It cannot be surpassed in fair Scotland,
> Especially the elegant Palace of Scone, in history renowned,
> Where some of Scotland's kings were crowned.
>
> And the Fair Maid of Perth's house is worthy to be seen,
> Which is well worth visiting by Duke, Lord or Queen;
> The Fair Maid of Perth caused the battle on the North Inch
> 'Twixt the Clans Chattan and Kay, and neither of them did flinch
> Until they were cut up inch by inch . . .

McGonagall certainly found the *mot juste* for **Scone**. It *is* elegant; the gorgeous rooms with their 17th- and 18th-century furniture, the superb Long Gallery with organ at the end (down which Charles II walked to be crowned King of Scotland in 1651), the whole set in a most beautiful park, overlie the tumultuous earlier history. Kenneth McAlpine brought the famous Stone of Scone here in 843, and Edward I removed it to Westminster in 1296. For a thousand years it was the crowning place of the Scottish kings, of whom Robert Bruce was one. There was an abbey here, burnt to the ground by followers of John Knox 430 years ago.

There was something familiar about its later splendour. Where had one seen similar taste, matched by the wealth to implement it? Ah yes, Kenwood House, Hampstead, London (see p. 65). Scone was given to Sir David Murray by James VI (of Scotland, later James I of England as well) for saving his life in something called the Gowrie Conspiracy, in 1604; and it was that same Sir William Murray, a direct descendant, who as we have seen became Lord Chancellor in the 18th century and who as the first Lord Mansfield lived at Kenwood. He was actually too busy to live at Scone; it was the 2nd and 3rd Earls whose admirable taste is now reflected by the building which was Gothicised in 1802, before this meant the Heavy Victorian that this word now suggests—when in fact it was a charming *light* fantasy. The present (8th) Earl lives there now with his family, and there are things which would doubtless have surprised his ancestors (even though he too read Law, at Oxford)—such as Fun for the Family at Scone Palace, with lucky dips, bookstall, flea market, greasy pole, highland dancing, trampoline display, pony rides, bicycle testing, bowling for pig, arrival of Fiona Kennedy by helicopter at 2.45 p.m. to open the Fayre . . .

Well, after this (oh, and there was no space to tell you about the *marvellous* porcelain) we were soon in motorway country and over the new Forth road bridge into—

Edinburgh

One must say either nothing or everything about Edinburgh. I myself do not think it is seen at its best on a hot August day when it is simply full of people eating ice-cream. There are not just pamphlets, not just books, there are libraries about Edinburgh, of which the essential attraction is of course the contrast between the old town, with its famous Royal Mile, dominated by the Castle, seen as the crowning glory of the fantastic skyline observed from Princes Street, the architecturally worthless boundary of the northern section, and that section, the New (i.e. 18th-century) Town, much better appreciated in the austere splendours of the parallel George Street and Queen Street behind it, and Charlotte Square, of which No. 7 is splendidly maintained by the National Trust for Scotland as a Typical Georgian House.

Certainly the Edinburgh Festival is a Good Thing, whether you have booked for months ahead to hear the World's Greatest Artists, Orchestras, Conductors, etc., or are prepared to take pot luck with the ever-expanding fringe events with, when we were doing our tour, such events as '*Gay Authors Workshop* (at Heriot Watt Theatres, 25 Grindlay Street)—New songs, fresh poems, different stories, outrageous sketches by forty women and men of G.A.W. in their second Edinburgh season. GOING GAY, G.A.W. Productions present a fast, merciless probe into the seamier side of straight life, and the funnier aspects of being gay.' Or *A Change of Sheets*. 'Three sets of sheets, from pure silk to Brentford Nylons. Pull back the covers to reveal a crate of cucumbers. There's a sex-doll in the cupboard, and she's getting hungry. Paper aeroplanes are flying out the window, but where the hell is South Yemen anyway? Why does a dead composer want to shoot himself, and why doesn't Oscar Wilde have time to wash his hair? There are no easy solutions for attempted answers you must see *A Change of Sheets*. Three explosive new

Edinburgh: 'Auld Reekie'

plays that force you out of bed.'

I'm not making this all up, you know. It's in an official booklet.

What we did, absurd really, was go into the National Gallery of Scotland largely to see the miraculous (and until the 1776 bicentenary exhibition in London unknown to us) Constable picture called *Dedham Vale* and buy six postcards and a slide of it. I noticed on the way, from our luckily-discovered parking meter in Charlotte Square, that Rose Street, just behind Princes Street, in my time there a very vulgar street indeed with some very notorious pubs, had been pedestrianised and was full of boutiques and very *smart* pubs. Two cheers. No, one and a half.

But the fact is, I believe Edinburgh is a *winter* city. That's when you get the true R. L. Stevenson atmosphere, that's when you are likely to see the Castle appear suddenly out of a *haar*, as we did those hills at Pitlochry. My favourite Edinburgh story is about the philosopher David Hume, who fell into the water which once filled the low ground between Princes Street and the Castle heights and, to my intense rage ever since I heard about it, was drained to make room for the mere *railway*. The man who rescued him, having heard that he was an atheist, held him by the hair and would not pull him out until he recited the Lord's Prayer.

The night at another friend's house, then the 'Lowlands' again. Down to **Peebles**, which has always been my idea of the classic small Scottish town. On a river, of course—the Tweed this time. At the local tourist office they give a very good Town Walk leaflet. Lovely wide High Street with the usual off-centre tower. Tontine Hotel, with a most lovely music room with lime-green walls, green swagged curtains, musicians' gallery supported by slim cast-iron pillars. Shop announcing that it sells 'paperbacked novels', many fine shop-fronts, Walter R. Davies, Chemist, has splendid gold pestle sign. You keep seeing river through alley arches, one is called Stinkin' Stair. Bank House, where John Buchan lived as a boy, now houses J. & W. Buchan, Writers (Scots for solicitors). A peaceful town.

Then beautiful, beautiful **Traquair House**, the oldest inhabited house in Scotland. Tall, spare, elegant but not posh (since the lairds of Traquair were always staunchly Catholic and Jacobite, a harder thing to be down here). Beautiful austere library with painted heads of classical writers, a room meant for *reading*, not show. Gates opening on grassy tree-lined avenue will not be opened till a Stuart reigns again. Rosary and crucifix of Mary Queen of Scots. Slightly French-château feeling, yet quintessentially Scottish. And can't leave without tasting incomparable home-brewed Traquair ale, of which I can only say that it is better than Adnam's, made in Southwold, Suffolk, and if you've ever drunk that you will know what praise this is.

Down over endless blue hills, through wooded valleys; much of Roxburghshire, very hedgeless and open, could be Burgundy if there were a few vineyards. But of course they just don't have moors in Abroad. Or that Air. Through Eskdale, criminal not to explore that too. Next tour, perhaps.

Lights of Carlisle ahead. Good heavens, England. No wonder the Scots have that song, *Will Ye No Come Back Again?*

Yes. Any time.

Index